ETHICAL ISSUES
IN CONTEMPORARY
HUMAN RESOURCE
MANAGEMENT

MANAGEMENT, WORK AND ORGANISATIONS

Series editors: **Gibson Burrell**, Warwick Business School
Mick Marchington, Manchester School of Management, UMIST
Paul Thompson, Department of Human Resource Management, University of Edinburgh

This series of new textbooks covers the areas of human resource management, employee relations, organisational behaviour and related business and management fields. Each text has been specially commissioned to be written by leading experts in a clear and accessible way. The books contain serious and challenging material, take an analytical rather than prescriptive approach and are particularly suitable for use by students with no prior specialist knowledge.

The series is relevant for many business and management courses, including MBA and post-experience courses, specialist masters and postgraduate diplomas, professional courses and final-year undergraduate courses. These texts have become essential reading at business and management schools worldwide.

Published

Forthcoming

Series Standing Order

If you would like to receive future titles in this series as they are published, you can make use of our standing order facility. To place a standing order please contact your bookseller or, in case of difficulty, write to us at the address below with your name and address and the name of the series. Please state with which title you wish to begin your standing order. (If you live outside the United Kingdom we may not have the rights for your area, in which case we will forward your order to the publisher concerned.)

Customer Services Department, Macmillan Distribution Ltd
Houndmills, Basingstoke, Hampshire RG21 6XS, England

ETHICAL ISSUES IN CONTEMPORARY HUMAN RESOURCE MANAGEMENT

Edited by

Diana Winstanley and Jean Woodall

Published by
PALGRAVE MACMILLAN
Houndmills, Basingstoke, Hampshire RG21 6XS and
175 Fifth Avenue, New York, N.Y. 10010
Companies and representatives throughout the world

PALGRAVE MACMILLAN is the global academic imprint of the Palgrave Macmillan division of St. Martin's Press, LLC and of Palgrave Macmillan Ltd. Macmillan® is a registered trademark in the United States, United Kingdom and other countries. Palgrave is a registered trademark in the European Union and other countries.

ISBN 0–333–73965–5 hardcover
ISBN 0–333–73966–3 paperback

This book is printed on paper suitable for recycling and made from fully managed and sustained forest sources.

A catalogue record for this book is available from the British Library.

Transferred to digital printing in 2002

Editing and origination by
Aardvark Editorial, Mendham, Suffolk

Printed and bound in Great Britain by
Antony Rowe Ltd, Chippenham and Eastbourne

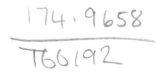

Contents

List of exhibits, figures and tables

Exhibits

Figures

Tables

Notes on the contributors

Barry R Baker, CPsychol, FIPM, MSc, BA(Hons), is Principal Lecturer in the Management of Human Resources at Cheltenham and Gloucester College of Higher Education.

Timothy J Claydon, BSocSci, MSc(Econ), PhD, is Head of the Department of Human Resource Management in the School of Business at De Montfort University, Leicester.

John N Cooper, BSc(Hons), MSc, CPsychol, is an occupational psychologist who runs his own practice in Cheltenham, specialising in psychometric training, selection, assessment and development. He is also a lecturer in organisational psychology at Bristol University.

Linda Dickens, BA(Kent), MA(Warwick), is Professor of Industrial Relations and Director of the MA Programmes in Industrial Relations at Warwick Business School.

Noeleen Doherty, BSc, MSc, is a Senior Research Fellow in the Human Resource Research Centre at Cranfield School of Management. Prior to this she worked at the Manpower Services Commission as an occupational psychologist.

Danielle Douglas, MSc, FIPD, FRSA, is a human resource specialist who runs her own management consultancy. She has worked with several blue chip multinational organisations, smaller companies and professional organisations. Danielle advises on strategic direction, cultural change and organisational transformation and personal transitions.

Edmund Heery, BA, MA, PhD, MIPD, is Professor of Industrial Relations at Cardiff Business School, Cardiff University.

Charles Jackson, BSc, MSc, PhD, CPsychol, is an independent researcher and consultant and an Industrial Fellow in the Centre for Stakeholding and Sustainable Enterprise at Kingston University. He advises organisations on strategies for career and employee development.

Peter L Jones, BA(Hons), FIPD, is a management consultant and also a partner in Transition Partnerships.

Karen Legge, MA(Oxon), DSAS, is Professor of Organisational Behaviour at Warwick Business School.

David Lewis, LLB(Hons), MA, MIPD, is a Reader in Employment Law at Middlesex University.

Sonia Liff, BA, MSc, PhD, is a Senior Lecturer in Industrial Relations and Organisational Behaviour at Warwick Business School.

Maria Sillanpää, MSc, MISEA, was Ethical Audit Team Manager responsible for social auditing within The Body Shop Group and is now principal consultant, Social Accountability, KPMG.

Ruth Simpson, BSc(Econ), MA(Econ), is a Senior Research Fellow in the Centre for Equality Research in Business and Senior Lecturer in Economics at the University of North London.

Laura J Spence, BSc, PhD, lectures in business ethics at Brunel University and is a member of the executive of the European Business Ethics Network (EBEN).

Celia Stanworth, MA, MIPD, FRSA, is a Senior Lecturer in Human Resources and Industrial Relations at Greenwich University and a Research Fellow at Westminster Business School.

Shaun Tyson, FIPD, FRSA, is a Professor of Human Resources at Cranfield School of Management.

Paul Taylor, BTech, MSc, MPhil, FIBMS, is a Consultant Clinical Scientist in the Microbiology Department at the Royal Brompton and Harefield NHS Trust.

Diana Winstanley, BSc(Hons), PhD, FIPD, FRSA, is a Senior Lecturer in human resource management at Imperial College Management School.

Jean Woodall, BA(Hons), PhD, FIPD, FRSA, is a Professor of Human Resource Development at Kingston Business School.

Acknowledgements

We would like to thank BUIRA (the British Universities Industrial Relations Association), and EBEN UK (European Business Ethics Network UK) for sponsoring and supporting our conferences on ethical issues in contemporary human resource management. We also appreciate the work of those organisations that sent delegates to our conferences or more generally promote ethical human resource practice, including the Involvement and Participation Association (IPA), Public Concern at Work, The Body Shop, Phoenix Human Resource Consultants, Transition Partnerships, GHN and Consultants.

We would also like to thank Roma Van Dam for word processing some of the manuscript and for her painstaking advice and guidance in using IT in this area.

Finally, both of us owe a debt to 'the great outdoors' – for moments of relaxation and inspiration on long-distance walks (Di on the coast-to-coast and West Highland Way walks) and on rockfaces (Jean hanging on to Tower Ridge on Ben Nevis). We both advocate these as ways for any aspiring writer to keep their sanity!

The authors and publisher would like to thank the following organizations and individuals for permission to use the following copyright material:

John Wiley and Sons Limited for Figure 4.1 from Robertson, I. and Smith, J. (1989) Personnel Selection Methods in Smith, J. and Robertson, I. (eds) *Advances in Selection and Assessment*, p. 107.
Elsevier Science for Figure 5.1 from Billing, Y. and Alvesson, M. (1989) 'Four Ways of Looking at Women and Leadership', *Scandinavian Journal of Management*, 5(1): 77.
Stephen Holman for Table 7.2.
Blackwell Publishers for material in Chapter 9.

European Foundation for Quality Mangement for Figure 11.1.

Harvard Business Review for Figure 11.2 from Kaplan, R. S. and Norton, D. P. 'The Balanced Scorecard – measures that drive performance', January–February 1992, p. 72. Copyright © 1992 by the President and Fellows of Harvard College; all rights reserved.

The Body Shop International plc for extracts from *The Body Shop Approach to Ethical Auditing* (1996) and *The Values Report* 1995 and 1997 in Chapter 13.

PART I

THE ETHICAL CONTEXT FOR HUMAN RESOURCE MANAGEMENT

CHAPTER 1

Introduction

Diana Winstanley and Jean Woodall

Origin of this book

The ideas for this book arose from our interest in the developing field of business ethics and from a concern that very little of the debate in this area seemed to have percolated into the field of human resource management (HRM). Although there have been some articles in the professional HRM literature and some in the academic literature (such as Legge, 1998a, 1998b; Miller, 1996a, 1996b), these are few and far between. A forum to enable human resource practitioners and academics to bring together these ideas and focus more specifically on human resource management was needed. Although some discussion of ethical issues and human resource management had taken place at conferences and seminars convened by the European Business Ethics Network (EBEN) UK, the Institute of Personnel and Development (IPD), the British Academy of Management (BAM), the British Universities Industrial Relations Association (BUIRA), the International Labour Process theorists, Jack Mahoney (now retired) at London Business School and the Royal Society of Arts Ethics in the Workplace network, there needed to be a conference dedicated to this area to enable a greater debate and synthesis of ideas. As a result two UK conferences on ethical issues in contemporary human resource management were organised, one at Imperial College in April 1996 and one at Kingston Business School in January 1998. The lively debate which followed the first conference has been reported in a special issue of *Personnel Review* (Vol. 25, No. 6, 1996) and a number of articles in journals such as *Business Ethics: A European Review* (see in particular Vol. 6, No. 1, 1997). Many of the evolving themes from both these conferences have been brought together in one collection in this book which is aimed primarily at making human resource professionals and academics aware of business ethics concepts and their relevance for understanding contemporary working practices. As a result this book uses many of these earlier conference papers, plus other chapters that have been commissioned to highlight the areas of greatest ethical concern.

This book is intended to raise ethical sensitivity and awareness of the latent ethical underpinnings in contemporary human resource management and to enable ethical analysis of HR policy and practice utilising traditional and newer ethical frameworks. Although many chapters do highlight actions that could be taken to promote ethical awareness and behaviour (particularly in Section 3), a pluralist approach was inevitably required in order to reflect the competing views of what constitutes ethical practice and whether this is at all possible.

The book is divided into three parts. The first draws together those ethical frameworks of most relevance to the changing nature and context of contemporary human resource management (this chapter) and examines more fully the context in which human resource management is enacted (Legge, Chapter 2). The second identifies some of the main areas of human resource management where ethical issues have the greatest significance, such as in recruitment and selection (Spence, Chapter 3), occupational testing and psychometric profiling (Baker and Cooper, Chapter 4), equal opportunities (Liff and Dickens, Chapter 5), employee well-being (Doherty and Tyson, Chapter 6), training and development (Woodall and Douglas, Chapter 7), flexibility (Stanworth, Chapter 8), working time (Simpson, Chapter 9), remuneration (Heery, Chapter 10), performance management (Winstanley, Chapter 11) and empowerment and participation (Claydon, Chapter 12). In this section we identify areas of both ethical concern and examples of good ethical practice. The third section draws together some of the initiatives and processes which have been developed as means of monitoring, assessing, addressing and developing ethical practice. These include social auditing (Sillanpää and Jackson, Chapter 13), employee charters (Taylor and Jones, Chapter 14) and whistleblowing (Lewis, Chapter 15). In Chapter 16 we draw together the key themes from the book and identify possible routes for ethical action in human resource management.

Earlier work on ethics and human resource management

What has been the traditional focus of ethical interest in human resource management, both in terms of academic investigation and professional practice? On the whole, ethical issues have been of marginal significance to the unfolding academic debates around HRM. The Harvard analytical framework for HRM (Beer *et al.*, 1984, p. 16) was one of the earlier academic models to suggest that as well as organisational well-being, HRM has also to concern itself with the promotion of individual and societal well-being. This reasserts the primacy of the stakeholder as opposed to the shareholder model of the firm, an issue on which the battle lines have been clearly drawn in business ethics literature. On the one side there are those such as Sternberg (1994, 1997), who draw on Friedman's (1962) argument that the primary responsibility of organisations is to its shareholders and so to make a profit – the 'business of business is business' view. On the other side there are those such as the Centre for Tomorrow's Company at the RSA, drawing on earlier work of the strategic management academic Freeman (1984), who suggest that organisations should meet the needs of a wider range of stakeholders, including employees.

Any emphasis on ethics and employee well-being within the HRM debate is therefore very contentious and has become more so as organisations have struggled for survival in the last 20 or so years. The ethical dimension of HR policy and practice has been downplayed in more recent texts on HRM, where the focus has shifted to 'strategic fit' and 'best practice' approaches (for example Tyson, 1998). See also the debate that took place in an ESRC/BUIRA Seminar Series on 'The Contribution of HR Strategy to Business Performance' (Guest, 1996; Purcell, 1996). However there are enough arguments to the contrary to suggest that employee well-being and ethical treatment are as justifiable a focus as 'strategic fit' and 'best practice'. Three in particular are pertinent. The enlightened self-interest model of business suggests that a business will be more successful if it pays attention to ethics as this will enhance reputation with customers and improve motivation among employees (for an example of the benefits of the social responsibility argument see Wilson, 1997). The economic argument is also not paramount for not-for-profit organisations, including much of the public sector, social businesses, non-governmental organisations (NGOs) and the voluntary sector. There is also the case that the economic system and thus ultimately business organisations within it are created to serve human and societal needs, rather than the other way around.

It is important to recollect the centrality of ethical concern in the past in HRM. The origins of HRM in personnel management and earlier welfare officer roles date back to the formation of the Welfare Workers' Association in 1913, a forerunner of the Institute of Personnel and Development, and to the early social reformers in the Industrial Revolution and Quaker industrialists such as Joseph Rowntree and Adrian Cadbury. Despite concerns that this welfare role has compromised the status and strategic base of human resource management, these activities have not been totally eclipsed. However, over time, the notion of employee well-being has become reduced to a more specific set of practices confined around 'wellness' programmes and health screening, rather than extended to the wider experience an individual has of organisational life. Doherty and Tyson (Chapter 6 in this book) discuss some of the wider implications of individual well-being posed by 'best-practice' HRM, work intensification and academic discussion of 'emotional labour'. Likewise Simpson (Chapter 9) explores the impact on managers of the long hours work culture and the consequences for employee well-being, particularly for those with children.

Another way in which the ethical treatment of workers and concern for their welfare has been addressed is in the area of job design and motivation. Through the influence of the human relations movement, the early work of Mayo (1933) and later work of Herzberg (1968) and Maslow (1987) and the Quality of Working Life (QWL) movement, there has been an ongoing interest in quality of life issues. These focus particularly on work systems promoting job design that satisfies the motivation needs of employees and issues such as self-actualisation, autonomy, variety and skill development. Nonetheless Claydon (Chapter 12) suggests that some of these concepts have been abused in the practice of high-performance work teams and empowerment, where the employee experience is rather one of work intensification and greater intrusion into and exploitation of the notion of self.

Certainly an ethical concern has survived in the enduring academic and professional interest in research and practice on issues of fairness and equal opportunity. Research has revealed in detail problems of discrimination, particularly in the areas of recruitment and career development. The translation of this knowledge into more ethical practice has been tackled by codes of professional practice and professional education. For example, organisations such as the IPD have advocated fair treatment in areas such as recruitment and selection, remuneration and promotion for groups felt to be disadvantaged. They have addressed issues of gender, marital status, race and ethnicity, disability and more recently age. Voluntary action by organisations, individuals and professional groups has been underpinned by earlier employment legislation, such as the Sex Discrimination Acts of 1975 and 1986 and the Race Relations Act 1976 – and even more recent legislation such as the Disability Discrimination Act 1995. Yet Liff and Dickens (Chapter 5) highlight the continuing dilemmas over how to translate equal opportunities into practice and the divergent approaches they outline illustrate that there is no one way to be ethical in this area.

Another ethical concern that has 'survived' is procedural justice. This has always been a strong theme in industrial relations literature and has underpinned work in theory and practice in areas such as collective bargaining, payment systems and job evaluation. Procedural justice is an abiding ethical concern and Heery (Chapter 10) and Spence (Chapter 3) highlight issues to do with fair process as well as fair outcome, in relation to recruitment and remuneration.

There has also been some interest in the role of the human resource specialist as a guardian of ethics, with the human resource function taking on the role of 'ethical stewardship'. Sporadic debate around this in professional

HRM journals is common. For example, some writers have stressed their role in raising awareness about ethical issues, in promoting ethical behaviour and in disseminating ethical practices more widely among line and project managers. The ethical role of HR professionals is also identified as communicating codes of ethical conduct, providing training in ethics, managing compliance and monitoring arrangements and taking a lead in enforcement proceedings (for example Arkin, 1996; Johns, 1995; Pickard, 1995; Wehrmeyer, 1996). Where ethical conduct is questioned, HR managers have traditionally overseen arrangements such as disciplinary and grievance procedures. Lewis (Chapter 15) takes this one step further in proposing they play a role in creating and overseeing whistleblowing procedures as well.

Other work on ethical leadership such as by Connock and Johns (1995) tend to stress the importance of this responsibility being placed with the senior management team and line managers and this parallels the moves to make human resource management something which is enacted by a wider group of organisational stakeholders.

While all these concerns are still relevant, the changes which have been taking place in human resource management over the last two decades raise new ethical concerns and call into question exactly what is meant by ethical approaches to human resource management and how possible and desirable it is to incorporate an ethical basis in human resource practice. Above all, questions arise about the nature of the relevant frameworks to inform ethical decision making in this area.

Ethical frameworks and their relevance to HRM

What is ethics?

To understand the relevance of ethical frameworks we need to have a definition of what exactly ethics is. Needless to say, this is problematic! Ethics could easily become a catch-all word representing all that is seen as 'good' or 'moral' in HRM. Many writers on ethics suggest that ethics and morality are in fact synonymous, (for example Maclagan, 1998, pp. 1–4), where morality concerns traditions of belief about right and wrong conduct, whether by an individual, a group or a society. Morality is defined by Petrick and Quinn (1997) as:

> the customary, sociolegal practices and activities that are considered importantly right and wrong; the rules that govern those activities; and the values that are embedded, fostered, or pursued by those conventional, sociolegal activities and practices. (Petrick and Quinn, 1997, p. 43)

Some writers (such as Beauchamp and Bowie, 1983, pp. 1–21; and Petrick and Quinn, 1997, pp. 42–5) suggest there is a difference between morality and ethics; Petrick and Quinn taking the study of ethics to be one step back in saying that:

> ethics is the study of individual and collective moral awareness, judgement, character, and conduct. (Petrick and Quinn, 1997, p. 42)

Beauchamp and Bowie (1983, pp. 1–2) likewise suggest that whereas morality is a social institution with a history and code of learnable rules distinguished from rules of prudence or self-interest, ethical theory refers to the 'philosophical study of the nature and justification of ethical principles, decisions and problems'.

Another distinction central to the approach adopted in this book is between ethical sensitivity and reasoning on the one hand and theory and ethical conduct and normative morality and ethics on the other. Ethical sensitivity is the ability to reflect on human resource management and be able to identify the ethical and moral dimensions and issues. Ethical reasoning is the ability to identify appropriate ethical frameworks with which to explore the ethics of those dimensions and issues. This book emphasises the importance of ethical sensitivity and reasoning by exposing the reader to the many different areas of HRM where we can identify ethical issues and by introducing a variety of relevant frameworks which can be used to analyse and understand the ethical dilemmas and ways of viewing the issues. Yet caution is needed. This book can only in part attempt to identify appropriate ethical conduct and suggest ethical solutions. Although some writers in this book may propose ethical actions, ultimately readers will utilise their own moral frames of reference to determine 'right' and 'wrong'.

When embarking upon ethical reasoning, depending on which ethical framework is being pursued at the time, it is very easy to become bogged down in a discussion of absolute versus relative values, of virtues, principles, rights and responsibilities and of concepts such as justice and equality. Is ethics an attitude, value or behaviour; is it a set of rules for correct conduct or a system for adopting a series of moral principles or virtues? Ethics is not about taking statements of morality at face value; it is a critical and challenging tool. There are no universally agreed ethical frameworks, but this is not to offer the excuse of collapsing in a morass of moral relativism. It will be clear from the ensuing chapters that some ethical frameworks are more relevant to the study of human resource management than others. Different situations require ethical insight and flexibility to enable us to encapsulate the grounds on which competing ethical claims are made. Decisions are judgements usually involving choices between alternatives, but rarely is the choice between right or wrong.

So, if the choice is not between absolute standards of right and wrong, on what, then, is it based? Unavoidably, human emotion comes into play. MacIntyre (1985) has identified how much of contemporary moral debate is founded on 'emotivism', where each ethical framework, when broken down to its first principles, leads to the ultimate defence of suasion, or 'because I believe it to be so'. Emotivism:

> is the doctrine that all evaluative judgements and more specifically all moral judgements are nothing but expressions of preference, expressions of attitude or feeling, insofar as they are moral or evaluative in character. (MacIntyre, 1985, p. 12)

Moral disagreement and judgements are concerned with attitudes and feelings, not facts, and to deny this would 'entail the obliteration of any genuine distinction between manipulative and non-manipulative social relations' (MacIntyre, 1985, p. 23). Ethical statements, by their nature, are subjective attempts to invoke agreement and adherence to one or other ethical framework, rather than objective statements of truth. However, a distinction can be made between this and relativism as a doctrine to be supported in itself. Thus we need to be ethically aware of how an individual's own dispositions affect the choice of an ethical frame of reference.

Another point of caution made by MacIntyre concerns the fact that:

> We all too often still treat the moral philosophers of the past as contributors to a single debate with a relatively unvarying subject matter, treating Plato and Hume and Mill as contemporaries both of ourselves and of each other. This leads to an abstraction of these writers from the cultural and social milieus in which they lived and thought so the history of their thought acquires a false independence from the rest of the culture. (MacIntyre,1985, p. 11).

So while we are respectful of the ground covered by the great philosophers, the intention in this book has been to bring the ethical frameworks up to date and to incorporate new perspectives which are more relevant to contemporary HRM practice.

It is difficult to know where to start in introducing ethical principles to those who do not normally spend their spare time in philosophical wrestling over concepts of 'justice', 'equality', 'rights, 'obligations' and so on. However, we have done so by starting with minimalist theories that place the rights of the individual as the 'unencumbered self' in prime position, before moving on to ethical theories that stress the importance of human obligations and interconnectedness.

Ethical egoism

One of the most minimalist of ethical positions is ethical egoism, based on the work of the seventeenth-century philosopher Thomas Hobbes, the *Leviathan*, written at the time of the English Civil War. Here the 'only valid standard of conduct is the obligation to promote one's own well-being above anyone else's' (Beauchamp and Bowie, 1983, p. 18), where one ought to act on the basis of maximising one's own self-interest. However, 'an ethical egoist does consider the interests of others when it suits his or her own interest, and usually it is in our interest to treat others well because it is in our advantage to do so' (Beauchamp and Bowie, 1983, p. 18). Otherwise, as Hobbes suggested, life could become 'solitary, poor, nasty, brutish and short'. Much work on business ethics is based on this premise and the view epitomised by Friedman (1962) of business working for the sole benefit of shareholders is countered by the stakeholding literature that follows, which suggests that an enlightened self-interested model of management would take into account the interests of others. Claydon (Chapter 12) is one writer in this book who takes up the ethical egoism approach in his discussion of empowerment, where he suggests that this is more feasible than other ethical positions due to the contradictory nature of the employment relationship. In this model, the ethical role of the human resources professional would be limited to supporting the enlightened self-interest of the employer, rather than the rights of employees for their own sake, which implies that the role in ethical stewardship is limited to those areas where it can be demonstrated to impact on organisational effectiveness.

Kantian rights-based ethics

Another approach places individual interest at the centre of all ethical consideration, but in contrast to ethical egoism's concern to limit infringement on action to support the employer's interests, it is preoccupied with a positive assertion of basic rights for all.

The most common rights-based frameworks tend to draw on the work of the eighteenth-century German philosopher Immanuel Kant and more specifically his categorical imperatives (see, for example, Paton 1948). The first imperative is that one should follow the principle that what is right for one person is right for everyone, and thus you must do to others as you would be done by – the principle of universalisability and reversibility. The second formulation of the categorical imperative is that there should be the principle of respect for all people and that they should be treated as ends in themselves, never as the means to an end.

A number of rights are commonly propounded and these usually embrace issues such as the right to life and safety and human rights of privacy, freedom of conscience, speech and to hold private property. A number of chapters in this book raise the relevance of rights-based frameworks to HRM, particularly Spence (Chapter 3, on selection interviewing), Baker and Cooper (Chapter 4, on occupational testing), Dickens and Liff (Chapter 5, on equal opportunities), Woodall and Douglas (Chapter 6 on employee development), Stanworth (Chapter 8, on flexibility), Simpson (Chapter 9 on working time), Taylor and Jones (Chapter 14, on staff charters) and Lewis (Chapter 15, on whistleblowing).

Justice-based ethical frameworks

Another rights-based ethical framework focuses upon the exercise of distributive justice, and the work of John Rawls (1971) is most commonly cited here. In his theory of justice, Rawls advocates two principles: that each individual has an equal right to basic liberty and that inequalities in distribution should be to the benefit of all or to the least advantaged. Justice ethics therefore emphasises fairness and equality and likewise asserts the golden rule of 'do unto others as you would have others do unto you'. Rawlsian justice rests upon social contract theory and emphasises societal and contractual agreements to ensure that justice and rights are upheld. Issues concerning procedural and distributive justice are particular relevant in the area of rewards, such as in Heery's Chapter 10, but are seldom pursued to their logical conclusion.

However, most conventional approaches to business ethics begin by juxtaposing the deontological theories (*deon* meaning duty in Greek) that start from the position that ethical justification rests with basic rights of individuals with the teleological theories (to do with the *telos* meaning the final purpose or issue or goal in Greek, see later) that justify ethical positions in terms of the consequences of action. This has often been the basis of distinguishing utilitarian (teleological) frameworks from the rights-based (deontological) frameworks already mentioned.

Teleological ethics and utilitarianism

Teleological frameworks consider teleological outcomes and ends. The nineteenth-century British philosophers such as Jeremy Bentham and John

Stuart Mill are particularly associated with utilitarianism, perhaps the best known teleological framework. Utilitarianism assumes an ethical commitment to the principle that the aim is to achieve 'the greatest good for the greatest number', and an 'act is right if it results in benefits for people, wrong if it damages or harms'. Two types of utilitarianism are usually distinguished. Act-based utilitarianism is where the decision maker would need to assess how the greatest good or utility could be achieved. Rule-based utilitarianism is where the individual would be required to adhere to rules which have been fashioned on utility, in order to achieve the greatest good. Although very well used in areas such as the assessment of health service provision and access to social benefits, these approaches have been less useful in HRM, although some reference is made to them in Chapter 3 where Spence discusses the balancing of individual rights to, for example, privacy, with the organisation's desire to make a fully informed decision, where the outcome utility is maximised and in Chapter 4 where Baker and Cooper discuss balancing the rights of test takers with those of test users.

Many textbooks make the distinction between deontological and teleological ethical theories the centre of their ethical classification and debate. In this book, however, the focus has shifted to other ethical frameworks which revolve around three themes:

- ethics in the process, epitomised by stakeholding, and discourse ethics
- welfare ethics, where the emphasis has moved away from paternalism towards a more contemporary view of 'ethics of care' which tends to focus on ethical acts and intention towards employees, (distinguished from 'the duty of care' framework which informs much health and safety legislation)
- ethics in the actor and approaches that tend to focus on ethical virtues or dispositions.

Although these three approaches are rooted in the earlier history of moral philosophy, the aim is to focus on their meaning when assessing contemporary practices.

Stakeholding

The concept of stakeholding has much relevance to human resource management and suggests an approach promoting greater involvement and voice of employees in managerial decision making, with more account taken of employee interests through a range of different consultation and participation methods.

The word 'stakeholding' has been in popular parlance since Freeman's seminal text (1984) on business strategy and management. It was a central element in the incoming Labour government's policy platform in 1997 and has taken centre stage more recently by virtue of its widespread utilisation in the political and public policy domains, where social inclusiveness is seen as an antidote to the problems produced by the rampant individualism of the Thatcherite era (for example see Hutton, 1995; Kelly *et al.*, 1997). This has also infiltrated the employment area, with political rhetoric and legislation around the area of partnership and mutuality in employment, as evidenced in the 'Fairness at Work' legislation culminating in the Employment Relations Bill 1999. There has also been an energetic debate in the business strategy and management area between those who reassert the primacy of the shareholder corporation, such as Sternberg (1994, 1997) on the one hand, and those who propose a stakeholding approach to management either for moral or effectiveness reasons, such as the Centre for Tomorrow's Company (RSA, 1995) and the New Academy of Business sponsored by The Body Shop (Wheeler and Sillanpää, 1997) on the other.

Some of the chapters in this book provide suggestions for promoting greater stakeholding. Sillanpää and Jackson's (Chapter 13) elaboration of The Body Shop social audit approach is one such attempt to secure feedback from employees and find ways of engaging and addressing their needs. Other chapters warn against taking too utopian a line. For example Legge (Chapter 2) identifies some of the barriers to stakeholding when operating in global markets. Claydon (Chapter 12) likewise suggests that approaches to involvement and participation based on stakeholding may be a form of duplicity which ties employees into a rhetoric of excellence and enterprise, with ethical egoism being a more realistic frame of reference.

The practical difficulties of applying stakeholding as an ethical concept in the workplace are considerable. The length of time required for competing claims to be recognised and addressed (Winstanley and Stoney, 1997) can lead to an undermining of profitability and effectiveness. An even more thorny problem for the utilisation of stakeholding as a concept to promote more ethical treatment of employees is that it undermines the primary relationship between employers and employees. Employees' needs may be balanced against those of customers, suppliers and other groups and little work has been done on how to adjudicate between such rival claims. It seems unlikely that stakeholding can succeed while the espoused rhetoric arouses suspicion of deceit and the outcome of what employees experience in practice is very different.

Discourse ethics

Discourse ethics is a normative moral theory which attempts to operationalise stakeholding by providing a framework for ethical decision making and conflict management (for example see French and Allbright, 1998). It draws upon the work of Karl-Otto Apel (1989, 1990), Jurgen Habermas (1989, 1990) and other critical theorists of the Frankfurt School (for a useful overview see Kettner, 1993). Although much of the work has been developed with public policy making and debate in the public domain and also with relation to the resolution of moral problems, it also has much relevance in identifying methodologies for consensus decision making among organisational stakeholders. Discourse ethics suggests that the role of ethicists is not to provide solutions to moral problems, but rather to provide a practical process and procedure which is both rational and consensus enhancing, through which issues can be debated and the discourse can take place. It is thus concerned with identifying processes through which decisions can be made and it asserts the moral requirements of including in the discourse all those affected by the issue or decision, the ability to challenge and evaluate the assertions of others and willingness to open one's own stance up to questioning, the neutralisation of power differentials (no easy matter) in the debate and openness and transparency of one's aims, goals and intentions (Kettner, 1993, pp. 34–5). Kettner sums it up with a quotation from John Stuart Mill:

> The only way in which a human being can make some approach to knowing the whole of a subject is by hearing what can be said about it by persons of every variety of opinion, and studying all modes in which it can be looked at by every character of mind.

However, it is not always clear how we could get stakeholders to act in this way in their discourse. For example, if the discourse is over the issue of pay differentials, how would we get employers to suspend their superior power position. Getting employers to rescind the managerial prerogative and relinquish power is at the heart of the problem for stakeholder approaches. Where it occurs at all in HRM, such as in dispute resolution procedures, it usually also requires employee representatives, such as trade unions, to relinquish some of their power, such as in no-strike agreements. Winstanley (Chapter 11) demonstrates an attempt to operationalise the principles of discourse ethics in the identification of performance indicators for one organisation, but recognises that for much performance management and objective setting, these principles are absent.

Inclusiveness and communitarianism

It is but a short step from specifying the conditions within which rational discourse can take place to arguing that individuals are part of a community to which they have obligations as well as rights. For inclusiveness to have any chance of working as an ethical approach, a condition for its effectiveness is the existence of a community of purpose, which some suggest requires an element of commitment to job security for employees to buy in to such a model (Coupar and Stevens, 1998; Monks, 1998). Communitarianism is one philosophy that focuses on the shared values of individuals in a community of purpose. As with stakeholding, this is a philosophy for life at the individual, group, organisational and societal level. Etzioni (1995) has been one of the most influential writers on this subject and advocates approaches based on the importance of rights and obligations. He suggests that the unbridled liberal defence of freedom is a fallacy; we are all members of overlapping communities and the workplace is one such community of purpose. Unlike stakeholding, which espouses diversity of values and a plurality of interests, communities of purpose emphasise shared values, a sense of belonging and inclusiveness.

Taylor and Jones (Chapter 14) acknowledge the need for mutuality in their outline of staff charters and enumerate rights to be balanced against responsibilities. However, Heery (Chapter 10), on the new pay, suggests that the balance of rights and responsibilities has shifted significantly in management's favour, to the extent that new HR systems in this area expect employees to take more of the risk and responsibility in the employment relationship. Likewise, part of the implicit contract in the long hours culture discussed by Simpson (Chapter 9) suggests there is more pressure on employees to give more in the employment relationship, a trend unlikely to be halted by new European working hours directives.

One problem with the community of interest, partnership or mutuality approach is that it focuses on harmony and consensus. The danger is that all too often the equilibrium of the community of purpose is disturbed by 'greedy' employers. This can be seen in the effort devoted to 'shaping' employee values, beliefs and corporate cultures (Woodall and Douglas, Chapter 7). Another danger is that the community could become too much of a moral community, too paternalistic and narrow in its perspective. Dickens and Liff (Chapter 5) suggest that at least two approaches to equal opportunities encompass diversity and alternative values and therefore a community of purpose view would need to reflect on how values of diversity and difference could be allowed to flourish rather than perish.

Ethics of care

Most of the preceding debate rests upon the primacy accorded to intellectual reason – feelings, intuitions and senses are seen as dysfunctional to ethical judgement. Gilligan's book (1982) *In a Different Voice* and her later work

(Gilligan, 1987) have highlighted in her ethical framework more subjective and intuitive approaches to ethical problem solving. She reasserts the role of feelings and empathy in ethical reasoning and takes us back to a more humanitarian basis for managing HRM. Unlike the formalistic theories of justice, deontology and consequentialism, she argues that the 'care' orientation rejects impartiality and believes that moral judgements should be sensitive to the needs of the situation and of other individuals. For Gilligan moral reasoning involves empathy and concern, emphasising responsiveness and responsibility in our relationships with others, where moral choices are made in relationship with others, not in isolation (Carse, 1996). Gilligan argues:

> As a framework for moral decision, care is grounded in the assumption that... detachment, whether from self or from others is morally problematic, since it breeds moral blindness or indifference – a failure to discern or respond to need. (Gilligan, 1987, p. 24)

Carse suggests that being impartial makes it difficult to imagine oneself in the other's position and thus adequately to understand the other's perspective or needs (Carse, 1996, p. 86).

Gilligan's approach arose out of research into the ethical reasoning processes used by women, whom she found more likely to adopt the 'care' approach. Aside from the issues raised by the gendered nature of much ethical debate, the ethics of care reasoning has much relevance to human resource management. Its incorporation of the role of feelings and emotions into organisational life has resonance with the growing literature on 'emotion in organisation' (see for example Fineman, 1993).

There is of course the danger that an ethic of care can become oppressive. We have already mentioned the strong welfare component in much personnel management, although diluted in some respects in contemporary human resource management. Warren's paper (1998) at the second of our conferences outlined paternalism as one alternative to the lack of care associated with contractarianism in management thinking. However, he highlighted some of the shortfalls of paternalism with its dominant parent–child metaphorical relationship, where employers take responsibility for decision making and safeguard their own interests. The lack of empowerment, autonomy and openness that can result can be detrimental to employees and raise questions about ethicality. Gilligan's outline of an ethics of care framework is very different from the paternalist and welfarist model of HRM that has dogged the care ethic in HRM over many years and moves a long way from seeing people as 'human resources'. Doherty and Tyson (Chapter 6), Woodall and Douglas (Chapter 7) and Winstanley (Chapter 11) go some way towards asserting this different view of the notion of care, incorporating more fully the notion of respect and empathy for the individual.

Virtue ethics

Concern with human intuition and empathy ultimately leads ethical argument to a focus upon individual characteristics and dispositions – or 'virtues' as they were called in fifth-century Greece at the time of Aristotle, the original proponent of virtue ethics. Little attention has been paid from those involved in human resource management to the resurgence of interest in the virtue ethics elsewhere. This has been heralded by Alistair MacIntyre's influential book on 'after virtue' (1985) and the work of Robert Solomon on virtue ethics and excellence for business (1992, 1993).

Aristotle's theory was grounded on the Greek notion of *arete* which means both virtue and 'excellence'. For him, virtue was a disposition and, so, rather than a behaviour we pick up and shed at will, it arises from a deeper state of being, with the requirement to 'lead the good life'. There is also a teleological aspect of aiming for 'the golden mean', an optimum amount rather than excess in all things. Implicit in this view is some notion of congruence: what we are exists both at home and at work. However, the reality of many people's experience of organisations is that there is a different standard for ethical behaviour at home from that at work and also that the virtues or, in today's terms, the competences expected of us at work may be at odds with our true selves and may be required to be taken on or shed as company policy changes.

Solomon (1993, p. 206) also suggested that there is no ultimate split or antagonism between business, the public good and the individual interest – to excel is to do so as a member of the larger community, the *polis*. This is also linked to a notion of what Aristotle and the ancient Greeks called *eudaimonia* – blessedness, happiness, prosperity – rather than focusing on pecuniary and financial advantage. Although this leads back to where we began, with the assertion of Beer *et al.* (1984) of the *telos* being individual, organisational and societal well-being, there is a question as to how much this was possible due to the nature of society at the time of Aristotle and how far it is still possible as an assertion today.

Another damper in applying virtues to contemporary work organisations is that the dispositions encouraged may not always be ethically pursued. For example, Claydon (Chapter 12) discusses the abuse of virtue ethics when it has been shackled to the harness of the cult of excellence and enterprise and, as with stakeholding, it suffers from its misuse as another way to achieve work intensification and an extension of the boundaries of work into the other lives of employees. Stanworth (Chapter 8, on flexibility) highlights another such concept that has suffered the same fate.

What, however, would be the virtues that a virtuous employer and employee would exhibit today? Historically, a variety of classical models dating back to ancient Greek and Athenian society has been used. The classical, heroic and 'Homeric' virtues, found in Homeric poems recited in public ceremonies in sixth-century Athens, emphasised competitive qualities such as excellence, courage, cunning, sense of shame in wrongdoing and honour, as well as fidelity and life (MacIntyre, 1985). Interestingly, MacIntyre also mentioned congruence as a 'Homeric' virtue – where people are their actions with no hidden depths. Congruence or integrity between a person or an organisation's rhetoric and espoused values, and how their behaviour is received in practice, is an area which has been highlighted for its absence in contemporary HRM by many critical writers (see for example Legge, 1995a, 1995b). However, not all organisations who propound ethical values lack congruence between the espoused values and the practice. Fidelity by organisations has also been marked by its absence, in the rise of literature on broken psychological contracts and the removal of job security. Alternatively, Athenian democracy is said to highlight more co-operative virtues such as justice, order, friendship, self-restraint, wisdom (see MacIntyre, 1985). As with the concept of leadership and competences, it becomes easy to generate list after list of competing qualities, with little consensus and agreement on what should be on the list and a lack of evidence to justify the choice. As a starting point, the virtues need to be embedded in the contemporary social, economic and political context.

Solomon (1992, 1993) draws on Aristotelian accounts of virtue to present a contemporary view of virtues for ethics in business. He identifies six: 'community, excellence, role identity, holism, integrity and judgement'. 'Community' is chosen because individuals are socially constituted and socially situated and whether we do well and lead happy and productive lives largely depends on the organisations of which we are a part. 'Excellence' relates to doing one's best and 'role identity' situates this within the duties and obligations of one's role at work. 'Holism' suggests the congruence mentioned earlier, with 'good employees' being 'good people'. 'Integrity' and 'judgement' are called for because of the difficulties of addressing rival loyalties in organisational life. Virtues in one arena may inevitably conflict with those in another, so that we may not make 'the right decision but rather make the decision in the right way, with good judgement and sensitivity' (Solomon, 1993, p. 216). Solomon's virtues clearly need elaboration and debate and there is also the question for this book of about whom we are talking. Are these virtues addressed to the members of organisations in general or should the debate here focus on those for human resource specialists and professionals? The discussion which takes place in the concluding chapter raises issues of how far the virtues and ethics of human resource professionals should be embodied in codes of practice.

There is a fair amount of mixing of models and conceptual confusion and overlap between ethical frameworks. If we turn to virtue ethics, we find that many of the principles being espoused in rights, justice, stakeholding and duty of care frameworks could equally be rephrased as individual or organisational 'virtues'.

Both Spence on selection interviewing (Chapter 3) and Winstanley on performance management (Chapter 11) outline the fundamental requirement for transparency in decision making and in the ethical stances taken. Paradoxically, even in ethical frameworks as far apart as stakeholding and ethical egoism, there does seem to be a virtue in ensuring that the fundamental needs of employees are met and that organisations can achieve some 'virtue' in attempting to solicit and address these needs. Communitarianism emphasises the virtues of inclusiveness and community, stakeholding that of involvement and participation in decision making. Care ethics emphasises the virtues of empathy and attachment and the rights frameworks throw up many more. Certainly there is much room for greater discussion on 'virtues' in human resource management.

Summary

This chapter has attempted to trace the origins of ethical interest in human resource management. It has been suggested that although there has been a history of work in this area, there needs to be a reorientation of work to take account of contemporary developments, both in human resource management practice and in the availability of ethical theories to explore these. It has also been asserted that the changing nature of contemporary HRM itself has paradoxically taken the focus away from ethics, towards issues such as strategy and effectiveness, while at the same time creating the conditions which make ethical exploration more urgent, as new ethical concerns and dilemmas emerge. An overview of relevant ethical theory and frameworks has been presented and, in ensuing chapters, these are used to elucidate the ethical dimensions in current HR practice. The concluding chapter of the book returns to discuss the question as to how far ethical action is desirable and possible.

Much of what is written in this book reasserts the humanistic view of the organisation. Many of the ethical problems raised here on the treatment of employees in work organisations derive from an overly contingent view of employees as 'human resources'. Although we recognise the dangers of a humanistic model in emphasising individual goals and unconstrained choice, relative to socio-political and economic determinism, we suggest that literature on human resource management has overly concentrated on the 'resources' aspect, to the detriment of the 'human', on objective rather than subjective relations and on what individuals can do for the organisation, rather than what the organisation can do for them. The language of management has illegitimised even the mention of words such as ethics and morality in the cult of business and we hope to get these words at least acknowledged as worthy of debate and inclusion in the management vocabulary.

References

Apel, K.-O. (1989) 'Normative Ethics and Strategic Rationality. The philosophical problem of political ethics' in Schurmann, R. (ed.) *The Public Realm, Essays on Discursive Types in Political Philosophy*, New York: State of New York Press, pp. 107–31

Apel, K.-O. (1990) 'Is Ethics of the Ideal Communication Community a Utopia?' in Benhabib, S. and Dallmayr, F. (eds) *The Communicative Ethics Controversy*, Cambridge, MA: MIT Press

Arkin, A. (1996) 'Open Business is Good for Business' *People Management*, 2(1): 24–7

Beauchamp, T.L. and Bowie, N.E. (1983) *Ethical Theory and Business* (2nd edn), New Jersey: Prentice Hall

Beer, M., Spector, B., Lawrence, P., Mills, Q. and Walton, R. (1984) *Managing Human Assets*, New York: Free Press

Carse, A. (1996) 'Facing Up To Moral Perils: the virtues of care in bioethics' in Gordon, S., Benner, P. and Noddings, N. (eds) *Caregiving: Readings in Knowledge, Practice, Ethics and Politics*, Philadelphia: University of Pennsylvania Press

Connock, S. and Johns, T. (1995) *Ethical Leadership*, London: IPD

Coupar, W. and Stevens, B. (1998) 'Towards a New Model of Industrial Partnership: beyond the "HRM versus industrial relations" Argument' in Sparrow, P. and Marchington, M. *Human Resource Management: The New Agenda*, London: Financial Times/Pitman Publishing, pp. 145–59

Etzioni, A. (ed.) (1995) *New Communitarian Thinking: Persons, Virtues, Institutions and Communities*, Virginia: University Press of Virginia

Fineman, S. (ed.) (1993) *Emotions in Organisations*, London: Sage

Freeman, E. (1984) *Strategic Management: A Stakeholder Approach*, London: Pitman

French, W. and Allbright, D. (1998) 'Resolving a Moral Conflict through Discourse' *Journal of Business Ethics*, 17:177–94

Friedman, M. (1962) *Capitalism and Freedom*, Chicago: University of Chicago Press

Gilligan, C. (1982) *In a Different Voice: Psychological Theory and Women's Development*, Cambridge, MA: Harvard University Press

Gilligan, C. (1987) 'Moral Orientation and Moral Development' in Kittay, E. F. and Meyers, D. T. *Women and Moral Theory*, Totowa, NJ: Rowman and Littlefield

Guest, D. (1996) 'Human Resource Management, Fit and Performance'. Paper presented at the ESRC/BUIRA Seminar Series on 'The Contribution of HR Strategy to Business Performance', Cranfield School of Management

Habermas, J. (1989) *Moral Consciousness and Communicative Action*, Cambridge, MA: MIT Press

Habermas, J. (1990) 'Discourse Ethics; Notes on a Program of Justification' in Benhabib, S. and Dallmayr, F. (eds), *The Communicative Ethics Controversy*, Cambridge, MA: MIT Press, pp. 60–110

Herzberg, F. (1968) 'One More Time: How Do You Motivate Employees?' *Harvard Business Review*, 46(1): 53–62

Hutton, W. (1995) *The State We Are In*, London: Jonathan Cape/Random House

Johns, T. (1995) 'Don't Be Afraid of the Moral Maze' *People Management*, 1(20): 32–5

Kelly G., Kelly, D. and Gamble, A. (eds) (1997) *Stakeholder Capitalism*, Basingstoke: Macmillan

Kettner, M. (1993) 'Scientific Knowledge, Discouse Ethics, and Consensus Formation in the Public Domain' in Winkler, E. and Coombs, J. (eds) *Applied Ethics: A Reader*, Oxford: Blackwell

Legge, K. (1995a) *Human Resource Management: Rhetorics and Realities*, Basingstoke: Macmillan

Legge, K. (1995b) 'HRM: Rhetoric, Reality and Hidden Agendas' in Storey, J. (ed.) *Human Resource Management: A Critical Text*, London: Routledge, pp. 33–62

Legge, K. (1998a) 'The Morality of HRM' in Mabey, C., Salaman, G. and Storey, J. (eds) *Strategic HRM: A Reader*, London: Open University Press/Sage, pp. 18–29

Legge, K. (1998b) 'The Morality of HRM' in Mabey, C., Skinner, D. and Clarke, T. (eds) *Experiencing HRM*, London: Sage

MacIntyre, A. (1985) *After Virtue: a Study in Moral Theory* (2nd edn), London: Duckworth

Maclagan, P. (1998) *Management and Morality: A Developmental Perspective*, London: Sage

Maslow, A. (1987) *Motivation and Personality* (3rd edn), New York: Harper & Row

Mayo, E. (1933) *The Human Problems of an Industrial Civilisation*, New York: Macmillan

Miller, P. (1996a) 'Strategy and The Ethical Management of Human Resources', *Human Resource Management Journal*, 6(1): 5–26

Miller, P. (1996b) 'Ethics, Strategy and Human Resource Management: Delivering Value to the Employee', in Towers, B. (ed.) *The Handbook of Human Resource Management* (2nd edn), Oxford: Blackwell, pp. 155–72

Monks, J. (1998) 'Trade Unions, Enterprise and the Future' in Sparrow, P. and Marchington, M. *Human Resource Management: The New Agenda*, London: Financial Times/Pitman Publishing, pp. 171–8

Paton, H.J. (1948) *The Moral Law*, London: Hutchinson

Petrick, J.A. and Quinn, J.F. (1997) Management Ethics: Integrity at Work, London: Sage

Pickard, J. (1995), 'Prepare to Make a Moral Judgement' *People Management*, 1(9): 22–5

Purcell, J. (1996) 'Human Resource Bundles of Best Practice: A Utopian Cul-de-sac?' Paper presented at the ESRC/BUIRA Seminar Series on 'The Contribution of HR Strategy to Business Performance', Cranfield School of Management

Rawls, J. (1971) *A Theory of Justice*, Cambridge MA: Harvard University Press

RSA (1995) *Tomorrow's Company: The Role of Business in a Changing World*, otherwise known as the 'Tomorrow's Company Report', London: Royal Society for Arts (Centre for Tomorrow's Company)

Solomon, R.C. (1992) *Ethics and Excellence: Cooperation and Integrity*, New York and Oxford: Oxford University Press

Solomon, R.C. (1993) 'Corporate Roles, Personal Virtues: An Aristotelian Approach to Business Ethics' in Winkler, E. and Coombs, J. (eds) *Applied Ethics: A Reader*, Oxford: Blackwell

Sternberg, E. (1994) *Just Business: Business Ethics in Action*, London: Little, Brown and Warner Books

Sternberg, E. (1997) 'The Defects of Stakeholder' Theory' *Corporate Governance: An International Review*, 5(1): 3–10

Tyson, S. (ed.) (1998) *The Practice of Human Resource Strategy*, London: Pitman

Warren, R. (1998) 'Between Contract and Paternalism: HRM in the Community of Purpose'. Paper presented at the 2nd UK Conference on 'Ethical Issues in Contemporary HRM', Kingston Business School, January

Wehrmeyer, W. (1996) 'Green Policies Can Help to Bear Fruit' *People Management*, **2**(4): 38–40

Wheeler, D. and Sillanpää, M. (1997) *The Stakeholder Corporation: A Blueprint for Maximising Stakeholder Value*, London: Pitman

Wilson, A. (1997) 'Business and its Social Responsibility' in Davies, P. (ed.) *Current Issues in Business Ethics*, London: Routledge

Winstanley, D. and Stoney, C. (1997) 'Stakeholder Management: A Critique and a Defense'. Paper given at 15th International Annual Labour Process Conference, University of Edinburgh, Scotland, 26–28 March

CHAPTER 2

The ethical context of HRM: the ethical organisation in the boundaryless world

Karen Legge

Introduction

This chapter examines postmodern trends in work organisations and takes an agnostic view of ethics, largely on the grounds that the trends identified broadly undermine the ethical treatment of people in the workplace. These trends also call into question any certainty about what ethical treatment might constitute.

These trends are partly reflective of an acceleration of those characteristic of modernism: an intensification of competition arising out of the contradictions of capitalism and strategies of amelioration that involve spatial displacement or the internationalisation of trade. They also involve an obsession with performativity, now termed 'a search for competitive advantage'; and an embracing of technologies, such as information and communication technologies (ICTs) that accelerate time–space compression; the final triumph of materialism in the promotion of 'customer sovereignty'. At the same time, the cultural, indeed the epistemological dimension of postmodernism, celebrates diversity and relativism (Harvey, 1989). Although this may serve to undermine the homogenising confidence of western globalising tendencies, its very commitment to relativism and deconstruction gives little basis for the assertion of ethical foundations to action.

The chapter identifies four important points with relation to understanding the limitations and possibilities for the ethical treatment of workers within the global marketplace.

First, a number of obstacles specific to the ethical control of employment practice are outlined in relation to the processes of globalisation itself. Issues related to international differentiation of the labour market, the potential mobility of foreign client investment, employment generation in the service sector and, particularly, in seasonal, temporary and part-time jobs and the development of flexible organisational forms and the 'virtual organisation', all give rise to difficulties in promoting and regulating ethical practice. Utilising a vignette of the football stitching industry these difficulties are traced, along with an exploration of the power of 'customer sovereignty' on the one hand to create unethical practice and, on the other, potentially to counter it.

Second, it is proposed that from an ethical universalism perspective organisations should fully consider the consequences of their actions through the whole supplier chain and embrace the principles of 'do unto others as you would be done by', emphasising the notion of human agency and the intention to act ethically.

Third, transcultural relativism, itself a form of act utilitarianism, leads to a questioning of what ethical practice may be. The fundamental paradox presented is that, given the relativism of postmodernism and its celebration of difference, how can it be possible to gain agreement over what counts as ethical treatment? In essence, postmodernism itself questions the validity of this endeavour.

Finally, the problems of ethical practice in a globalised work environment are exacerbated when we examine more specifically the features of 'good practice' HRM. It is suggested that it has in-built tendencies towards exploitation, particularly in relation to the use of core and periphery workforces, temporary working, casualisation and 'performativity'.

The boundaryless organisation thus makes the identification of human agency and the promotion of ethical practice an epistemological conundrum and a practical minefield. The implications for the agenda of this book are very serious and raises limits on the likely success of those chapters proposing various forms of ethical intervention.

EXHIBIT 2.1

CHILD LABOUR IN THE STITCHING OF FOOTBALLS

The following vignette is used to illustrate how postmodern trends may impact on the ethical content of HRM. It summarises material from a news report by Julian West entitled 'Children Still Sweat Over World Cup Balls' (*Sunday Telegraph*, 10 May 1998, p. 3). The report states that despite a two-year agreement to end child labour, Pakistani youngsters continue to make footballs for international firms. The story goes roughly like this:

Between 5000 and 7000 children are believed to work in the football manufacturing industry in Sialkot, an army town near the Kashmir border, which supplies about 80 per cent of the world's footballs to international companies such as Nike, Reebok and Adidas. Although the world's big football manufacturers agreed that no child labour would be used in the manufacture of their footballs by March 1999, and the phasing out began in October 1997, by the time the World Cup began, only 25 per cent of the footballs were guaranteed to have been produced by adult workers.

A few large manufacturers built special stitching centres which do not employ children. But about 80 per cent of the work is still subcontracted to outlying villages. They are so many and so difficult to monitor that no one is certain how many children are employed. Child welfare agencies, including Britain's Save the Children Fund (SCF) have so far surveyed only 173 of more than 1000 villages involved. Fawad Usman Sudar, who works with SCF said: 'After the crackdown they moved workshops into the back alleys, and companies running stitching centres are now very wary of inquiries. The fact is children are still working at home – we don't know how many.'

The report goes on to say that most children work alongside their parents, to supplement the family income and pay for their school fees, as only primary education is free in Pakistan and Muslim welfare schemes rarely filter down to the poor. 'But some of them are orphans or primary school dropouts working full-time: many are barely old enough to handle the thick hexagons of plastic cloth, course waxed thread and complicated stitches which go into the making of match grade footballs.'

The report adds that a skilled stitcher can expect to make 60p for a ball that will fetch 20 times that much in Europe. The most expert adult worker cannot make more than five balls a day. However, the workers are paid for each football stitched and children receive the same pay as adults, so there is little reason for large manufacturers to flout the ban. However, child labour is commonplace in the sub-continent, and there is likely to be pressure from families affected by a substantial loss of income, and subcontractors, to re-employ children.

Agencies feared that unless adequate credit and employment schemes were in place by March 1999, children may either return to stitching footballs or turn to more hazardous jobs in Sialkot's tanneries and surgical instrument factories.

'Above all, we don't want to see children going into worse work or even prostitution,' said David Husslebee of Save the Children Fund.

Globalisation, competitive advantage and consumer sovereignty

It is a cliché that we now all live in a 'global village', as Marshall McLuhan put it in the 1960s (McLuhan, 1967 and 1973, first published 1966). The image of a village is a reassuring one, of intimacy with neighbours and a common language. And, to some extent, this is true – there is increasingly a common language of consumerism. As one of the child footballer stitchers put it, 'I don't play with the footballs I make. I just work. But I'd love to watch a match on television. I want to see the footballs stitched by me being used in the matches. It makes me feel proud.' Here indeed is the vicarious enjoyment of the media and leisure, two essential elements in the process of globalisation. Globalisation may be defined as the 'intensification of worldwide social relations which link distant localities in such a way that local happenings are shaped by events occurring many miles away and vice versa' (Giddens, 1990, p. 64). Thus, in this example, events that took place in France in 1998 are affecting a town and villages in Pakistan, but non-governmental organisations (NGOs) campaigning in these villages are reciprocally affecting the behaviour of international companies through the conduit of international media. And this reciprocity extends to products and services. The homogenising effect of world brands such as Coca-Cola, Levi's, McDonald's, Disneyland and Microsoft are counteracted by a hybridising effect as consumers in the West, partly as a result of tourism and immigration, experiment with new foods, wines and lifestyles. The manufacture and service of 'Indian' food is now a bigger industry (in both employment and financial terms) than the steel industry in the UK and drugs-trafficking, from production in the Third World to marketing and consumption in the First, is the fastest growing industry on earth. But this reciprocity between peoples and different cultures raises the question: does this mean that as globalisation intensifies we can negotiate generally accepted ethical parameters or are cultural divisions too deep? Or, will we arrive at a *modus vivendi* that suits all parties, but, in reflecting the unacceptable face of capitalism, can hardly be called ethical?

The ethical issues become even more problematic when we consider both the impetus for and facilitators of the internationalisation of trade. The search for competitive advantage, in the context of the breakdown of the Keynesian settlement and the consequent deregulation of financial markets, at the level of the nation state, has led to a global division of labour and socio-politico-cultural effects which have been characterised in terms of 'disorganised capitalism' (Lash and Urry, 1987). In other words, a global division of labour is emerging, not at the level of job tasks, but in regional specialisations in terms of industry, skills and production of raw materials (Giddens, 1990, p. 76). The extraction and realisation of surplus value by globalised capitalism stimulates the development of a world economic order. On the one hand we have Third World countries specialising as providers of cheap labour and commodities (our football stitchers in Exhibit 2.1 being an example of cheap labour), and, on the other, countries within the First World developing the skills that enable the production of high value-added goods and services. Sophisticated differentiation occurs within these broad categories: note the alarm in erstwhile First World countries, such as the UK, at the rise of a super league of industrial powers, for example, USA, Germany and Japan, and their subsequent fear of relegation to the ranks of a 'screwdriver' economy. Note, too, the even greater alarm among workers in such 'screwdriver' factories when news reports highlight the potential mobility of the foreign direct investment on which they depend. As I was writing this, Nissan Europe's president, Norio Matsumara, stated in an interview with the Economist Intelligence Unit's Motor Business Europe:

> If the current strength of sterling continued, then clearly we would have to think about investment elsewhere in the future – we are in the process of selecting suppliers for Almera production and clearly the current exchange rate is influencing the process. (Segall, 1998, p. 27)

'Disorganised capitalism' carries other connotations – of 'winners' as well as 'losers'. In the First World, with the shift away from labour-intensive manufacturing to the service sector, there has been a decline in traditional class consciousness and loyalties, a decline in the nation state and the 'death' of the inner cities. Compensationally, there has been the rise of two distinctive classes of globally oriented knowledge workers – 'symbolic analysts' (Reich, 1991) and the 'transnational organisation man' [sic] (Ohmae, 1989) in information-thirsty industries, often media based. The 'symbolic analysts' are globally oriented in that their highly valued skills, in theory at least, are autonomous of fixed organisational or national perspectives, for example, a Stephen Spielberg or a Richard Rogers. The 'transnational organisational man' is globally oriented in that he or she is mobile between the multiple locations of a transnational corporation, possessing skills that are at a premium in relation to that corporation and, hence, whose sense of identity and solidarity is bound up with the life of that corporation rather than with any national or regional identities, for example, the managerial cadre of a BP, Coca-Cola or Ford.

The rise of knowledge workers in this vision of global, 'disorganised capitalism' reflects the crucial role of information and communication technologies (ICTs) in facilitating the process. Globalisation of social, cultural and economic institutions and values rests on the annihilation of space by time. All globalisation depends on the rapid and simultaneous access to pooled information on the part of individuals widely separated from each other (Giddens, 1990, p. 78). What is new is not so much that international trade is an important part of each nation's economy (cf. Hirst and Thompson, 1996) but that national economies now work as units at the world scale in real time (Carnoy *et al.*, 1993). The Football World Cup would not generate the demand for millions of footballs if there were no real-time TV reportage and media hyping of the event. ICTs allow instantaneous electronic/communication transactions with the accelerated distribution of physical goods through just-in-time delivery systems, themselves heavily dependent on ICTs. ICTs lie at the heart of ideas about lean production and business process re-engineering and facilitate Panopticon-like surveillance of producers and consumers alike. ICTs are now a taken-for-granted tool in keeping up with the competition, let alone in securing competitive advantage (as most players with similar resources will have similar ICT systems).

A knowledge/media-based service sector is increasingly relevant to globalisation in the context of customer sovereignty. Consumers in a global marketplace want world products, so long as they are customised in line with their cultural preferences. Competition between regions and cities is not just for inward investment in 'screwdriver' manufacturing plants. It is also in the media/leisure industries of the postmodern world: for 'world' events such as the Olympic Games, or World Cup Football; for knowledge dissemination events such as the international conference business and prestigious cultural events; and for Disneyworld-type theme parks. In summary, competition exists for the tourist and entertainment dollar. In Spain, for example, consider the promotion of Barcelona as Cultural Capital of Europe and home to the 1992 Olympics. Similarly, the new Guggenheim museum in Bilbao is being promoted as a magnet for tourism with 2.5 million visitors in its first six months after opening. It is also seen as a means of regenerating a depressed industrial area.

However, a point to note is that much of the employment generated by such investment in the service sector is in either seasonal, temporary, or part-time jobs and what Reich (1991) would term involving low-skill, in-person services. The sex tourism of Thailand and the Philippines, where First World tourists exploit the poor and vulnerable of the Third World, is the most shameful example of a flexible, deregulated (save for criminal regulation) labour market and labour process. Yet it also typifies entrepreneurial responsiveness to consumer demand and sovereignty.

Finally, these interrelated postmodern trends of globalisation, the rise of media-based industries and knowledge working, of the use of ever more sophisticated ICTs, the search for competitive advantage and the acknowledgement of customer sovereignty, both precipitate and facilitate the development of flexible organisational forms (Drucker, 1988; Kanter, 1989). ICTs are central to business process re-engineering. Here the logic is to cut out anything within the organisation or along its supply chain that does not add value, as, in theory at least, they lie at the heart of the redesign of work processes to achieve market responsiveness while substantially reducing costs. This is believed to be one route to competitive advantage. In theory, it means a move from function-centred to process-oriented organisational forms and practices;

from linear/sequential work organisation towards parallel processing and multi-disciplinary teamworking; towards integrating previously fragmented tasks so that fewer people take less time to perform the process in question. It also allows decentralisation at the operating level with a centralisation of control. If the inevitable corollaries are massive downsizing and delayering, in theory at least, the up-side is contained in a rhetoric of responsiveness and flexibility (customer sovereignty and the elimination of bureaucracy) and empowerment (Willmott, 1994, 1995; Grey and Mitev, 1995).

The links between customer sovereignty, competitive advantage and flexible organisational forms are also apparent in arguments about organisations' core competences or distinctive capabilities. Following Kay (1993), organisational success may be measured in terms of an organisation's ability to add value to its inputs, particularly in the light of the intensification of competition due to globalisation. This is achieved, so the argument goes, through developing distinctive capabilities, such as reputation or innovation, often derived from the unique character of the organisation's relationships with its suppliers, customers or employees, precisely identified and aimed at relevant markets.

One distinctive capability identified is the 'architecture' of supplier and employee relations, that is, the development of appropriate relational forms, be it trust in interpersonal relations, or involving subcontracting or networking organisational forms (which may depend on trust or contract). Similarly, if an organisation's core competences relate to employee know-how that cannot just be bought in, but represents job and organisational knowledge that is unique to the organisation, can only be learned inside and is only valuable to the firm itself (cf. Ohmae's 'transnational organisational man' – or woman) or know-how that might be transferable but is difficult to secure and retain (cf. Reich's 'symbolic analysts'), an appropriate cost effective organisational form might be a minimalist organisation supported by a network of subcontractors (outsourcing) and contract labour agencies (insourcing). In other words, these characteristics of the postmodern world are giving rise to the 'virtual organisation' (Handy, 1994), where it may no longer be possible to define an organisation just by reference to those it employs permanently.

So what implications does this boundaryless world have for the ethical management of people at work? And, in the postmodern world of relativism and deconstruction, can we establish any consensus on ethical criteria for HRM?

The morality of child football stitching

The foregoing analysis raises the issue that, if an organisation is concerned to act in an ethical manner (and many do so, even if only for the pragmatic reasons of image and reputation with potential shareholders, employees, customers and suppliers), then ethical considerations cannot be limited to within the organisation's own legal boundaries, but must embrace its whole supply chain. In a world of increasingly international trade and faster, more public, communication, this will involve concern for the child football stitchers who (see Exhibit 2.1), while not direct employees, are implicated in the supply chain.

There is evidence that organisations are aware of the negative image a lack of concern can present, hence, in the football stitching case, the efforts of major companies to ban the use of child labour. And this is not an isolated case. It was reported in May 1998, that after talks with CAFOD (the UK Roman Catholic aid agency), Clarks, the UK's second largest shoe retailer and by tradition a Quaker family-run company, well known for its paternalistic, welfare-oriented management style, had agreed to introduce an independently verified code of conduct for its Third World suppliers. It is also to join the Ethical Trading Initiative, a new grouping of retailers (such as Boots and Sainsbury, again companies well known for their history of benevolent paternalism), aid agencies, trades unions and the UK Government. Clarks is working on developing methods for monitoring Third World suppliers' labour standards. Further, the growing popularity and good performance of ethical investment and unit trusts is frequently reported in the financial press.

But just how ethical are these behaviours? To return to the football stitching example, it would be somewhat naive to believe that the international companies are motivated by the Kantian ideal of the necessity to treat people with respect and as ends in their own right, not solely as means to others' ends. If this were the case, one would have expected the companies either to have used some of their vast profits to invest in schools for the children or to have offered higher wages for the labour employed (as organisations such as 'Traidcraft', allied to aid agencies, advocate and enact). Footballs sell in Europe at 20 times the cost of direct labour. Clearly too, the contracting companies appear unmoved by stakeholder ethics. In their alliance with the retailers, it is not only the football stitchers that are exploited, but also the gullible customers.

However, the international companies could conceivably make a case for their actions in terms of teleological ethical theories. Utilitarianism, by justifying actions in terms of their consequences, and 'the greatest good to the greatest number', does allow for people to be used as means to ends, if it is to the advantage of the majority. At first sight this may appear to undermine rather than support the companies' case. Surely it is the minority (that is the shareholders) who benefit most from the use of cheap Third World labour, not the majority, the workers themselves and the equally ripped off customers? A response might be that, from a Kantian perspective, we must treat the customers as autonomous beings capable of making rational choices, who freely choose to buy footballs at the price the market will bear. We might, of course, question this 'freedom', given large companies' manipulation via the media of our tastes and preferences or, in this case, of our children's insatiable demand for peer-approved fashion items. Further, from a utilitarian perspective, the Third World football stitchers (whether adults or children) are better off due to First World investment than they would be without it, given the alternatives of either no paid work or harder, more dangerous work (in the tanneries or surgical instruments factories) or dangerous and degrading work (prostitution). It could also be argued that if the international companies had to pay wages approaching those of the First World there would be no incentive for them to bring such work to the Third World. In addition, paying First World wages would have an extremely deleterious effect on the local economy.

Taking the spirit of Aristotelian teleology, that ethics should be based on the achievement of human beings' mental, moral and social potential, as part of a broader social community, it might even be argued (somewhat speciously, in my view) that the money the children earn contributes not only to their education and, therefore, to their mental development, but also to their moral development. This would occur through the contribution their work makes to the survival of their family, particularly to even younger and older family members who may be unable to earn.

Even if we can justify the treatment of the football stitchers in terms of teleological ethical theories, although the arguments are somewhat strained, there is another difficulty. The part played by large western companies in the Third World is arguably a form of economic imperialism. While it may be appropriate to evaluate such organisations' actions in terms of western ethical theory, insofar as they are western companies, to judge the behaviours of Third World subcontractors in these terms could be argued to be a form of ethical imperialism, a twenty-first-century variant on missionary work. This is implied in Clarks' attempt to introduce a code of conduct on labour standards for its Third World suppliers. Certainly, if one takes an ethical position of transcultural relativism:

> one would hold that judgements of right and wrong are culturally determined and that transcultural judgements make no more sense in questions of morality than they do in judgements about whether one language is better than another. (de George, 1995, p. 42)

The counter argument to this, of course, from a Judeo-Christian tradition, is the absolutist view that moral judgement applies to all members of the moral community and that, if the moral community includes all human beings, then the moral judgement of an action extends to all. If all people are my brothers and sisters, then I am my brothers' and sisters' keeper. Rather than ethical imperialism, what is being practised is ethical universalism.

In the spirit of such ethical universalism we might propose two criteria for an ethical approach to HRM along a supply chain that may embrace subcontracted and agency workers, who are not employed by the ethical organisation, as well as its core employees. These are:

1. In our actions towards all organisational stakeholders, we should accept the moral obligation to consider fully the consequences of our actions, particularly towards those who appear to bear the costs rather than the benefits. Also to resist the exclusionary and sometimes exploitative dictates of an instrumental, technical rationality.
2. To embrace the values of a Judeo-Christian tradition, not a million miles away from Rawlsian ethics or even Aristotelianism, that ' I am my brothers' and sisters' keeper' and 'Do as you would be done by'. With utilitarian overtones, this may be accepted, not in a Kantian sense, but as sound business principles for the building of long-term, mutually beneficial relational contracts (Kay, 1993) or of reciprocal high trust relationships (Fox, 1974).

What evidence do we have that such criteria for an ethical approach to managing people at work are being enacted in our boundaryless world?

Three scenarios: the good, the bad and the ugly

In western terms at least, there is a widespread assumption that 'High Commitment Management' (HCM) bundles of practices represent 'best practice' HRM and, by inference, an ethical way of managing people at work (see Guest, 1996; Huselid, 1995; Legge, 1998; MacDuffie, 1995; Purcell, 1996; Walton, 1985; Whitfield and Poole, 1997; Wood, 1996; Wood and Albanese, 1995). These practices embrace:

- Careful recruitment and selection, with an emphasis on traits and competency
- Extensive use of systems of communication
- Teamworking with flexible job design
- Emphasis on training and learning
- Involvement in decision making with responsibility
- Performance appraisal linked to reward systems.

But, as Purcell has pointed out, it is improbable that 'best practice' can be universally applied: 'Would every firm adopting HCM for all its employees survive and prosper in markets frequently marked by over capacity (Schoenberger, 1997) with very short-run pressures on costs?'(Purcell, 1997, p. 5; see also Purcell, 1996). Rather, he suggests, HCM is applicable only in very distinct sets of circumstances and is liable to be focused on a relatively small number of workplaces and, within them, on core employees. Here, employee discretion is crucial to the delivery of added value and reciprocal high trust relations are essential to organisational performance. These are the knowledge workers who possess either job or organisational knowledge that is unique to the organisation. It can only be learned inside and is only valuable to the firm itself. Alternatively, the knowledge might be transferable but is difficult to secure and retain. This may include not only that of the professional and managerial élites identified as 'transnational organisational man' (Ohmae, 1989) or 'symbolic analysts' (Reich, 1991), but any employee who possesses skills and knowledge that cannot easily be bought in and yet on which the organisation is highly dependent for achieving success. Thus, in lean production systems, with the time–space compression implied in speeding up the order-to-delivery cycle as well as in the JIT systems (all reflective of the intensification of competition), the very vulnerability of the system creates management dependency on the knowledge and skills of direct operatives and on their motivation to apply such skills, through discretionary effort, in managerial interests.

For such groups of employees, life may be good, involving empowerment, high rewards and some element of job security. But it is at the cost of a workaholic lifestyle for the élites and labour intensification for the direct operatives in lean production systems. In order to maintain a high-trust psychological contract, such employees cannot be treated purely as a means to an end, but must be offered rational arguments for acting in a particular way and, assuming their rationality, to leave it to them to evaluate the argument and to decide on a course of action. This is the premise on which genuine empowerment and the harnessing of discretionary effort rests.

The good life of the core knowledge workers, however, may be bought at the cost of inferior, not to say exploitative, employment conditions for what Reich (1991) terms routine production or in-person service workers, or those on the periphery of the flexible firm (Purcell, 1997). There is much evidence in the UK and in Europe, let alone in the US, where labour markets are traditionally less regulated, that temporary contracts appear to becoming increasingly attractive to large employers in a range of situations (Beatson, 1995; Brewster, 1998; Colling, 1995; Hutchinson, 1996; Purcell, 1997). It applies where jobs require little skill or where the skill is generic and easy to buy in or replace, such as with routine ICT skills such as word processing, data inputting, telesales. Or, alternatively, it applies where there is pressure to reduce headcount (for example see Geary, 1992) or to cut labour costs by employing labour on cheaper contracts.

Temporary contracts can take three forms. First, there is the case where the organisation directly employs the worker, but on a fixed and limited term contract. Such fixed-term contracts are often the only practicable option short of incurring 'unnecessary' redundancy costs in the UK public sector. Here funding may be dependent on fixed-term research grants or a limited period, renegotiable, competitive tender or subject to uncertainty or continual cutback in government funding in real terms.

Second, there is 'outsourcing'. This may take two forms: straightforward subcontracting or buying in of products, or 'facilities management', where the subcontractor takes over in-house facilities and often the staff, to provide a service (for example catering, security, transport, building maintenance) previously undertaken by the organisation. Either way, the ethical HCM policies the organisation extends towards its core employees may be predicated on driving such hard bargains with subcontractors that the latter may be pushed into treating their own employees, working for, if not employed by the purchasing (client) organisation, as a variable and minimisable cost (Blyton and Turnbull, 1994; Mitter, 1985).

Finally, there is 'insourcing', as described by the Purcells (see Purcell, 1996, 1997; Purcell and Purcell, 1996). This is where an employment agency sources people to work alongside the client organisation's existing staff. In the case of big contracts, the contract agency will place a manager on site to deal with issues of labour supply, such as absenteeism, lateness, payroll and replacement, while the client organisation remains in control of workspace allocation, allocation of work and quality.

The implications of this for the achievement of ethical HRM practices are twofold. First, large, often multinational, organisations are increasingly having their work performed, their value added, by workers who are not technically their employees, yet the quality of whose employment is an indirect outcome of the former's policies and decision making. This has worrying echoes. The longer the supply chain, the more the workers are placed contractually outside the boundaries of the organisation, the more proximity is replaced by physical, social and psychological distance, the more there is a danger that responsibility breaks down. It is also more likely that fellow human beings are transformed into objects different from ourselves for whom we feel no responsibility (cf. Bauman, 1991). How many purchasers of footballs either know about or give a second thought to the children, half a world away, who stitched them?

Second, the evidence we have from the UK (never mind from the Third World subcontractors) is that such temporary contracts generate little but second-class employment for the employee. For those holding fixed-term contracts there is the insecurity of contract renewal and the frustration that the conditions of contract renewal (awarding of research grants, school budgets, successful competitive tendering, up-turn in the economy) are largely out of the employee's hands. There are also the costs of unemployment if there is a discontinuity between contract renewal or the securing of another job/contract with another employer. In addition, those on fixed-term contracts generally have differential access to fringe benefits and employment opportunities than those on permanent full-time contracts. Finally, there is the disruption to working and personal life by frequent, often forced, moves between organisations and, possibly, geographical areas.

If such costs are evident for employees whose fixed-term contract is held with the employer of the organisation for which they work, they become magnified under conditions of outsourcing and insourcing. The whole point of subcontracting, the movement from hierarchy to market contract (Colling, 1995), is to reduce costs. In the case of insourcing, for example, Purcell and Purcell (1996) write vividly of the drawbacks. First, agency staff rarely receive the same pay, let alone fringe benefits, as the non-agency staff alongside whom they often work and at the same task. Sometimes such workers may be receiving as little as half the hourly rate. Indeed, this can present a problem for the purchaser of agency labour. Geary's (1992) study of the relationship between temporary and permanent employees working on the same tasks, reported frequent animosity between the two groups and it does not require formal knowledge of Adams' (1965) equity theory to understand why. The employer may incur a number of indirect costs from employing temporary staff, such as time-consuming intervention from supervision, taking them away from more productive tasks. This can lead to such strategies as separating temporary staff into a distinct unit and even with a distinctive uniform, to avoid problems between the two groups. Thereby, no doubt, highlighting the second-class status of this group of employees.

Second, according to Purcell and Purcell (1996), agency contracts are frequently more concerned with cost rather than with quality, hence there is often minimal investment by agency or client organisations in training. There is real pressure for continual cost reduction. A worst case scenario is where the client organisation's 'labour procurement' function itself becomes outsourced and needs to prove its worth by securing a reduction of agency charges in order to secure its own contract renewal. Further, because contracts between agencies and a client company rarely last longer than a year, the agency cannot offer its employees more than one year's contract at a time. Hence, many agency contracts of temporary work are doubly insecure. Not only can an agency employee's contract often be terminated at an hour's or a week's notice, with no fringe benefits or compensation, but the agency as employer cannot offer any type of long-term security since their commercial contract can be, and often is, terminated at the end of the contract period of one, at most, two years. Purcell and Purcell (1996) cite the example of NatWest Bank switching contract from Brook Street to Adia Alfred Marks in January 1996. The employee's 'employability' is not obviously enhanced as the insecurities that surround such contracts do not encourage the agencies, let alone the organisation in which the agency employee works, to invest in anything more than minimal training.

The ethicality of such insourcing, whether from a Kantian or stakeholder perspective must be suspect. The exploitative nature of the relationship, from the employee's perspective, is contained in the text of the overhead transparencies used in a presentation by the now Addeco Alfred Marks, suggesting the key benefits (naturally from the contracting client's perspective):

1. Enhances flexibility (turn on and off like a tap)
2. No legal or psychological contract with the individual
3. You outsource the management problems associated with non-core staff
4. Greater cost efficiency (on average 15 to 20 per cent). (cited in Purcell, 1997)

This illustrates in a nutshell the point made earlier that placing workers contractually outside the boundaries of the organisation, encourages that organisation to treat people like commodities ('turn on and off like a tap'), to wash its hands of responsibilities toward people who work for them ('no legal or psychological contract', 'outsource management problems'), all in the interests of an instrumental and technical rationality. Shades again of Bauman (1991)!

In this context, the words of an employment agency director (cited in Purcell and Purcell, 1996) point to the likely ethicality of organisations in a boundaryless world:

> There is a close relationship between E and F in the alphabet. E is for exploitation and F is for flexibility.

But there is an uglier scenario forecast for employment in the boundaryless world at the societal level. In an admittedly polemical piece, Angell (1995) forecasts a world of global corporations that pay no heed to national boundaries or regulation in their construction of profitable alliances with such local firms and regions that can provide expertise and markets, along an information superhighway. In this world, Angell argues, it will be recognised that it is the knowledge workers who are the true generators of wealth and that the underclass of the uneducated and ageing are a liability. For global companies, routine production can be automated or exported to wherever labour costs are cheapest. This will have the effect, ultimately, of wages in this sector converging worldwide to Third World levels. Similarly, low-skill in-service workers will now be expected to add far more value to the company, or face downsizing and reduced wage levels. This is already happening in the financial services, aided by ICTs.

If a nation's wealth depends on its acquisition and retention of wealth-generating knowledge workers, a taxation system that seeks to redistribute some of their wealth to a growing underclass will not be condoned, as the knowledge workers and their global companies can move to more congenial climes. Because of the political need to employ local workers, states will compete to attract global companies to partner local firms and will have little choice but to acquiesce to the will of the global companies. In a world where competition is represented as inevitable and as a good thing, state will compete against state, area against area, to attract global employers; nation states will fragment as rich areas seek to dump poor areas, as in Italy. While nations and areas will compete to attract wealth-generating knowledge workers, equally they will seek to export their own underclass and erect barriers against uneducated migrant workers from other parts of the world. All this, so Angell argues, will have deleterious effects on the survival of democracy as states themselves take on the characteristics of corporations, with concern for wealth maximisation, but diminishing commitment to equality and social justice. In such a context, will ethical HRM survive for any other than the élite of knowledge workers?

It could well be argued that although some of the trends Angell identifies are clearly apparent, this scenario is exaggerated. While undoubtedly there are important and accelerating globalising tendencies in the world today, the evidence suggests that a world run by global corporations is still some way off. For example, Hirst and Thompson (1996) provide persuasive evidence that genuinely transnational companies are relatively rare, most companies still being nationally based and trading mutinationally on the strength of a major national location of production and sales. Further, capital mobility is not producing a massive shift of investment from the advanced to the developing countries. Rather, foreign direct investment, with the exception of a small minority of newly industrialised countries (and these mainly the now wobbling Asian Tigers) is highly concentrated among advanced industrial economies, while trade, investment and financial flows are still concentrated in the triad of Europe, Japan and North America. In spite of sometimes dire threats to uproot foreign direct investment, short of major structural disincentives, most existing investment stays put because companies become entrenched in specific national markets with local dealers and suppliers. Even in the Nissan Europe example cited earlier, the threat was for the removal of continued investment rather than complete withdrawal. Hirst and Thompson, on the basis of this analysis, argue that the major economic powers thus have the capacity, especially if they co-ordinate policy, to exert powerful governance pressures over financial and other markets. Global markets, they suggest, are by no means beyond regulation and control, 'even although the current scope and objectives of economic governance are limited by the divergent interests of the great powers and economic doctrines prevalent among the élites' (Hirst and Thompson, 1996, p. 3). A big 'if', particularly when it comes to implementation, is, of course, these divergent political interests, as is only too apparent in the implementation of EU directives. However, the dangers posed for the world economy by the recent financial crises in the erstwhile 'Tiger' economies of Asia (not to mention meltdown in Russia and turbulence in Latin America) have given added impetus and legitimacy to the search for effective means of regulating at least global financial institutions.

Conclusion

There does seem to be some evidence, if perhaps rather trenchantly drawn, that an ethical HRM is more likely to be offered to core knowledge workers, employed within an organisation's boundaries, than to routine production or in-service workers, who may contribute to that organisation's profitability, but who are not directly employed by it. The major incentive for such organisations to press for ethical HRM for those who work for them, but beyond their legal boundaries, is customer power. If customers boycott footballs stitched by child labour, if such products no longer have the right politically correct image, then there is a chance that influence can be exerted. Customer boycotts can be effective, as is evidenced by Shell's behaviour over the Brent Spar incident. But here I'm left with a doubt. If it takes consumer boycotts to persuade multinational companies to act ethically, their 'morality' is not truly ethical, at least from a Kantian viewpoint, as it is motivated by self-interest. As Eliot (1969) wrote in *Murder in the Cathedral*:

> The last temptation is the greatest treason:
> To do the right deed for the wrong reason.

Further, the ethical context discussed in this chapter, the socio-politico-economic tendencies of the so-called postmodern world, cannot be divorced from the cultural-epistemological directions of postmodernism. The latter rejects the notion of fundamental truths and considers that 'truth' is created from discourses emergent from power/knowledge relationships embedded in different language communities. Thus, in an enterprise culture, the insecurities and costs of temporary, marginalised, employment may be presented as both an outcome and reinforcement of one's 'employability' and, hence, for the macro-economy, as a 'good' thing. No doubt when Hammer and Champy (1993) admitted that, as a result of BPR, there would be those that would have to 'man the lifeboats', their ethical position was one of carefully thought out utilitarianism, certainly not any Kantian position or a Rawlsian one of 'minimisation of regret' (Keeley, 1978).

The point is that the relativism of postmodernism, while through deconstruction analysis has the potential to highlight the marginalised and to celebrate difference, in practice provides no firm basis for devising any generalisable ethical code, whether in relation to HRM or any other area of activity. The end result is supportive of the status quo (Eagleton, 1996). Hence we have a paradox. The trend towards globalisation and virtual organisation, both part of a postmodern world, call for some agreement as to what counts as ethical treatment of people at work. The epistemology of postmodernism not only offers no assistance, but questions the validity of this endeavour.

References

Adams, J.S. (1965) 'Inequity in Social Exchange', in Berkowitz, L. (ed.) *Advances in Experimental Social Psychology*, Vol. 2, New York: Academic Press, pp. 267–99

Angell, I. (1995) 'Winners and losers in the information age', *LSE Magazine*, 7(1): 10–12

Bauman, Z. (1991) *Modernity and the Holocaust*, Oxford: Polity

Beatson, M. (1995) Labour Market Flexibility, Employment Department Research Paper No. 48, Sheffield: Employment Department

Blyton, P. and Turnbull, P. (1994) *The Dynamics of Employee Relations*, Basingstoke: Macmillan

Brewster, C. (1998) 'Flexible working in Europe: extent, growth and the challenge for HRM' in Sparrow, P. and Marchington, M. (eds) *Human Resource Management, The New Agenda*, London: Financial Times/Pitman Publishing, pp. 245–58

Carnoy, M., Castells, M., Cohen, S. and Cardoso, F.H. (1993) *The New Global Economy in the Information Age*, University Park, PA: Pennsylvania State University Press

Colling, T. (1995) From hierarchy to contract? Subcontracting and employment in the service economy, Warwick Papers in Industrial Relations No. 52, Industrial Relations Research Unit, University of Warwick

Drucker P. F. (1988) 'The coming of the new organization', *Harvard Business Review*, 66(1): 45–53

Eagleton, T. (1996) *The Illusions of Postmodernism*, Oxford: Polity

Eliot, T.S. (1969) *The Complete Poems and Plays of T.S. Eliot*, London: Faber and Faber, p. 258, lines 6–7 (*Murder in the Cathedral*, part 1, first published, Faber, 1935)

Fox, A. (1974) *Beyond Contract: Work, Trust and Power Relations*, London: Faber and Faber

Geary, J. (1992) 'Employment flexibility and human resource management', *Work, Employment and Society*, 6(2): 251–70

de George, R. T. (1995) *Business Ethics* (4th edn), New York: Macmillan

Giddens, A. (1990) *The Consequences of Modernity*, Oxford: Polity

Grey, C. and Mitev, N. (1995) 'Re-engineering organizations: a critical appraisal', *Personnel Review*, 24(1): 6–18

Guest, D. E. (1996) 'Human resource management, fit and performance'. Paper presented to the ESRC Seminar Series, 'Contribution of HR Strategy to Business Performance', Cranfield, 1 February

Hammer, M. and Champy, J. (1993) *Re-engineering the Corporation: A Manifesto for Business Revolution*, London: Nicholas Brealey

Handy, C. (1994) *The Empty Raincoat*, London: Hutchinson

Harvey, D. (1989) *The Condition of Postmodernity*, Oxford: Blackwell

Hirst, P. and Thompson, G. (1996) *Globalization in Question*, Oxford: Polity

Huselid, M. (1995) 'The impact of human resource management practices on turnover, productivity and corporate financial performance', *Academy of Management* 38(3): 635–72

Hutchinson, S. (1996) 'The changing nature of employment in the UK: employment flexibility'. Paper presented to the ESRC/IPD seminar on Flexibility in Employment, Manchester Metropolitan University, 27 September

Kanter, R.M. (1989) *When Giants Learn to Dance*, New York: Simon & Schuster

Kay, J. (1993) *Foundations of Corporate Success. How Business Strategies Add Value*, Oxford: Oxford University Press

Keeley, M. (1978) 'A social-justice approach to organizational evaluation' *Administrative Science Quarterly*, **23**: 273–92

Lash, S. and Urry, J. (1987) *The End of Organized Capitalism*, Oxford: Polity

Legge, K. (1998) 'Flexibility: The Gift-Wrapping of Employment Degradation?' in Sparrow, P. and Marchington M. (eds) *Human Resource Management, The New Agenda*, London: Financial Times/Pitman Publishing, pp. 286–95

MacDuffie, J.P. (1995) 'Human resource bundles and manufacturing performance: organizational logic and flexible production systems in the world auto industry', *Industrial and Labor Relations Review*, **48**(2): 197–221

McLuhan, M. (1967) *The Gutenberg Galaxy*, London: Routledge & Kegan Paul

McLuhan, M. (1973) *Understanding Media: the Extension of Man*, London: Routledge & Kegan Paul (first published 1966)

Mitter, S. (1985) 'Industrial restructuring and manufacturing homework: immigrant women in the UK clothing industry', *Capital and Class*, 27: 37–80

Ohmae, K. (1989) 'Managing in a borderless world', *Harvard Business Review*, **67**(3): 52–61

Purcell, J. (1996) 'Contingent workers and human resource strategy: rediscovering the core/periphery dimension', *Journal of Professional Human Resource Management*, 5 October, pp. 16–23

Purcell, J. (1997) 'Pulling up the drawbridge: high commitment management and the exclusive corporation'. Paper presented to the Cornell Conference, 'Research and Theory in SHRM: An Agenda for the 21st Century', October 1997

Purcell, J. and Purcell, K. (1996) 'Responding to competition: insourcing, outsourcing and the growth of contingent labour'. Paper given to the conference on 'The Globalization of Production and Regulation of Labour' University of Warwick, 12 September

Reich, R.B. (1991) *The Work of Nations*, New York: Knopf

Schoenberger, E. (1997) *The Cultural Crisis of the Firm*, Cambridge, MA: Blackwell

Segall, A. (1998) 'Tietmayer in warning over interference', *Daily Telegraph*, p. 27

Walton, R.E. (1985) 'From control to commitment in the workplace', *Harvard Business Review*, **63**(2): 76–84

Whitfield, K. and Poole, M. (1997) 'Organizing employment for high performance', *Organization Studies*, **18**(5): 745–63

Willmott, H. (1994) 'Business process re-engineering and human resource management', *Personnel Review*, **23**(3): 34–46

Willmott, H. (1995)'The odd couple?: re-engineering business processes; managing human relations', *New Technology, Work and Employment*, **10**(2): 89–98

Wood, S. (1996) 'High commitment management and payment systems', *Journal of Management Studies*, **33**(1): 53–78

Wood, S. and Albanese, M.T. (1995) 'Can we speak of high commitment management on the shopfloor?', *Journal of Management Studies*, **32**(2): 215–47

PART II

AREAS OF ETHICAL INQUIRY IN HUMAN RESOURCE MANAGEMENT

CHAPTER 3

What ethics in the employment interview?

Laura Spence

Introduction

Despite the active investigation of business ethics at an academic level since the 1960s, there remains a gap between the work of academics and the application of business ethics in the workplace. In 1993 Andrew Stark made a vociferous and widely cited attack on business ethics academics in his article 'What's the Matter with Business Ethics?' (Stark, 1993). He claims that business ethicists fail to offer concrete assistance to managers, instead occupying 'a rarefied moral high ground, removed from the real concerns and real-world problems of the vast majority of managers'. (p. 38). While Stark's article has been widely critiqued and his arguments undermined by business ethicists (see in particular Monast, 1994) his basic premise remains evident: there is still a gulf between academia and practice. Indeed, unless business ethics academics reinvent themselves as business consultants, there will always be a distinction between theoretical discussions and practical application, with some justification. This is not to say, however, that business ethicists should lose sight of the end product to which they make a contribution: practice in organisations.

Academics *can* help practitioners grapple with ethics by assisting in the clarification of the moral perspective in practices. This in turn can advance the familiar business benchmark of 'best practice', helping to define 'best practice' inclusive of ethical considerations. 'Best practice' can hence be a point of conversion for business academics and business practice. In this chapter, established notions of 'best practice' in a key area of human resource management, recruitment interviewing, are reconsidered in light of ethical analysis of empirical employment interview data.

The employment interview is often the first point of contact between the potential employee and employer representative. Raisig (1991) suggests that even those who after entering an employment procedure are not actually selected should be considered to have a relationship with the company which must be carefully handled. The interview can set the tone of the employment relationship, and represents the attitude and values of the firm and its members. What goes on in the interview is thus an indication of a firm's ethics and a process with which organisational managers, through their HR policies and practices, should actively be concerned. As a result of the investigation of ethics in employment interviewing, a revised model of 'best practice' is presented at the end of the chapter.

Some notions of 'best practice' in the employment interview

The employment interview remains the most widely used selection tool (Anderson and Shackleton, 1993, p. 15; Kumra and Beech, 1994). Different types of interview are used, the one-to-one, the sequential interview, the panel interview and group interviews depending on the needs, customs and time constraints of the employing organisation (for discussion see Anderson and Shackleton, 1993, pp. 74–6; Langtry, 1994, pp. 232–3; Torrington and Hall, 1987, pp. 255–8). In this case, we are concerned with the one-to-one interview as the most used interview form, especially as the likely first point of face-to-face contact between candidate and company representative.

Within the one-to-one interview itself, different practices may be employed. Bingham (1988, pp. 150–2) identifies the following forms of interviewing and why they might be used:

1. Stress interviews which use aggression to pressurise the candidate. This may be adopted where it reflects the tough company environment, to test speed of reactions, sensitivity and to break through to the 'real' nature of the candidate.
2. Unstructured interviews are characterised by very open questions which allow the candidates to present themselves freely. Hence the interview is flexible and can be tailored to the individual.
3. Structured interviews with pre-set questions which each candidate must answer. This interview style allows for standardisation across interviews, and hence is considered fair because each candidate has the same opportunity. In this way, the potential for interviewer bias is reduced, and the possibility of comparison between candidate (responses) enhanced.

In more recent years, the forms of interview recommended have tended to be increasingly sophisticated and highly structured. Anderson and Shackleton

(1993, p. 71) summarise a continuum of interview structure as follows: unstructured, semi-unstructured; focused; semi-structured; structured. At the unstructured end of the continuum the interview is unplanned, not directed or controlled by the interviewer and characterised by bilateral communication flow. Where the interview is focused, the discussion points and major topic areas may be pre-scheduled, so that the discussion is directed but flexible. Finally, at the more structured end of the spectrum, the interview questions are pre-planned, the interview being strongly directed by the interviewer and standardised across interviews. Structured interviews are hence characterised by the unilateral flow of information and are inflexible due to the requirement to be standardised.

The structured interview has been a focus of attention since the early 1980s (Eder and Ferris, 1989, pp. 27–8). It is intended to make the interview a more scientific process and improve its reliability and validity. In this way, it is suggested that the structured interview is a fair way of interviewing because it gives everyone the same opportunity and helps minimise interviewer bias which can creep in to more flexible, unstructured interview styles. This intention of fairness is typically achieved by standardising the interactions across interviews, with the same questions asked of each candidate and the quantifying of replies by the interviewer on given scales relating to sought-after characteristics (Anderson and Shackleton, 1993, p. 72). Proponents of this interview style argue that these results are scientifically reached and allow objective measurement and comparison of candidate suitability for the position. In further developments of the categorising of interviews, particular forms of structured interview which have emerged are situational interviews and patterned behaviour description interviews. In situational interviews candidates are asked to give their responses to hypothetical situations. In patterned behaviour description interviews candidates are required to describe their actions in previous situations which relate to sought-after characteristics. On the whole, the structured interview is increasingly viewed as the most sophisticated, fair and efficient form of selection interviewing.

The advances in selection interviewing described are intended to improve the success of the interview as a tool for selecting appropriate candidates for vacant positions. In addition to the wide-ranging discussions about efficiency of the interview as a selection tool some work has been done on ethical aspects of the interview. In part this is identified as a self-interest factor for companies, with recognition that the candidate's perception of the company will be heavily influenced by the first contact of the interview. As Langtry notes, 'identifying the best candidate for the job is only one side of a coin' (Langtry, 1994, p. 231). The interview is also an opportunity for the candidate to assess the company and may influence his or her decision on whether to join it if an offer is made (Robertson *et al.*, 1991; Welch, 1996). More subtly, the perception of the candidate about the company which the candidate develops in the interview may influence his or her performance in the interview.

Hence in the consideration of how the employment interview should best be done the question emerges 'best practice for whom?' Attention only to efficiency in recruitment may be a rather short-sighted approach for recruiters to take, since this does not necessarily take into account the (potentially negative) impact which different recruitment methods have on the candidate. The importance of this to the company may of course vary according to the state of the labour market and available capable candidates. Herriot and Fletcher (1990) argue that there is a strong case for what they call 'candidate friendly' selection even when skills are not in short supply. From the candidate's point of view particularly, 'best practice' is likely to mean more than efficiency alone, also including the manner of treatment received and the fairness of the interview.

A body of work does exist on the fairness of the interview. To date, however, the emphasis in this work has been on discrimination in the interview, resulting in selection decisions being unduly influenced by factors unrelated to ability to do the job. The irrelevant factors most heavily focused on tend also to be regulated and are race, colour, nationality, gender, age, disability and religion (see for example Anderson and Shackleton, 1993; Arvey, 1979, pp. 155–85; Arvey and Sackett, 1993, pp. 171–202; Kuip, 1992; Schmidt, 1989). Most consideration of fairness in the employment interview thus focuses on the reduced likelihood of minority groups being selected for further progression in the recruitment process. Pearn (1989) points out, however, that much of the debate on fairness in selection comes from the United States and the findings may not be applicable elsewhere.

It is inherent in selection that some individuals will be chosen over others. Where this is done on job-related criteria, it is considered to be fair (Silvester and Chapman, 1996). Where the selection procedure systematically biases against particular groups, the discrimination can be considered to be unfair. Pearn and Seear (1988, pp. 73–6) suggest the following measures to help avoid such discrimination and unfair recruitment practices:

1. Interviews should be properly conducted along professional lines.
2. Interviewers should be properly trained.
3. Interviews should be as consistent as possible.
4. Interviews should only be used to assess abilities which cannot be more directly and accurately assessed by other means.

The second point which Pearn and Seear recommend, that interviewers should be properly trained, is a critical one. It is important to note that in fact much of the criticism about interviewing as a selection method is based on the inadequacies of interviewers rather than the process itself (Langtry, 1994, p. 235).

Issues of fairness in employment interviewing go beyond discrimination against particular groups (Arvey and Sackett, 1993, pp. 171–202). Furthermore, it is unclear what is meant by 'fairness', since it can have different meanings for all stakeholders (Silvester and Chapman, 1996). When it is also considered that fairness is just one element of the ethics of the interview, this area of analysis becomes even more vague. Some limited work has been done on ethics in the interview, for example Fletcher (1992) and Barclay (1993), highlighting areas such as honesty, intrusive or persistent questioning, power use and abuse and the relevance of the criteria used.

A further aspect in ethics and employment interviewing is the influence of cultural differences – not just in terms of the impact on minority groups, but in relation to cross-cultural recruitment and the multinational firm. Silvester and Chapman (1996) note that there is a growing demand for insights into fair practices in cross-cultural selection. A company's ability to recruit across cultures is likely to be a significant aspect of staff selection in the future (Langtry, 1994). Some work has been done on comparing tools of recruitment and structural barriers in different cultures (see Molle and van Mourik, 1990; Shackleton and Newell, 1994; Sieveking, 1990). Tixier (1996) includes considerations of differences in what can be expected in the interview in different Nordic countries suggesting that practices and expectations reflect differing underlying managerial values. Investigating different practices, it is suggested, helps in the understanding of different underlying values. After decades of research into the employment interview, however, it seems that there remains a lack of empirical evidence and ethical analysis of employment interviewing practice, particularly in conjunction with cultural comparisons.

Empirical research

In response to the need for empirical research on employment interviewing across different cultures research has been completed which investigates employment interviewing in three cultures. The data are drawn from a single company interviewing for graduates to join a pool of 'international' employees, carried out in Germany, the Netherlands and the UK in 1995. One company was used in order to minimise variables other than the culture of the participants. All the interviewers had undergone the same training in employment interviewing and were given guidelines in structured patterned behaviour description interviewing (see above). A total of 30 observed and transcribed interviews constitute the core of the data, complemented by interviews with participants, informal observation and documents gathered. The data have been analysed using Erving Goffman's (1974) frame analysis, which is concerned with identifying the different ways in which participants organise their experience in a given strip of activity. Sifting through these data and applying frame analysis leads to the identification of four main ways or 'frames' of understanding what is going on in the employment interview. The four frames identified are the bureaucratic test frame, the life-buoy frame, the hangman frame and the reciprocity frame. Each frame may occur during the course of a single interview and can be identified by the form of the interview dialogue.

The bureaucratic test frame closely mirrors the standard guidelines for interviewing in which all the interviewees have been trained. The clinical asking of questions by the interviewer ensures the standard application of procedures, with information flow being predominantly from candidate to interviewer. This frame was identified through the types of comments and feelings expressed by participants in the interviews as follows in relation to four candidates:

Candidate: 'She's leading the interview, reading down her list of questions, I have to answer with a list of answers. I could direct for a while, but then she got it back on her line.'

Candidate: 'It is professional and a bit distant. Like meeting your girl-friend's parents for the first time. You know you are being analysed and checked out, and that it will benefit you to be approved, to pass the test.'

Candidate: 'The focus in the interview was on me. I'm here for them to see whether I'm [company name] material, not vice versa.'

Candidate: 'The whole process was very mass – next one, next one – it is just like a production line. It makes me feel just one of many. I had the idea that no one will notice if I sit there all day. It's a strange feeling, just like waiting in a long queue at Tropicana [an adventure swimming pool]; you don't know what is over the edge, but you all accept the wait.'

The life-buoy frame incorporates the response by the interviewer to the individual candidate, and for the candidate to be helped out in the provision of the evidence for which the interviewer is looking. Indicative quotations from the interview participants of this frame are:

Interviewer: '[The more general first part of the interview was impressive, the patterned behaviour description interviewing section] was OK but could have been better, I expected more of her. I have a gut feeling to recommend her, you have to go with that sometimes.'

Candidate: 'The interviewer was nice, he helped me out when I got stuck.'

Interviewer: 'Sometimes it is hard to remember that people are individuals. That they are not worthless just because they didn't get through the interview. For example I had one candidate a few weeks ago who was a very able learner, but had a very solitary character. His biggest achievement was to get over his shyness. I ended up just helping him along. If people start to look uncomfortable I just leave them alone. If they have nothing to say at all, I just try to guide them through. They are not interesting from [company name]'s point of view, so I just try to help them.'

Conversely to the life-buoy frame, in the hangman frame the interviewer catches the candidate out, contradicting and undermining his or her answers, exposing any weaknesses. Where this occurs it is most apparent in the dialogue of the employment interview itself, but indicative comments by the participants of the existence of this frame are:

Candidate: 'It's like playing tennis with the umpire, you think the game's going well, and then suddenly he catches the ball and says "You lose that point", and there's nothing you can do about it.'

Candidate: 'I felt like a schoolboy who hadn't done his homework.'

In the reciprocity frame, the interview is a two-way exchange, in which each party is assessing the possibility and value of an employment relationship between candidate and company. Some of the participants identified this as follows:

Candidate: 'I and they must learn enough to register further interest.'

Interviewer: 'The interview is like a mating dance before you get married. You need to find out whether you like each other, because you intend to make a long-term commitment.'

These frames or ways of understanding employment interviewing can be viewed from an ethical perspective. The purpose of applying ethical theory is to use the structure of assessment provided by the theories to analyse how the practices observed might be evaluated from a normative perspective. No intentional judgements are made about the validity of particular theories as being ultimate determinants of right or wrong. The theoretical approaches drawn upon in this study are those most commonly used in business ethics in Europe: Kantian theory, utilitarianism, social contract theory, virtue ethics and discourse ethics. Brief summaries of these theories are given in Table 3.1, and they are discussed in part in Chapter 1, or see also Beauchamp and Childress (1994), Raphael (1994) and Winkler and Coombs (1993) for good summaries of ethical theories and illustrations of applied ethics.

TABLE 3.1   **Summary of ethical theories**

Theoretical base	Type	Perspective	Brief description
Kantian Theory	a) Universalisability and reversibility	Rule based	You must abide by the categorical imperative such that what is right for one person is right for everyone, and do to others as you would be done by
	b) Respect for persons	Rule based	Second formulation of the categorical imperative: people should be treated as ends in themselves, never as means to ends
Utilitarian Theory	a) Act utilitarianism	Act based	Assess the act that will be for the greater good (or utility) as being ethical – the ends of the act justify the means. Aim is to achieve the greatest good for the greatest number
	b) Rule utilitarianism	Act/rule based	Focus on the utility of a rule rather than the act: rules are fashioned on utility, conduct on rules. Assess tendency for an act to improve happiness or utility if acts of this type are generally done rather than not done
Social Contract Theory		Contract based	Societal or contractual agreements must be abided by to ensure justice and rights of individuals
Virtue Ethics		Character based	Assess a person's character such that a good, virtuous person exhibits virtues such as honesty, kindness, generosity
Discourse Ethics		Communication based	Assess the process by which decisions are arrived at. An ethical discourse is open, honest with suspension of power differentials and inclusion of all relevant view points

The following discussion was developed by reconsidering the observed actions and transcriptions of employment interviewing and coupling these with other types of ethnographic data gathered to assess what the meaning of the perceived frames might be from an ethical standpoint. Assuming that the bureaucratic test frame did exist, for example, what might the ethical implications of its existence be? Put simply, from the perspective of existing ethical theories, is the bureaucratic test frame a good or bad thing in itself and for whom is it good or bad? In Table 3.2, the characteristics of the frames of the employment interview observed are summarised and ethical theories which could defend those types of behaviour noted.

TABLE 3.2   Interview frame characteristics and ethical defences

Frame	Characteristics	Ethical theories defending frame main defence (secondary defence)
Bureaucratic Test Frame	Guidelines followed (patterned behaviour description interviews). One way flow of information from candidate to interviewer. Power held by interviewer, highly structured, no personal interaction	Social Contract Theory (Kantian Reversibility and Universalisability, Rule Utilitarianism)
Life-buoy Frame	Interviewer reacts more individually to the candidate to his or her advantage. Help and prompts given in answering questions, may be due to preferential treatment (positive 'gut feeling' or sympathy)	Act Utilitarianism (Kantian respect for persons, Virtue Theory, Discourse Theory)
Hangman Frame	Interviewer reacts more individually to the candidate to his or her disadvantage. Rules of the exchange are changed mid-way by the interviewer and the candidate is caught out. Power held by the interviewer. May be motivated by negative 'gut feeling'. Candidate accepts disadvantaged role	Act Utilitarianism
Reciprocity Frame	Two-way conversation flow. Power in guiding interview shared	Discourse Theory (Kantian respect for persons, Virtue Theory)

The interpretations made and shown in Table 3.2 demonstrate that different ethical perspectives may pervade business practices. The choice of ethical theories associated with the defence of each frame is now more clearly explained.

Where the bureaucratic test frame is adopted the candidate and interviewers have agreed to comply with the guidelines set by the company and carry out the interview in the specified way. The standardisation of the agreed practice is considered just and ethical, hence the frame is an ethical form of behaviour when considered from the perspective of social contract theory. Similarly, the repeating of the same model in interviewing is ethical from the point of view of Kantian reversibility and universalisability as well as rule utilitarianism, that is all the rule-based theoretical ethical perspectives. The dry repeating of questions and the discomfort caused to the candidate would suggest, however, that the bureaucratic test frame is unethical when viewed from the perspective of virtue theory or Kantian respect for persons. Also, the one-way nature of the discussion and the holding of the power by the interviewer means that from the point of view of discourse theory the frame is unethical.

The life-buoy frame and the hangman frame are both primarily defensible on the grounds that they are driven, in part at least, by concern about the outcome of the interview from the company's perspective. In this respect they can be considered ethical from the point of view of act utilitarianism. In the life-buoy frame, the interviewer perceives that the candidate is a good one and assists him or her in order to ensure that they can be selected to continue in the interview process. In the hangman frame, the interviewer perceives that the candidate is a poor one and prevents him or her from performing well in the interview. Each of these acts may have a useful outcome, although the pragmatic means of achieving that outcome imply that these frames are unethical from the point of view of all the rule-based theories.

The life-buoy frame may be carried out for other reasons, for example out of sympathy to the struggling candidate. In such cases the frame can be considered ethical from the perspective of Kantian respect for persons and virtue theory. Where the frame is somewhat more discursive and more of an open conversation than in the bureaucratic test frame, it may be considered ethical from the perspective of discourse theory to a degree.

The reciprocity frame encompasses the most equitable sharing of power over the form of the interview dialogue, resulting in a much more open and two-way conversation than would be observed in the other three frames. Full discussion and the suspension of power differentials are characteristic of an exchange which would be considered ethical from the point of view of discourse theory. In this respect also, the reciprocity frame can be considered to be in keeping with stakeholding approaches (see Chapter 1). The responsiveness of the interviewer to the individual candidate suggests that the reciprocity frame would be considered ethical from the perspective of Kantian respect for person and virtue theory. As a result of the unique question asking in response to each individual candidate, the same questions will not be asked in each interview and hence the reciprocity approach may be considered unfair. The lack of standardisation in the reciprocity frame would mean that the type of behaviour is considered unethical from the perspective of the rule-based theories such as social contract theory and Kantian universalisability and reversibility. The focus is on the discursive and individualised process of the interview and thus would not be considered ethical from an act utilitarian point of view, although may be ethically defensible if adopted as a rule (rule utilitarianism).

It becomes clear in this analysis that judgement of actions as ethical or otherwise is by no means an exact science. Even the interpretations made could be differently argued. However, what the process does do is enable us to begin to understand the ethical perspective of actions observed in this sample of employment interviews. As noted above the interview sample was taken from interviewing in Germany, the Netherlands and the UK. Hence there are further implications to these findings from a cross-cultural perspective.

Interviewing in different cultures

When considering the frequency of frame adoption in Dutch, UK and German interviews, the frame adopted in all cases with overwhelming dominance was the bureaucratic test frame. Hence the main frame used in employment interviewing in each of the samples was that intended by the company. However, other frames were adopted at times during the interviews. The reciprocity frame was adopted at some stage in each of the German interviews. In the UK interviews the strict guidelines were often rejected in favour of a more pragmatic, utilitarian approach in which the life-buoy or hangman frame could be observed. In the Dutch interviews the bureaucratic test frame was most consistently adopted when compared with the other two countries. Although it is difficult to be sure of a causal relationship, it seems likely that these factors influenced the higher recommendation rate for German and UK candidates to remain in the recruitment process compared with Dutch ones.

Langtry (1994) has pointed out that the inadequacies of the interviewer are as important as the inadequacies of the interview. This research supports that finding, although the emphasis is not so much on the inadequacies of the interviewers as the individual influences which even trained professional interviewers will have on the interview. Across cultural divides this influence is bound to be particularly crucial.

The sample in this case is too small and the company too specific an example to make any claims of generalisability. Nevertheless, the findings indicate a tendency for different ethical approaches to employment interviewing, which may be linked to national characteristics. There are three particular implications in this. First, 'good' interviewing from an ethical perspective may be perceived differently by interviewers from different cultures. Second, these differences may influence the likelihood of selection of candidates of different cultures. The third point is that these differences persist *despite* the efforts of the company to interview 'fairly' across cultures. A specific aim of this company, as with many multinationals, is to recruit a diverse workforce. According to the results of this study, standardising procedures and using sophisticated structured interview techniques is not sufficient to achieve a diverse workforce.

If we return to Pearn and Seear's (1988, pp. 73–6) criteria for avoidance of unfair recruitment practices, the interviewing in this company appears to satisfy them. Interviews in the case study company are professionally conducted, along clear written guidelines, all interviewers are fully trained and the highly structured approach means that interviews are as consistent as possible. The interview is also only one step in a series of recruitment procedures, so other methods are used at later stages to measure other characteristics. However, if candidates do not pass this first interview stage they do not proceed in the system. Furthermore, even when the interview is carried out as in the intended bureaucratic test frame, it can be considered unethical and disrespectful to the candidate, as illustrated in the foregoing discussion. It seems that the approach taken by this company may be a good example of aspiring to 'best practice' but still an ethical interview is not guaranteed.

Given the findings of this research it may be tempting to descend into a relativistic stance which simply accepts different approaches to interviewing as equally valid. This is of course an option, but is less helpful than ever for the business person trying to assess what should be done in order to interview ethically and to identify what 'best practice' would be. For the ethically concerned recruiter there remains a dilemma of how to interview.

The recruiter's dilemma

In response to Stark's (1993) criticisms of business ethics research, some practical suggestions, rooted in empirical research, are made. It should be kept in mind, however, that far from offering concrete solutions to ethical problems, the work of ethics is in many senses to 'help disprove some suggestions and throw up some confusions' (Raphael, 1994, p. 10). There are nevertheless lessons in this empirical work which might help recruiters solve the dilemma of how best to carry out employment interviews both nationally and across different cultures. The three-point plan shown in Table 3.3 is suggested for companies with a serious commitment to improving employment interviewing.

TABLE 3.3   **Steps towards 'best practice'**
ethical employment interviewing

Step	Action
ONE	Acknowledge individual interviewer influence on interviewing and identify actual practices
TWO	Understand the reasons for those practices
THREE	Clarify and communicate with all participants in interviewing the preferred ethical stance of the firm

The first point, the acknowledgement that individuals and members of different cultures do different things in employment interviews, may seem obvious but, it is suggested, is under-recognised in practice. For companies wishing to improve their employment interviewing practices, the starting place must be to find out empirically what their practices really are, whether recruitment is done in different cultures or domestically. Without this knowledge as a starting point, managers will not know what they are tackling. In a commentary on different views on international business ethics, Enderle (1997, p. 1) notes that 'before asking for ethical guidance in international business, it is crucial to become aware of, and familiar with, the resistant diversity in space and time that characterises business environment and business behaviour'. The importance of understanding practices, then, is a critical concept for all manner of business operations, not just interviewing.

Second, having 'discovered' what they do, recruiters must pinpoint why they do it. In this research, this has taken the form of looking to ethical theories which justify perspectives adopted, and actions taken, in employment interviews. Such an academic analysis may not be necessary in practice in order to uncover the motives behind actions. It would be important, however, to do some kind of independent research which investigates recruiter's motives for action. The care needed at this stage is significant because it will be difficult to influence or change practice unless the reasons for those practices are known and understood.

The third stage is the need for companies and their recruiters to decide what they want to happen in employment interviews, that is determine what the ethical underpinnings would ideally be; such as justice and equal opportunity, or discourse and respect for persons, or the prioritising of consequences and outcomes of the interview. The interviewer, at the sharp end of any recommended policies and procedures, will inevitably maintain some discretion in how interviewing is carried out. Being explicit about the preferred perspective, and incorporating this in training, should help the recruiter achieve the practice considered best in the organisation.

It is intended that such a three-stage process will be of help to recruiters and others in HR to determine their perceptions of best ethical practice. Business ethics cannot offer any easy blueprints for action for practitioners, but can help raise ethics onto the agenda and support the sensitising of business people to the ethical perspective in their actions.

Summary

Business ethicists are sometimes criticised for doing work which does not offer any help to business people seeking guidance in relation to business ethics. In this chapter, the employment interview is focused on as an example of how theoretical, empirical ethics research can be useful in determining 'best ethical practice'.

'Best practice' in interviewing has tended to be seen in terms of standard-ising and objectifying the employment interview. Some reference has been made in existing literature to notions of fairness and avoidance of discrimina-tion. However, there is little recognition that even where sophisticated inter-view techniques are adopted, interviewers can apply and interpret interview procedures differently.

Different types of observed behaviour in standardised employment inter-viewing have been analysed from the perspective of ethical theory, demon-strating that distinct forms of behaviour can be perceived as ethical depending on the theoretical perspective taken. There are indications that cultural differ-ences directly impact upon the preferred form of behaviour in the interview and differing underlying values are demonstrated. Recognition and under-standing of this difference is an essential step for those seeking to interview ethically. It is proposed that 'best practice' will be different according to organ-isational and national culture, values and requirements. The approach to iden-tifying 'best ethical practice' as outlined in Table 3.3 is recommended.

References

Anderson, N. and Shackleton, V. (1993) *Successful Selection Interviewing*, Oxford: Blackwell

Arvey, R. (1979) *Fairness in Selecting Employees*, London: Addison-Wesley

Arvey, R. and Sackett, P. (1993) 'Fairness in Selection: Current Developments and Perspectives' in Schmidt, N. and Borman, W.C. (eds) *Personnel Selection in Organizations*, New York: Jossey Bass, pp. 171–202

Barclay, J.M. (1993) 'Making the "Right" Choice: Some Considerations of the Ethics of Selection at the Workplace', *Recruitment, Selection and Retention* 2(3): 17–22

Beauchamp, T.L. and Childress, J.F. (eds) (1994) *Principles of Biomedical Ethics* (4th edn), Oxford: Oxford University Press

Bingham, V. (1988) 'The Selection Interview' in Sidney, E. and Ungerson, B. (eds) *Managing Recruitment* (4th edn), Aldershot: Gower, pp. 138–56

Eder, R.W. and Ferris, G.R. (eds) (1989) *The Employment Interview: Theory, Research, and Practice*, London: Sage

Enderle, G. (1997) 'Five Views on International Business Ethics: an introduction', *Business Ethics Quarterly* 7(3): 1–4

Fletcher, C. (1992) 'Ethical Issues in the Selection Interview', *Journal of Business Ethics* 11: 361–7

Goffman, E. (1974) *Frame Analysis: An Essay on the Organization of Experience*, Boston: Northern University Press

Herriot, P. and Fletcher, C. (1990) 'Candidate Friendly Selection in the 1990s', *Personnel Management* February 22(2): 32–5

Kuip, R. (1992) 'De gekleurde bril van de selecteur', *PW Vakblad voor Personeelsmanagement* November, pp. 18–23

Kumra, S. and Beech, N. (1994) 'The Selection Interview: an investigation of contemporary usage'. Paper presented at British Academy of Management Conference, Lancaster University, 12–14 September

Langtry, R. (1994) 'Selection' in Beardwell, I. and Holden, L. *Human Resource Management: A Contemporary Perspective*, London: Pitman, pp. 230–63

Molle, W. and van Mourik, A. (1990) 'Labour Mobility' in Wolters, M. and Coffey, P. (eds) *The Netherlands and EC Membership Evaluated*, London: Pinter, pp. 160–7

Monast, J.H. (1994) 'What is (and isn't) the Matter with "What's the Matter…"', *Business Ethics Quarterly* 4(4): 499–512

Pearn, M. (1989) 'Fairness in Employment Selection: a comparison of UK and USA' in Smith, M. and Robertson, I. (eds) *Advances in Selection and Assessment*, Chichester: John Wiley & Sons, pp. 155–65

Pearn, M. and Seear, N. (1988) 'Selection within the Law' in Sidney, E. and Ungerson, B. (eds) *Managing Recruitment* (4th edn), Aldershot: Gower, pp. 64–81

Raisig, G.J. (1991) 'Die Ehre des Bewerbers und der Umgang mit ihm und seinem Interesse', *Personalführung* 12: 896–900

Raphael, D.D. (1994) *Moral Philosophy* (2nd edn), Oxford: Oxford University Press

Robertson, I.T., Iles, P.A., Gratton, L. and Sharpley, D. (1991) 'The Impact of Personnel Selection and Assessment Methods on Candidates', *Human Relations* 44(9): 963–82

Schmidt, N. (1989) 'Fairness in Employment Selection' in Smith, M. and Robertson, I. (eds) *Advances in Selection and Assessment*, Chichester: John Wiley & Sons, pp. 133–55

Shackleton, V. and Newell, S. (1994) 'European Management Selection Methods: A comparison of five countries', *International Journal of Selection and Assessment* 2(2): 91–102

Sieveking, K. (1990) 'Free movement of European citizens' in Schweitzer, C.C. and Karsten, D. (eds) *Federal Republic of Germany and EC Membership Evaluated*, London: Pinter, pp. 197–206

Silvester J. and Chapman, A.J. (1996) 'Unfair Discrimination in the Selection Interview: an attributional account' *International Journal of Selection and Assessment*, 4(2): 63–70

Stark, A. (1993) 'What's the Matter with Business Ethics?' *Harvard Business Review* **71**(3): 38–48

Tixier, M. (1996) 'Cross-Cultural Study of Managerial Recruitment Tools in Nordic Countries', *The International Journal of Human Resource Management* **7**(3): 753–74

Torrington, D. and Hall, L. (1987) *Personnel Management: A New Approach*, London: Prentice Hall

Welch, J. (1996) 'Recruiters Face up to the Moral Imperative', *People Management* **2**(12):16

Winkler, E.R. and Coombs, J.R. (1993) *Applied Ethics: a Reader*, Oxford: Blackwell

CHAPTER 4

Occupational testing and psychometric instruments: an ethical perspective

Barry Baker and John Cooper

Introduction

The ethics of occupational testing is one area of human resource management where there has already been substantial ethical debate. In this chapter we trace the increasing use of occupational tests and psychometric instruments, both in the UK and elsewhere, and their utility to organisations. We go on to outline the existing ethical concerns raised over the use of these instruments, and then link these concerns to the ethical frameworks and perspectives raised in Chapter 1. It is suggested that a valuable ethical approach could be to balance a 'rights' perspective, with a 'limiting principle' applied within a stakeholder framework where no one stakeholder can uphold their own 'rights' to the detriment of others. We also highlight the extent to which codes of practice produced by professional bodies and others have highlighted ethical issues.

In the next part of the chapter, we report on the findings of our own empirical study into the espoused values of testers and their views on test taker's rights, compared to their reported practice in testing. This research throws up some interesting information over those areas where there are strong ethical values and practice, and also over aspects where the practice does not live up to the espoused values. The survey raises some concerns over the likely success of ethical codes of practice in promoting ethical practice which, given the predominance of codes of practice as a way of regulating tester ethics, begs the question what else do we need to do to promote ethical awareness and ethical practice in this area? Finally, we provide our tentative rationale as to why the conduct of testing may not live up to suggested good practice and we provide an outline of an organisational mindset which may undermine ethical approaches in this area. We conclude by providing a list of questions which we believe the organisation or tester need to ask to check their own ethics in testing practice.

The usage of occupational testing

Occupational testing or psychometrics refers to the use of ability and aptitude tests and personality and motivation questionnaires used in the context of recruitment and selection, development, career guidance, team building and outplacement. There are literally thousands of occupational tests on the market and, in the UK, occupational testing is a multi-million pound business. Established as a powerful tool for occupational selection since World War Two there are now many thousands of trained test users in the UK (Cooper, 1997a).

The extent of usage is well documented. In the UK the use of occupational tests is widespread and growing, although the actual figures for usage do differ. Saville and Holdsworth claim around 70 per cent of large organisations say they use personality and cognitive measures some of the time for selection (Saville and Holdsworth, 1993), yet Baker and Cooper (1995) found, in their sample of 217 organisations with employees in excess of 200, a lower reported figure of 47 per cent actively using testing. When asked if they had 'ever used testing' the figure rose to 58.5 per cent. The differences in reported figures may reflect the different sample frames and difference in the degree of specificity in the questions.

Psychometric tests, it is argued, have a number of benefits. In the UK the massive increase in their popularity in recruitment and selection in the last decade is largely because of their objectivity, speed and capacity to predict job success when compared with subjective techniques such as the interview. Many advocates of psychological testing have argued that quantitative selection techniques are valuable predictors of work behaviour and job performance (for example Cook, 1990, pp. 237–41; Cooper and Robertson, 1995, p. 129). Usually, such advice is tempered by caveats such as 'used properly and in a professional manner' (Melamed and Jackson, 1995, p. 11). In summary, the main benefits of psychometric tests are that:

- Tests can generate objective, benchmarked and impartial results (see Beardwell and Holden, 1997, Chapter 6; Bolger, 1997; Toplis *et al.*, 1997)

- Tests can provide a common and neutral language to discuss and understand differences between people
- Tests can provide powerful results in a short time span
- Tests can offer an idea of strengths and development areas and give a good starting point for open discussion
- Tests can provide a focus for changing behaviour
- Tests can offer people a way to understand themselves better.

Turning from UK use to examine usage elsewhere, such as in the rest of Europe, there are variations. In Belgium tests are well established yet in Italy and Germany reported frequency of usage for large companies is about 20 per cent (Shackleton and Newell, 1997). In the USA around 33 per cent of companies estimated using personality measures and 50 per cent cognitive measures.

In some countries there are significant concerns about the use of tests. In Sweden concerns are being raised about tests and invasion of individual privacy, while in Cyprus it is a legal requirement to use a fully qualified psychologist when undertaking testing. Cultural, social, political and religious aspects may also have a strong part to play; for example the Catholic Church tends to disapprove of psychological testing (Shackleton and Newell, 1997, cited in Anderson and Herriot, 1997, pp. 81–2).

Across the world then there are different approaches to regulating and controlling occupational testing. Some recent work undertaken by Bartram (1997) on behalf of the European Federation of Professional Psychological Associations (EFPPA) has explored similarities and differences across cultures and the International Test Commission (ITC) is working on developing and implementing common standards.

Applications of psychometric instruments in HRM

In recruitment and selection tests are often used in pre-selection or screening, as part of a staged process, as an important component of an assessment centre or extended selection event and as a special profiling activity for important posts.

Occupational tests can also add value in development settings and Cooper (1997b) suggests that in the last few years there has been greater emphasis and push towards the use of psychometrics as a tool in development contexts. This is strongly associated with the general shift in organisations to valuing and developing people, for example through initiatives such as Investors in People.

Commentators, notably Maddocks (1998), have identified a general shift of emphasis in the way tests are being designed, promoted and used. In practice new psychological tools are becoming 'softer' and more user friendly, often focused more on learning and work-related skills than on ability and aptitude. The predicted shift from more traditional, educational approaches to assessment will probably result in the growth of alternative approaches to assessment.

There are many hundreds of different measures in the marketplace and some lend themselves to particular uses or roles. Indeed, some measures have been specifically designed for particular uses, such as occupational interest inventories for careers counselling, ability and aptitude tests to identify level of potential and personality questionnaires to help understand a person's preferences and style of working. For a fuller appreciation of this diversity see Anastasi (1990), Jackson (1996) and Toplis *et al.* (1997). Frequent uses may include:

- Pre-selection or screening and initial assessment
- Selection: part of a staged process
- Selection: clinical and comprehensive assessment, usually on final shortlist and for senior managers
- A means of providing a realistic job/role preview
- Capacity to learn and re-learn, and trainability
- Management development potential, needs analysis or prospective assessment
- Personal development and self-awareness
- Careers counselling and vocational guidance
- Interpersonal conflict
- Team building
- Counselling.

Psychometric tools are used differently for development and selection. Used for developmental purposes psychometric tools are concerned less with statistical prediction of performance and more with the process of using the data for discussion and focusing. Broadly speaking, in developmental contexts the individual 'owns' the results and is the primary stakeholder in the process and in their own development. The resistance which is faced from participants in psychometric assessment mostly disappears when they share or own the results. In selection the organisation 'owns' and 'uses' psychometric data to aid decisions about people. The implication of this difference is that assessment for development is a less threatening, more positive and a more involving process for people than being assessed for selection. Clearly the difference in the two perspectives may in some cases be more apparent than real. The contrast can become blurred when, in development for example, the ownership locale is forgotten or where selection is masked by a developmental facade.

Emerging ethical concerns in the use of psychometric testing

In 1986 Wilfrado R. Manese wrote a book entitled *Fair and Effective Employment Testing*. Its age and US focus notwithstanding the book addresses many of the issues currently being voiced concerning ethical issues in occupation testing. Since 1986 the literature on occupational testing has grown rapidly with particular reference to ethical behaviour and good practice, (see Arvey and Renz, 1992; Baker and Cooper, 1995; Barclay, 1993; Cooper *et al.*, 1996; Fletcher, 1993; Herriot and Fletcher, 1990; Iles and Robertson, 1997; Lord, 1994; Melamed and Jackson, 1995; Newell and Shackleton, 1992, 1993; Robertson *et al.*, 1991).

A number of UK studies have suggested that the occupational testing practice of some employers may not follow suggested guidelines of 'good practice' as well as they might (see for example Baker and Cooper, 1995; Commission for Racial Equality, 1990, 1993; Newell and Shackleton, 1992). High-profile cases have led to a growing awareness of legal and equal opportunity issues and has led to questions being raised about the fairness, appropriateness and ethical use of tests. As psychometric techniques become increasingly embedded in human resource practices there are more concerns voiced by stakeholders in the process, from test publishers, candidates, psychologists, lawyers, practitioners, journalists and academics.

In the UK practitioner and quality press many articles have appeared over the last few years which provide testament to the 'concerns' about tests. For example over test usage and fairness, cross-cultural issues and biases of race and gender, test selling practice, the computer interface with tests, types of test such as integrity and honesty tests, facets of testing practice and testing practice and disabled candidates to name but a few of the expressed concerns (see for example Becket, 1997, p. 31; British Psychological Society, 1997a, p. 16; Cramp, 1996, p. 21; Donkin, 1998, p. 14; Finn, 1998, pp. 37–8; Fowler, 1997, pp. 45–6; Institute of Personnel and Development, 1997; Kellaway, 1994; Kent, 1997, pp. 24–7; McHenry, 1997, pp. 32–7; North, 1994, pp. 18–22; Palmer, 1997; Pickard , 1996a, pp. 20–5, 1996b, p. 7; Rich and Donkin, 1994; Sheppard, 1995, pp. 23–6; Smith, 1996, pp. 25–30; Wood, 1996, pp. 27–33).

The concept of 'adverse impact', although originally linked to unfair discrimination within the realms of the UK laws, has also been used to refer to the deliberate or unintentional selective disadvantage arising out of the application of a test or process of testing. In the USA Mello (1996) has commented on the increasing number of legal cases being brought under federal, state and common law that relate to an individual's right to privacy. Recently, Davidson (1997) has commented on the ethical issues and responsibilities of test users in Australia.

Trades unions are increasingly sensitive to issues concerning the use of testing by employers as cases of alleged misuse, unfairness and adverse impact grow. Wheatley (1996) has described the increasing awareness of test takers in regard to their rights and the growing impetus of union support.

Iles and Robertson (1997, p. 562) sound a further note of caution when they suggest that 'selection methods that have good criterion-related validity may be a necessary but not sufficient condition for effective personnel selection'. There is now a further concept of 'impact validity ' which refers very much to the psychological and behavioural affects emanating from testing experiences and outcomes (see the earlier discussion centred around the social process paradigm and the work of Baker and Cooper, 1995; Robertson and Smith, 1989; Robertson *et al.*, 1991). Fletcher (1991, p. 558) argues that 'experiences with selection outcomes or decisions appear to have major impact on candidate and organisational health'. Robertson and Smith (1988) initially coined the phrase 'Impact Validity' to express the extent to which processes of testing may have negatively influenced the psychological characteristics of candidates.

Some examples of where this may be particularly relevant is in the areas of genetic testing, honesty testing and computer-based testing. Various writers have highlighted the growing interest in genetic testing and are beginning to question some of the motives and impact such testing can have (see Bower, 1997, p. 25; Iles and Robertson, 1997). Iles and Robertson (1997) cite the work of various authors in discussing the trend in use of honesty and integrity testing, drug testing and the use of polygraphs. The discussion takes in the evidence for their respective 'worth' and touches on the kind of ethical impact issues that can arise. Deriving primarily from the US they concluded that there are growing concerns about the intrusiveness and impact of these techniques. Yet another shift in the use of tests is the growing use of computerised or IT-driven processes. The scope for a process that is de-personalised, heavy on technocratic determinism and open to non-qualified users must be recognised.

Figure 4.1 is adapted from the work of Robertson and Smith (1989) and captures the notion of impact validity in a model which attempts to suggest potential consequences associated with poor testing practice. The model conceptualises 'consequences 'of testing practice which may arise through a process of participants' perception of their testing experience. Thus, there may be potential for some form of negative impact.

Codes of professional practice have generally been based in the psychometric paradigm and the emphasis on impact validity on candidates has not been strongly emphasised outside of the legal focus of 'adverse impact' through forms of unfair or unlawful discrimination. The influence of the process of testing on candidates' well-being and the organisation's attitude to testing and assessment needs greater recognition within the codes of practice and research. Iles and Robertson (1997, p. 562) discuss the evidence for impact validity and conclude that the impact model is conceptually useful but remains speculative since research has been inconsistent in offering support, and thus more fieldwork is required.

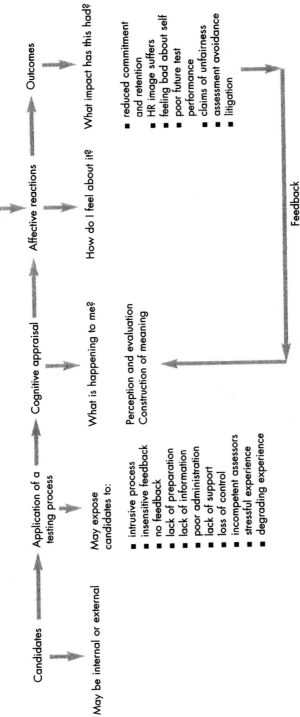

FIGURE 4.1   The consequences of poor testing practice
(Adapted from Robertson, I. and Smith, J. (1989)

There is growing evidence that changing emphasis in HRM and the business context may be driving testing practice away from the 'traditional usage', and this raises new ethical concerns. Storey (1995, p. 5) sees HRM as representing a 'new orthodoxy' in managing human resources where competitive advantage is gained through the strategic deployment of a committed, capable workforce. Furthermore, this is achieved through integrated HR techniques. Assessment including testing would be an important part of the HR strategy. Testing here becomes part of a much more strategically viewed assessment process supporting and fitting with business strategy. Assessment may also become part of a wider process of leverage for change or sustaining some preferred organisational characteristics (see Anderson and Herriot, 1997; Legge, 1995; Mabey and Salaman, 1995; Sisson, 1994; Townley, 1991, 1993).

Sisson (1994) discusses the 'hard and soft' versions of HRM and of the hard version suggests:

> the impression given is that flexibility is everything and the desired state is that management can do and should do anything it likes. (pp. 13–15)

The implications for testing practice arising out of a mindset predicated on a 'hard' version of HRM are profound. For example, a number of organisations have recently been in the public eye for using tests as part of a process for selection for redundancy in supporting cost-reduction business strategies (see Becket, 1997; North, 1994). Testing was used to support decisions not to offer jobs to existing employees after re-structuring and reduction in staffing levels. In this way testing is used not to predict success, but rather as a means to justify exclusion often against cultural values and other organisational level criteria. For a discussion on assessment and 'downsizing and deselection', see Jackson (1997). Critics have alleged that the use of psychometric tests in these contexts was inappropriate as they were measuring constructs that were arguably not genuine occupational or job requirements. For example, where existing data input clerks re-applying for similar jobs were rejected on the grounds of not displaying enough 'creativity'.

Iles and Robertson (1997) discuss other trends in assessment and suggest that some organisations have shifted from the traditional job/role and person fit to a cultural values person fit. In part this may reflect the shift in assessment focus as part of a strategic integrated process of HRM (see Baird and Meshoulam, 1988; Mabey and Iles, 1993). One consequence of this has been to express 'core values/competencies' as organisational level selection criteria as part of a wider processes of cultural fitting and 'careful selection' (Townley, 1991).

Another way in which testing can be used to support HR strategies is where it is used to identify the different characteristics required in core and peripheral workforces to sustain the flexible firm models (Purcell, 1996). Such differential treatment has also led to ethical concerns. ·Testing can also be applied in competitive contexts to focus on qualities needed in employees post restructuring, to support a futuristic orientation rather than focusing on current demands (Mabey and Salaman, 1995, pp. 19–67; Rothwell, 1995; Schenieder and Konz, 1989).

Iles and Robertson (1997) draw attention to the growing dissatisfaction with the psychometric paradigm as a framework for assessing the 'worth' of testing and argue that the full impact of testing can only be understood through a 'social perspective'. They build on the early ideas of Foucault, and latterly Townley (1993), and argue that assessment (testing) as a process of 'government' within the organisation is capable of impacting on a person's identity and self-concept. Furthermore, that testing when viewed as a 'technology of organisational government' is a process which regulates the power and knowledge relationship within the organisation (see Figure 4.2).

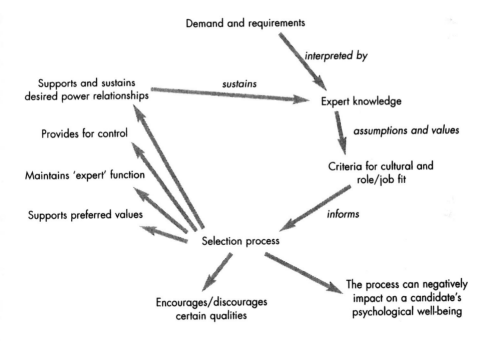

FIGURE 4.2   Testing as a social and psychological process within a power and control paradigm

(Drawn from Iles and Robertson, 1997)

The issue then is about the exercise of power, as Legge (1995) writes discussing the work of Foucault and Townley:

> Power then is relational and becomes apparent when exercised through the practices, techniques and procedures that give it effect... [such as in testing processes]. (Legge, 1995, p. 305)

One line of thought is that a certain amount of 'post hoc' rationalisation may be evident as organisations legitimise and support 'preferred' decisions through the rationale of 'scientific and objective' testing. Such a process can de-personalise decisions and present the person with unequivocal evidence about their unsuitability in a situation where they are relatively powerless to challenge the decision.

Thus far we have attempted to put current occupational test use into context and to look at some of the current and likely future tensions which may arise in the use of testing. We will now consider in more depth some of the potential ethical issues which can arise with the use of tests against a number of ethical reasoning frameworks.

Ethical perspectives and occupational testing

In Chapter 1 the various approaches to ethical reasoning were discussed. In the context of testing, the different threads of ethical thinking enable a range of self-justifying rationales to be employed. For example, a utilitarian focus might view the occasional mistake or adverse impact on a candidate as regrettable, but overall as acceptable, providing the use of testing has utility for the system as a whole. Likewise, the 'false negative' (wrongly rejected) candidate who is disadvantaged as a result of some dubious testing prediction might be satisfied to know that despite being disadvantaged themselves the testing process still manages to pick 'correct positives' (from the test cut-off points) in sufficient numbers to serve the interests of the organisation. Thus a consequential approach which may advocate utility for the greater good or greater number of people.

A deontological approach might stress the 'rights' and avoidance of 'harm' to others. This approach heavily influences the regulatory processes through codes of professional practice, and underpins statutory discrimination laws, and thus has provided one focus for ethical debate in the domain of testing, (see Baker and Cooper, 1995).

A Kantian 'universalism' perspective might focus on testing processes and products meeting stringent criteria in the sense of 'doing unto others as you would have done unto you'. This is the much cited golden rule discussed by

Carrol (1990) and espoused by his sample of managers as one of the most important ethical principles that guide their behaviour. This universalism often exists as a principle to be applied across the spectrum.

Social justice arguments in testing might stress egalitarianism, equity, distributive justice and equality of opportunity. Indeed, procedural and distributive justice arguments underpin much of the US work on ethical assessment. Perceived fairness of both the procedure used for testing and the justice accorded to the outcomes are considered significant drivers of subsequent organisational behaviour (see Iles and Robertson, 1997, pp. 556–8). Clearly, this perspective underpins much of the legal framework associated with the prescriptive area of statutory instruments which aim to regulate the processes of discrimination. Of course, it is perfectly possible to operate legally yet still offend the ethical 'ought' statement where ethical concerns go beyond the prescriptive edicts of the law.

A growing area of analysis in testing ethically owes its popularity to the interest in stakeholder analysis where a 'community of purpose' evokes a perspective which attempts to balance the often competing interests of the parties in the testing process. For example, key stakeholders in the occupational testing area whose interests need to be taken into account, include:

- Academics
- Human resource professionals
- Legislators
- Occupational psychologists
- Managers
- Peers of test takers (for example other employees, family)
- Professional bodies
- Test takers – successful
- Test takers – unsuccessful
- Test suppliers
- Wider employer community.

This balancing of stakeholders' interests necessarily evokes a deontological expression about respective rights and the relative legitimate claims that follow the rights. HR professional will rightly seek to justify the use of tests which may be viewed by potential test takers as intrusive and of doubtful validity given the job for which they are selecting. Managers may delight in being able to support selection decisions through a 'scientific rationale' and if such testing reduces the uncertainty associated with selection and lowers the likelihood of wrong selection decisions then the concerns of other parties may be secondary to the interests of the organisation.

Green's 'limiting principle' (Green, 1994) is discussed by Baker and Cooper (1995). The limiting principle seeks to stress that the parties' rights cannot exist in absolute terms such that each party might unreasonably seek to uphold their rights even in the face of the rights of other parties. In the testing arena, an employer might reasonably seek to create the 'transparent' candidate where their personal characteristics and qualities are entirely in the public domain, in order to reduce the organisation's uncertainty and the likelihood of making a wrong selection decision. Action to reduce uncertainty in assessment can often be argued and supported through the utilitarian approach as well as 'rights'. The candidate too might reasonably seek to maintain privacy and freedom from unwarranted intrusion. Can such rights be reconciled?

The limiting principle argues for recognition of mutual obligations and recognition of each party's rights and concerns. Given the imbalance in power that often exists in the assessment and selection domain (see Fletcher, 1991; Herriot, 1993, cited in Iles and Robertson, 1997), the mutuality may be more apparent than real. Yet proper recognition by both parties may offer a way forward. In return for giving up the absolute right to privacy and freedom from intrusion, prospective test takers might reasonably expect the testing organisation to respect their other rights which can easily be offended in the assessment process. These could include the right:

- not to be harmed by the process of assessment
- to be fully informed of purpose and results of assessment
- to be suitably prepared for the process of assessment
- not to be subjected to assessment processes which have systematic bias or unwarranted discrimination
- not to be adversely and unfairly disadvantaged by the process of assessment.

In safeguarding the interests of the organisation, users of testing should be mindful to safeguard the interests of candidates.

On the one hand, it is difficult to admit any one approach to ethical reasoning in testing practice as holding any advantage. It is entirely possible to construct an eclectic approach which draws on various threads of reasoning especially when attempting to prescribe a series of 'ought' statements which attempt to reconcile the parties positions. On the other hand, when defending a preferred approach to testing it is entirely possible to engage a mindset which attempts to legitimise the approach through an ethical rationale.

The regulation of occupational testing

Aside of the legislative discrimination laws, the primary approach to regulation is through voluntary codes of practice, for example the Institute of Personnel and Development's *Code of Practice for Occupational Testing* (IPD, 1995b) and British Psychological Society's Code of Practice *Psychological*

Testing Guidance for the User (BPS, 1989, 1991, 1997b). These are usually backed up by advisory and guidance notes prescribing 'good practice' from regulatory bodies such as the Equal Opportunities Commission and Commission for Racial Equality along with literature from test suppliers (see Commission for Racial Equality, 1984, 1992, 1993; Equal Opportunities Commission, 1988; the Publishers Association, 1994).

Typically the codes of practice express good practice centred around:

- supply of tests
- competence of test users
- selection of tests and related job/role analysis – relevance of occupational criteria
- the provision of organisational policy on testing
- ensuring testing is appropriate and piloting new applications
- use of test information, manuals, validity and reliability data from suppliers
- administering, scoring and interpretation of tests
- physical environment of the testing process
- feedback and support to test takers
- confidentiality and access to results
- monitoring test use for impact, unintended bias and forms of adverse impact
- working with publishers to sustain and build quality practice
- storage and security of test materials and data
- data protection
- preparation of test takers
- information about the place of testing in a wider selection strategy; uses to which test data will be put
- divulging test results to third parties
- respecting the rights of test takers.

These codes express a series of normative statements which reflect accepted good practice. However, codes are evolving themselves. For example, the 1992 IPD Code on Occupational Testing suggests 'if candidates are to be offered feedback they should be informed' (IPD, 1992), whereas the 1996 update is more unequivocal in stating 'that candidates should be given feedback unless there are compelling reasons why feedback should not be given'. So codes of practice may not only reflect good practice but may also be restricted in time to what is considered reasonable and practicable. This has led to a debate which suggests codes of practice may be expressed as a 'minimal' level. There is scope for expression at higher 'aspirational levels' which may better support test takers ethical rights. Such aspirational statements seek to exceed minimum standards and afford targets for organisations to aspire to. For a fuller debate see Raiborn and Payne (1990), Stevens (1994), Smith *et al.* (1995), Dean (1992) and Liedtka (1991). However, we have already also alluded to the possibility that the content of existing codes of practice may be tied too tightly to the prevalent psychometric paradigm in assessment.

Encouragingly, there is a high level of knowledge of test codes of practice in the UK. Of those employers reporting use of tests in a 1995 survey (Baker and Cooper, 1995) only 5 per cent had no knowledge of the IPD *Code of Practice on Occupational Testing* and 40 per cent claimed to have made direct use of it to inform their own test practice. At the European level there has been an attempt to standardise good testing practice across Europe which has started with an examination of test practice (see Bartram, 1997).

Much faith is placed on BPS-accredited training for test user schemes and the restrictions placed by test publishers on supply to non-holders of qualifications or accreditation certificates. Front-loaded training and accreditation schemes (those requiring qualifications before a person is eligible to use the tests) are clearly important in ensuring test users are initially competent to use testing relative to the demands of 'good testing practice'. More recently the need for targeted continuing professional development specifically for test users has been highlighted by Cooper *et al.* (1996).

Professional education for occupational psychologists and human resource professionals enables opportunities for 'students' to major in selection and assessment. Equally, the last few years has seen a growing interest in professional ethics particularly in the domain of human resource management (Wood, 1997). Over time therefore, HR ethics should begin to have some impact on the agenda and priorities of human resource professionals (see Trezise, 1996; Winstanley *et al.*, 1996).

A growing number of organisations are turning to internally generated codes of practice to underpin management policy and practice (Smith *et al.*, 1995; Stevens, 1994). Stevens suggests that internally generated codes of practice should bring about higher levels of conformity than externalised ones such as the professional codes of practice and those of the regulatory bodies. The argument centres around the possibilities for managerial involvement in evolving and refining the internal codes. This it is argued would promote a stronger organisational rationale, ownership, identity and internalisation of the standards and hopefully lead to effective behaviour.

However, Stevens (1994) and others have observed that the 'motives' behind establishing an internal ethical code may be more about self-interest, mitigation and public relations than a concern for the 'rights' of stakeholders. In addition, forces within the organisation which promote contradictions and contrary pulls may serve to reduce or negate the potential benefits of ownership, (Pickard, 1995; 1996b; Raiborn and Payne, 1990; Sims, 1992). These conflicting pressures can be identified as:

- pragmatism/expediency versus maintenance of ethical principles in testing
- cost-reduction pressures versus sustained ethical testing practice
- inconsistency versus consistent and coherent application of ethical testing behaviour
- time is of the essence versus time to ensure the interests of test takers are observed

- managerial mixed messages about importance of ethics versus consistent example the action
- secretive and defensive organisations versus openness
- hidden agenda driving testing practice versus declared reasons.

Figure 4.3 attempts to capture the main elements which seek to inform and guide professional practice in occupational testing.

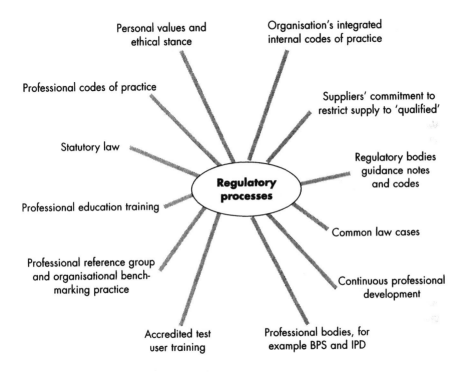

FIGURE 4.3   Sources of guidance and regulation for ethical and professional practice in occupational testing

The growing interest in external benchmarking offers other opportunities for organisations to assess the extent to which their testing practices match what other 'reasonable' employers are doing. Thus a relative assessment of practice becomes entirely possible as well as an absolute check on compliance with the regulatory stances. Texts on HR quality and external benchmarking can provide useful guidance on this (see Bramham, 1997; Matthewman, 1993).

A UK survey of employers testing practice

The authors undertook a national survey of 207 firms to ascertain the extent to which employers with greater than 200 employees were using occupational tests and in particular the extent to which existing codes of professional and occupational testing practice informed their own test practice. The results of the study are reported in full elsewhere (Baker and Cooper, 1995, 1996). However, some of the findings are relevant here.

Espoused values of testers

Personnel managers in the companies surveyed were asked about the beliefs and values underpinning their test practice to compare with those given in the IPD (1995b) and BPS (1989, 1997b) codes of practice and guidelines for occupational testing. The ethical deontological notion of 'rights ' was adopted as a means of structuring the 12 'testers' rights', which fits closely with the underpinning values within the professional codes. Not surprisingly, a very significant proportion of employers (over 95 per cent) agreed with the notion of basic 'test taking rights'.

Having obtained data on the espoused values of respondents on testing practice it was possible to compare these with their actual reported testing practice for 108 organisations. One might reasonably expect a high degree of congruence between their espoused values on test takers' rights and their reported testing practice. In some very important ways there was congruence but also a number of important contradictions. More importantly, lack of conformity to 'good practice' had potential to harm both the organisation and test takers and was not consistent with espoused concern for test takers' rights. What follows provides some flavour of the issues (see Baker and Cooper, 1995, 1996 for a more detailed discussion) and Table 4.1 summarises the findings.

Provision of feedback and support

Codes of practice allude to the process of feedback for test takers and Lord (1994) has written at some length about the necessity for test users to provide candidate-centred feedback. Interestingly, at the time of the survey neither the BPS nor IPD code of practice expressly required test users to provide feedback.

TABLE 4.1   A summary of the findings of the 1995 survey on the espoused values and reported practice of test users

Espoused values *(n = 207)*			*Reported practice* *(n = 108)*	
Test takers have the right to receive feedback			Feedback to internal candidates	96%
	Agree	87%	Feedback to external candidates	89%
Test takers have the right to receive post-testing support and counselling (where needed)			Provide support and counselling to internal candidates	55%
	Agree	77%	Provide support and counselling to external candidates	12%
Test takers have the right to expect competence in test users and test users' competence should be monitored			Use a systematic monitoring process of users continuing competence	14%
	Agree	99.5%	The monitoring of test users' performance seen as 'unnecessary'	37%
Test takers have the right to receive fairness and equal treatment			No monitoring of test results for bias	49%
	Agree	95%	Undertake systematic monitoring of test results for bias	16%
			Undertake monitoring by exception	35%

Note: All respondents on 'reported practice' were drawn from respondents to the baseline questionnaire on 'espoused values'.

Later codes have been more directive in this respect. Table 4.1 shows that there would appear to be a common mindset where the overwhelming majority of employers supported both in values and practice the right to feedback, although 11 per cent of test users in the survey did not provide feedback to external candidates. Given the greater emphasis in codes of practice since the survey on giving feedback it is likely that more test users are providing this feedback.

In relation to the data on testers provision of post testing support and counselling, the biggest disparity concerns the differential treatment of internal to external candidates (see Table 4.1).

Monitoring continuing competence of test users

Employers were asked whether a candidate could reasonably expect those responsible for testing to be competent in testing practice and 99.5 per cent agreed or strongly agreed that people who take occupational tests have this right. Initial training to accredited standard by verified trainers appeared to be well established. Despite the fact that the IPD (1995a) has a policy on continuing professional development, few employers in the survey reported monitoring the continuing test practice performance of those conducting the testing process and their ongoing competence in administering tests, scoring and interpreting results, accurate report writing and in feedback and support processes.

Against the declared value placed on a test takers rights to expect competency in test users these results were surprising. There are links between monitoring competence and the notion of continuing professional development. Monitoring, reflecting and learning form an important part of professional obligations, particularly in testing, where the consequences associated with testing decisions and processes can have profound affects on employees and the public as potential candidates and employees (Brien,1994; Lindley, 1995). This could take the form of peer assessment, manager assessment, self-assessment and perhaps even external benchmarking.

Fairness and equality: monitoring for unintended bias

Employers were asked in the survey to comment on the extent to which they monitored their test use to check whether the testing process unintentionally disadvantaged any specific group of people, for example, with relation to gender, ethnicity, disability or age. Although 95 per cent of organisations agreed that candidates should receive fairness and equal treatment, for over half of the organisations no monitoring took place (see Table 4.1). Few respondents could report systematic monitoring, yet all the advisory literature and codes of practice recommend that test users monitor their test use for unintended effects with relation to adverse and unintended impact. With relation to adverse and unintended impact, of the test users who reported undertaking no monitoring, 76 per cent reported being fully aware of the IPD and BPS codes of practice on occupational testing, and therefore should be aware of the dangers of not so doing.

Conclusions from the 1995 survey

The 1995 Baker and Cooper survey showed that there was a fair degree of correspondence between test users' espoused values about people's rights and their reported good practice. However, it was also apparent that in a number of important areas there was a contradiction between the reported practice of test users and their declared values about testing and people's rights. If the moral and social imperatives are uninviting to employers then one might have thought that the legal, contractual, public relations and quality pressures might promote sufficient self-enlightenment and self-interest to drive testing behaviour in the direction of good practice.

There is also a need to focus on the efficacy of the professional codes of practice as instruments of control, guidance and conduct and the role of HR professionals as purveyors and custodians of good testing practice. As survey results have shown, there appears to be little guarantee that knowledge of the codes of practice and the expectations that arise out of them are sufficient to promote the kind of widespread good practice that they intended.

Pressures on ethical thinking and testing practice

In an earlier paper (Baker and Cooper, 1996) we considered some of the possible reasons why test users may personally disregard or be expedient with what is claimed to be 'good testing practice'. More importantly, having acknowledged the legitimacy of test takers' 'rights', why, in some important respects, are some test users not providing for those 'rights'? In the space of this chapter it is only possible to summarise the issues. Many points of argument and conjecture remain since in the domain of occupational testing relatively little work has been done in field settings to establish evidence. However, at least three CRE and EOC cases have raised some important issues. Poor practice was claimed to prevail in these cases in part or because of 'time being seen of the essence', costs of selection needing to dictate assessment strategy, organisational need and interest prevailing above all other considerations, poor test selection and job/role analysis. Common to all is a rationale centred around pragmatics, self-interest and costs.

Three of Carrol's (1990) operational definitions of ethical mindsets are the 'means to an end ethic', the 'organisational self-interest ethic' and the power driven 'might equals right ethic'. All represent the exercise of an organisational imperative, relating to self-interest and power. We need to ask whether there is an 'organisational mindset' which undermines ethical good practice in testing. Such a mindset may, for example, accord with the following statements:

- Organisational pragmatics and short-term focus lead to short cuts in test selection and testing processes to save time and money/resources
- Where 'time is considered of the essence', short cuts can be justified
- The organisational self-ethic is so strong that means can always be justified by the preferred ends
- There is little ethical thinking or no debate in the organisation about ethical behaviour
- Managers are confused by inconsistency in ethical policy and practice, mixed messages and contradictions within the organisation
- Where ethical codes or testing policy exist, the policy and practice is not 'managed' to ensure consistency in application
- Externally prescribed codes of practice have little conformity pressure
- Voluntary codes of professional practice have minimum influence since they have very little real sanction
- Professional codes of practice are not written in aspirational language, they do not sufficiently adopt a social process/impact perspective
- The codes of practice fail to recognise the 'real' organisational milieu as a source of pressure, tension and contradiction for ethical behaviour in testing
- The 'new' directions in HR; in particular 'hard HRM' have led to the abandonment of moral/ethical thinking in the management of human resources in the organisation
- In an effort to gain greater influence and centrality in the organisation, HR managers have lost sight of 'justice', 'rights' and their professional roots
- HR managers have little real power and influence over the standard of testing practice within the organisation.

Although it is unlikely that any one manager or organisation would confirm all these statements, it seems likely that general agreement with this mindset is likely to reduce the impact of ethical codes of practice on testing behaviour. Certainly these tentative propositions require further research.

Summary

The chapter has discussed the contemporary use of occupational testing and the emerging trends in use. Tensions and questions about legal compliance, 'good practice' and ethical considerations have been addressed. The analysis has attempted to relate occupational testing policy and practice to ethical frameworks and it has been suggested that legal compliance is not necessarily the same as behaving ethically. As to which approach to ethical thinking is best adopted in the domain of testing, the deontological 'rights', 'harm' and consequence perspectives continue to be useful along with concerns for procedural and distributive justice. Although different commentators and practitioners may choose to adopt different ethical perspectives, there does seem to be a consensus about test taker rights in theory, but which is departed from in practice, as we have shown in the survey. An important point arises as to whether there is a particular organisational mindset associated with pragmatism, self-interest and pressures for cost reduction, which leads to a divorce of practice from espoused ethical rights and values. If this is so, we can also question whether such a mindset is a deeply held conviction or a philosophy of convenience adopted to support pre-conceived and preferred policy and practice on testing. As Pickard (1996b) said 'psychological measures are not easy to use well, they are just easy to use badly'.

The survey data suggest that in some important domains of testing there were significant differences between espoused policy and practice and practice in action. Some of these observed differences suggest that external professional 'codes of practice' may not in themselves be sufficient to drive 'good testing practice'. Although outside the scope of this chapter the questions raised in it may suggest fruitful avenues for further research, possibly through case studies.

We conclude by asking what guidance is needed to enable organisations to be more ethical in occupational testing? The various 'codes of practice' and guidance notes on occupational testing offer useful frameworks and, building on these, we have set out (Table 4.2) some self-check questions that may enable a review of ethical thinking and practice within the organisation.

TABLE 4.2   Self-check questions to review ethical thinking and practice within the organisation

- What is the prevailing 'organisation ethic' on occupational testing ? How consistent is the practice with the espoused ethic? Where contradictions exist – why? Can you do anything about these?

- Has 'organisational ethics' been addressed in the organisation with testing as part of the debate? Would an internally derived and managed 'Ethical Code of Practice' help focus on the issues of ethical behaviour?

- How well is the test assessing aspects demonstrably related to the job and job performance?

- How thorough is the job/role analysis? Could you show and defend how the criteria are linked to job/role/organisational performance or development?

- How comfortable are you with the ethics of the testing business? What sort of image is your organisation giving out by using the techniques?

- How well are your testers acting as 'ambassadors' to your organisation? How do you know? Do you evaluate/monitor?

TABLE 4.2 (cont'd)

- Are you sure your test predicts job/role/organisational success? What evidence do you have?

- Does your organisation use tests in a systematic, professional, value-for-money way? For example how competent are the test users? How do you know? Do you monitor stakeholders' opinions? Do you attempt to get a feel for the impact the process is having, intended and unintended?

- How does the information from tests and other sources really get used, as opposed to how you say it is used, to make decisions?

- Are you aware of some of the problems with using personality measures in selection? For example intrusiveness, face validity, evidence of value in prediction? Can you defend your use of these measures?

- How in tune is your use of testing with good/best practice principles? For example, would it stand up to a compliance check with codes of occupational testing practice?

- Internal 'quality audits' of practice are essential but what are other organisations doing from which you may learn? Some organisations have found external benchmarking useful. Have you considered this?

- How well trained are your test users (initial and with relation to continuing professional development) and is their performance monitored over time?

- Legal compliance with the 'discrimination laws' is one form of compliance check. However, ethical compliance may go beyond what is legal. Have you had this debate?

- To what extent do you have an 'independent' source of advice and expertise to draw on?

- In testing practice managers exercise choices: choice of assessment strategy, criteria, assessment instruments and assessment processes. The question remains, how central are the concerns for test takers in the wider context of organisational self-interests, tensions and pressures?

References

Anastasi, A. (1990) *Psychological Testing* (6th edn), Singapore: Maxwell McMillian

Anderson, N. and Herriot, P. (eds) (1997) *International Handbook of Selection and Assessment*, Chichester: John Wiley

Arvey, R. and Renz, C. (1992) Fairness in the selection of employees, *Journal of Business Ethics* **11**: 331–40

Baird, L. and Meshoulam, I. (1988) Managing the two fits of strategic human resource management, *Academy of Management Review* **13**(1): 116–28

Baker, B.R. and Cooper, J.N. (1995) Fair play or foul? A survey of occupational test practices in the UK, *Personnel Review* 24(3): 3–18

Baker, B.R. and Cooper, J.N. (1996) Occupational Testing Practice: Why might theory and practice contradict? Paper delivered to the First Conference on Ethical Issues in Contemporary Human Resource Management, Imperial College Management School, London, 3 April

Barclay, J. (1993) 'Making the right choice: some considerations of the ethics of selection at the workplace, *Recruitment, Selection and Retention* 2(3): 17–23

Bartram, D. (1997) The ITC/EFPPA Survey of Testing and Test Use Worldwide. Paper presented to the 1998 Division of Occupational Psychology Conference, Eastbourne, BPS

Beardwell, I. and Holden, L. (1997) *Human Resource Management: A Contemporary Perspective*, London: Pitman

Becket, M. (1997) 'Psychometric tests that are not the full shilling', *Daily Telegraph*, 27 October, p. 31

Bolger, A. (1997) 'A test for the right selection', *Financial Times*, 15 January, p. 12

Bower, H. (1997) 'Gene dreams', *Personnel Today*, 13 November, pp. 23–6

Bramham, J. (1997) *Benchmarking for People Managers*, London: IPD

Brien, A. (1994) 'Creating and maintaining an ethical profession', *Chartered Accountant Journal of New Zealand*, May, pp. 34–40

British Psychological Society (1989) *Psychological Testing Guidance for the User*, Leicester: British Psychological Society

British Psychological Society (1991) *Code of Conduct Ethical Principles and Guidelines*, Leicester: British Psychological Society

British Psychological Society (1997a) 'Experts hit out at test cowboys', *People Management* 23(2): 16

British Psychological Society (1997b) *'Level "A" Occupational Testing Information Pack'*, Leicester: British Psychological Society

Carrol, A. (1990) 'Principles of business ethics: their role in decision making and an initial consensus', *Management Decisions* 28(8): 20–5

Commission for Racial Equality (1984) *Code of Practice*, London: HMSO

Commission for Racial Equality (1990) *Lines of Progress: An Enquiry into Selection Tests and Equal Opportunities in London Underground*, London: HMSO

Commission For Racial Equality (1992) *Psychometric Tests and Racial Equality*, London: HMSO

Commission For Racial Equality (1993) *Towards Fair Selection: A Survey of Test Practice and Thirteen Case Studies*, London: HMSO

Cook, M. (1990) *Personnel Selection and Productivity*, Chichester: John Wiley, pp. 236–9

Cooper, D. and Robertson, I. (1995) *The Psychology of Personnel Selection*, London: Routledge, pp. 111–30

Cooper, J. (1997a) 'Selection testing: getting it right', *Recruitment Selection Induction Briefing*, Issue No. 2 February, London: Croner Publications, pp. 10–11

Cooper, J. (1997b) 'Psychometrics for development', *Training and Development Briefing*, Issue No. 13, London: Croner Publications, pp. 12–14

Cooper, J., Baker, B. and Maddocks, J. (1996) 'Occupational testing practice: sustaining quality testing processes through CPD: a case study' *Journal of European Industrial Training* 20(7): 3–9

Cramp, L. (1996) 'A test of character' *People Management* 2(24): 21

Davidson, G. (1997) 'The ethical use of psychological testing: Australia' *European Journal of Psychological Assessment* **13**(2): 132–9

Dean, P. (1992) 'Making codes of ethics real' *Journal of Business Ethics* **11**: 285–90

Donkin, R. (1998) 'The wrong tools for the job: new research questions the effectiveness of psychological tests' *Financial Times*, 14 January, p. 14

Equal Opportunities Commission (1988) *Avoiding Sex Bias in Selection Testing*, Manchester: EOC

Finn, W. (1998) 'On an equal footing', *Personnel Today*, 12 March, pp. 37–8

Fowler, A. (1997) 'How to select and use psychometric tests', *People Management* **3**(19): 45–6

Fletcher, C. (1991) 'Candidate reactions to assessment centres and their outcomes, a longitudinal study' in Anderson, N. and Herriot, P. (eds) *International Handbook of Assessment and Selection*, Chichester: John Wiley, pp. 559–62

Fletcher, C. (1993) 'Testing times for the world of psychometrics', *People Management* **25**(12): 47–50

Green, R. (1994) *The Ethical Manager*, New York: Macmillan

Herriot, P. (1993) 'A paradigm busting at the seams', *Journal of Occupational Behaviour* **14**(4): 371–6

Herriot, P. and Fletcher, C. (1990) 'Candidate friendly selection for the 1990s', *Personnel Management* **22**(2): 32–5

Iles, P. and Robertson, I. (1997) 'Impact of selection procedures' in Anderson, N. and Herriot, P. (eds) *International Handbook of Assessment and Selection*, Chichester: John Wiley, pp. 543–66

Institute of Personnel and Development (1992) *Code of Practice on Occupational Testing*, London: IPD

Institute of Personnel and Development (1995a) 'The IPD policy on continuing professional development' in *Codes of Practice*, London: IPD, pp. 63–8

Institute of Personnel and Development (1995b) 'Code of practice on psychological testing' in *Codes of Practice*, London: IPD, pp. 27–32

Institute of Personnel and Development (1997) 'IPD advises employers not to base recruitment decisions solely on the results of personality tests', *Journal of Management Psychology* **12**(3–4): 220–2

Jackson, C. (1996) *Understanding Psychological Testing*, Leicester: BPS

Jackson, P. (1997) 'Downsizing and deselection' in Anderson, N. and Herriot, P. (eds) *International Handbook of Assessment and Selection*, Chichester: John Wiley, pp. 619–36

Kellaway, L. (1994) 'Tests on trial: psychometric testing of job candidates is objective, true or false?' *Financial Times*, 28 March, p. 9

Kent, S. (1997) 'Mettle fatigue', *Personnel Today*, 16 January, pp. 24–7

Legge, K. (1995) *Human Resource Management: Rhetorics and Realities*, Basingstoke: Macmillan, p. 305

Liedtka, J. (1991) 'Organisational value contention and managerial mindsets', *Journal of Business Ethics* **10**: 543–57

Lindley, P. (1995) 'Continuing professional development', *The Psychologist* **8**: 5

Lord, W. (1994) 'The face behind the figures', *Personnel Management* **26**(12): 30–3

Mabey, C. and Iles, P. (1993) 'The strategic integration of assessment and development practices: succession planning and the new manager development', *Human Resource Management Journal* **4**(3): 16–35

Mabey, C. and Salaman, G. (1995) *Strategic Human Resource Management*, Oxford: Blackwell, pp. 19–67

Maddocks, J. (1998) 'Thinking ahead: the future of psychometrics and other approaches to assessment', *Assessment Matters*, Spring 7: 3–4

Manese, W.R. (1986) *Fair and Effective Testing*, London: Quorum

Matthewman, J. (1993) *HR Effectiveness*, London: IPD

McHenry, R. (1997) 'Tried and tested', *People Management* 3(2): 32–7

Melamed, T. and Jackson, D. (1995) 'Psychological instruments: the potential benefits and practical issues', *Industrial and Commercial Training* 27(4): 11–16

Mello, J.A. (1996) 'Personality tests and privacy rights', *HR Focus*, March, pp. 22–3

Newell, S. and Shackleton, V. (1992) 'Are psychological tests being used ethically in British industry and commerce?', *Selection Development Review* 8(6): 5–7

Newell, S. and Shackleton, V. (1993) 'The use and abuse of psychometric tests in British industry and commerce', *Human Resource Management Journal* 4(1): 14–23

North, S. (1994) 'Mind readers (psychometric testing)', *Personnel Today*, 5 April, pp. 18–22

Palmer, C. (1997) 'Workplace: biased, intrusive, manipulative', *The Observer*, 3 August, p. 8

Pickard, J. (1995) 'Prepare to make a moral judgement', *People Management* 1(9): 22–7

Pickard, J. (1996a) 'The wrong turns to avoid with tests', *People Management* 2(16): 20–5

Pickard, J. (1996b) 'Misuse of tests leads to unfair recruitment', *People Management* 2(25): 7

Publishers' Association (1994) *Responsible Test Use: Guidelines for Test Ppublishers and Test Users*, London: Publishers Association

Purcell, J. (1996) Introduction paper 'Ethics in a Boundaryless World' presented to the first Conference on Ethical Issues in Contemporary HRM, Imperial College Management School, 3 April

Raiborn, C. and Payne, D. (1990) 'Corporate codes of conduct: a collective conscience and continuum', *Journal of Business Ethics* 9: 879–89

Rich, M. and Donkin, R. (1994) 'A testing time in the job market', *Financial Times*, 19 December, p. 10

Robertson, I. and Smith, J. (1989) 'Personnel selection methods', in Smith, J. and Robertson, I. (eds) *Advances in Selection and Assessment*, Chichester: John Wiley

Robertson, I., Iles, P., Gratton, L. and Sharpley, D. (1991) 'The impact of personnel selection and assessment methods on candidates', *Human Relations* 44(9): 963–82

Rothwell, S. (1995) 'Human resource planning', in Storey, J. (ed.) *Human Resource Management: A Critical Text*, London: Routledge, pp. 167–202

Saville, P. and Holdsworth, R. (1993) 'Equal Opportunities Guidelines for Best Practice', in *Occupational Testing* Esher, Surrey: Saville and Holdsworth

Schenieder, B. and Konz, A.Z. (1989) 'Strategic job analysis', *Human Resource Management* 28(1): 51–63

Shackleton, V. and Newell, S. (1997) 'International assessment and selection', in Anderson, N. and Herriot, P. (eds) *International Handbook of Assessment and Selection*, Chichester: John Wiley, pp. 821–82

Sheppard, G. (1995) 'Tests of character' *Personnel Today*, 11 April, pp. 23–6

Sims, R. (1992) 'The challenge of ethical behaviour in organisation', *Journal of Business Ethics* 11: 505–13

Sisson, K. (1994) 'Paradigms, practice and prospects' in Sisson, K. (ed.) *Personnel Management: A Comprehensive Guide to Theory and Practice in Britain* (2nd edn), Oxford: Blackwell, pp. 3–50

Smith, K., Johnson, P. and Cassell, C. (1995) Corporate Codes in Their Organisational Context: Issues of Implementation. Paper given to the BPS Occupational Psychology Conference, Warwick University, January

Smith, S. (1996) 'A fair test?', *Personnel Today*, 16 January, pp. 25–30

Stevens, B. (1994) 'An analysis of corporate ethical code studies: where do we go from here?', *Journal of Business Ethics* 13: 63–9

Storey, J. (ed.) (1995) 'HRM: still marching on, or marching out?', in *Human Resource Management: A Critical Text*, London: Routledge, pp. 3–22

Toplis, J., Dulewicz, V. and Fletcher, C. (1997) *Psychological Testing: An Introductory Manager's Guide* (3rd edn), London: IPD

Townley, B. (1991) 'Selection and appraisal: reconstituting "social relations"' in Storey, J. (ed.) *New Perspectives on Human Resource Management*, London: Routledge, pp. 92–108

Townley, B. (1993) 'Foucault, power/knowledge and its relevance for human resource management', *Academy of Management Review* 18(3): 518–45

Trezise, E. (1996) 'An introduction to business ethics for HRM teaching and research', *Personnel Review*, 25(6): 85–9

Winstanley, D., Woodall, J. and Heery, E. (1996) 'Business ethics and human resource management', *Personnel Review* 25(6): 5–12

Wood, M. (1997) 'Human resource specialists: guardians of ethical conduct?', *Journal of European Industrial Training* 21(3): 110–16

Wood, R. (1996) 'Psychometrics should make assessment fairer', *Equal Opportunity Review*, May–June 67: 27–33

Wheatley, M. (1996) 'Are psychometric tests racially biased?', *Human Resources*, 26: 45–9

CHAPTER 5

Ethics and equality: reconciling false dilemmas

Sonia Liff and Linda Dickens

Introduction

Equal opportunity, with its links to concerns of social and organisational justice and to individual rights (embodied in European and national legislation) is one area of human resource management which appears to have an 'obvious' ethical dimension. It is an area where codes of practice from the equality agencies provide guiding principles for best practice and where human resource professionals have been encouraged by their professional body, the Institute of Personnel and Development (IPD), to operate as change agents.

The emphasis placed on the social justice and individual rights dimension of equality action, however, has waned in recent years and rationales for action based on promoting business interests are increasingly being presented. Equality action is argued for as a means to enhance the functioning of the organisation and to further its goals. 'Business case' arguments, rather than appeals to social justice and/or ethical standards, fit with the particular free market political context of the 1980s and early 90s, while the reduced emphasis on individual legal rights reflects the limited achievements in practice of legal compliance approaches and the deregulationary climate. It was a context which appeared to shift the ethical basis for equality action from the Kantian position of treating people with respect as end in itself, to a more utilitarian approach.

At the same time we are witnessing a shift in terminology from promoting 'equal opportunities' to 'managing diversity' (IPD, 1996). Diversity approaches explicitly acknowledge difference whereas most practical equality interventions (and the predominant legislative approach) have been underpinned by the view that men and women are fundamentally the same and thus should be treated the same (that is, the Aristotelian notion that like should be treated alike). The diversity approach argues that valuing differences between people can bring positive benefits to the organisation.

The nature of these developments and critical engagement with the diversity concept is provided by the authors, separately, elsewhere (Dickens, 1994a; Liff, 1997). In this chapter our aim is to deal with them in the context of exploring some ethical issues which are raised in pursuing equality. In particular we discuss the way in which equality interventions have been conceived and presented so that 'ethical dilemmas' or clashes of moral principles appear to arise. These are the social justice case versus the business case for equality action, and valuing diversity versus meritocracy as competing 'ethical bases' for action.

A model is outlined to demonstrate the main ethical dilemmas already indicated and these are then further discussed to highlight some problems. We then seek to show that the apparently contradictory aspects pose not necessarily an either/or choice but rather a challenge of integration.

Our argument is that the business case need not be at the expense of a social justice case for equality and that the perception that such a choice has to be made needs to be located in the particular context in which the business case has been emphasised. Further, we argue that, rather than having to choose between the ethical 'goods' of the merit principle and the recognition of diversity, it is precisely the failure to recognise diversity which makes it so difficult to challenge the notion of merit as a social construction working against minority groups and women. Also, if diversity were genuinely accepted the apparent incompatibility between it and the assessment of merit would be less problematic.

The apparent dilemmas

Social justice case versus the business case

Put starkly this poses an argument that the justification for equality is that it is morally right and should be pursued for this reason (with state imposed sanctions if necessary) regardless of the costs or inefficiencies it occasions for business (reflecting a deontological perspective), against one which argues that the goal of equality (the ethical 'good') can be better served by downplaying moral exhortations and instead stressing that equality action can serve organisational ends.

Diversity versus merit

Treating people fairly on merit is a fundamental moral value which has wide-spread legitimacy as an approach. It is an approach underpinned by the assumption that men and women are fundamentally the same. Thus treating people equally by judging individuals on their particular merits against the same standards is the best way to pursue equality and any deviation from this (for example, group-perspective positive action) is argued to be special treatment which undermines equality claims. Counterposed to this is the argument that inequality is the result, at least in part, of a failure to accept differences and to respond to them, and that meritocracy is not a neutral concept but rather embodies standards which favour the dominant group.

The false choices which emerge from counterposing these different moral principles can be illustrated by drawing on a model developed by Billing and Alvesson (1989) to map approaches to understanding women's absence from management positions (see Figure 5.1).

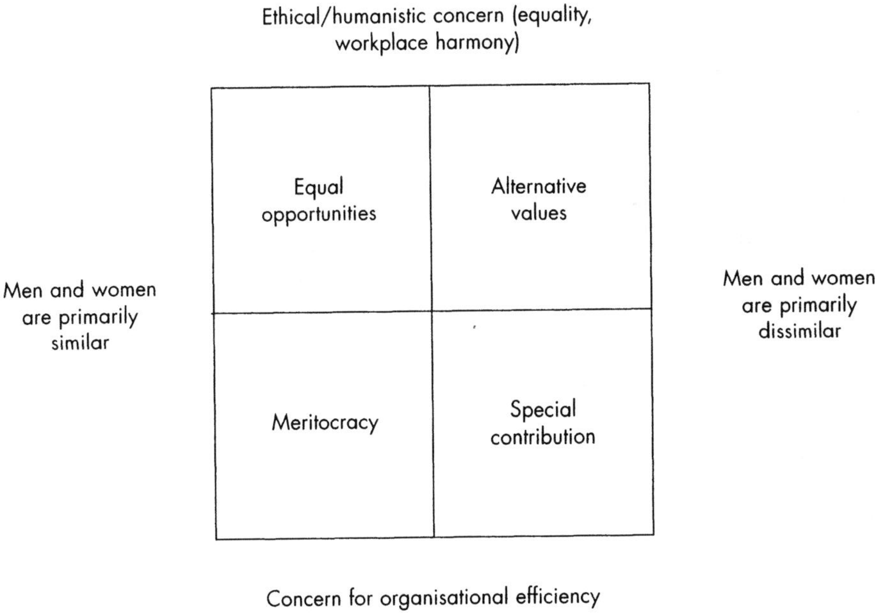

Ethical/humanistic concern (equality, workplace harmony)

Equal opportunities	Alternative values
Meritocracy	Special contribution

Men and women are primarily similar

Men and women are primarily dissimilar

Concern for organisational efficiency

FIGURE 5.1   Four ways of looking at women and leadership
(Billing and Alvesson, 1989)

This model was constructed from a review of the literature on women and management but its underlying principles have a broader purchase. It shows the ways in which the dilemmas identified earlier are reproduced in this mapping of equality approaches. As a consequence it would appear that advocating a particular approach to equality involves coming down on one side or the other of the two dilemmas: social justice or business efficiency; meritocratic or recognising diversity approaches. Billing and Alvesson (1989) sketch out the four types of explanations of why women fail to reach senior management positions which are indicated in the matrix as follows.

Equal opportunities perspective

The perception of the problem is that women are stereotyped and discriminated against. As a result of this they are denied opportunities to reach senior positions. This can be demonstrated in part by evidence that men and women with similar 'human capital' progress differentially. But men and women are basically similar, or would be if they were not channelled into different experiences and education. So if prejudice were tackled and discrimination removed equal outcomes for men and women would result. This should be pursued by senior management (with broader social support via legislation) because it is morally right.

Meritocratic perspective

The problem to be addressed is not discrimination per se but rather the under-utilisation of resources. Men and women are basically the same and so if organisations behaved rationally then decisions based on sex would disappear (for the most part). Unequal achievement by women and men is a problem that should be addressed primarily because it is inefficient rather than because it is wrong or unjust.

Special contribution perspective

Men and women have minor but significant differences. This does not make women worse than men in terms of the contribution they could make to management. Women possess complementary qualifications and thus a potential to contribute to business efficiency. So once women's difference in terms of experience, ways of behaviour, feeling and thinking are recognised their promotion will be accepted on business terms.

Alternative values perspective

This stresses difference more strongly than the special contribution perspective. Men and women are different and want different things from management, organisations and so on. There is a problem of fit between the female role and organisational expectations, as a result of which women exclude themselves from certain positions or opt out when they reach them. But this needs to be understood not simply as a loss for women (or an effective choice) but as a problem for organisations. There is a need to recognise that the alternative values that women possess could transform business and ways of working towards more ethical forms of organisation and work practices for all. There is therefore a moral incentive to pursue this.

The different perspectives depicted in these ideal types provide alternative explanations of women's exclusion. The kind of HR interventions taken to promote equality are likely to reflect these different understandings. Where the problem is seen to be that of the equal opportunity perspective one might expect measures such as awareness training to counter prejudice in, for example, recruitment and promotion and requirements to adhere to formalised policies and procedures designed to minimise scope for discrimination. The merit perspective leads to an emphasis on the objective identification of qualifications and skills necessary for particular jobs (through job analysis) so candidates may be measured against them using various valid selection techniques paying no attention to gender, class, race and so on. The HR interventions suggested by these two approaches are those which are commonly recommended in good practice equality guidance (Dickens, 1994b).

Human resource initiatives to recognise the value of women's different attributes, similar to those that reflect the special contribution perspective, can be found, for example, in job evaluation schemes (such as that developed for manual workers in local government, Lodge, 1987). These include factors typically found in work done by women such as caring skills and responsibility for people alongside the more usual male-oriented factors such as physical strength and responsibility for material things. A further example could be in rethinking competency profiles as they relate to leadership and team working. The alternative values perspective would give rise to much more radical organisational change designed to interest women in staying and contributing without a requirement for them to adapt to pre-existing organisational structures, norms and values. Such change would impact on all HR practices which currently tend to be gender blind (Dickens, 1998; Woodall, 1996) and might involve, for example, reconceptualising working time and rethinking career trajectories.

Having outlined the way in which social justice and business efficiency concerns are counterposed in equality debates, as are meritocratic and difference approaches, we move on to look at the development of current approaches to workplace equality, their limitations and the way they embody the ethical dilemmas outlined earlier.

The growth of 'business case' arguments

The 1980s saw the growth of equality discourses that stressed business case arguments for equality action. Rather than appeals to social justice (or the need for compliance with anti-discrimination legislation) arguments were based on business self-interest as a rationale for equality action. The business case strategy provided the keystone for Opportunity 2000 (a campaign to improve the quantity and quality of women's employment) from the time of its launch in 1991; and is at the centre of the Commission for Racial Equality's promotion of its Racial Equality Standard (Commission for Racial Equality, 1995). The Equal Opportunity Commission has sponsored projects on the 'economics of equal opportunity' (Humphries and Rubery, 1995) which attempt to quantify the costs and benefits of various equality initiatives.

Arguments about positive organisational benefits from equality initiatives have always played a part in attempts to get equality action, but in the 1980s and 90s it became the dominant rationale. This can be seen as a pragmatic response to the economic and political environment of the time. In an increasingly competitive world it does not seem plausible to expect businesses to do something just because it is morally right. They also need to be convinced that equality action will not undermine their efficiency or effectiveness or, even better, that it will contribute to the 'bottom line'. Conservative governments from 1979 saw the free market as compatible with the promotion of equality (Forbes, 1996). The reliance on a business case for equality, with its focus on economic efficiency, fitted the neo-liberal market model.

Increased emphasis on the business case rationale arose also in the context of acknowledged weakness in the legislative levers for equality and an appreciation that these would not be strengthened by Conservative governments with a policy of deregulation. Given the unwillingness to impose extra 'burdens' on businesses in the form of increased legislation or monitoring, change had to be achieved via persuasion. The move to a business case approach could also be argued to reflect a recognition that the traditional personnel management approach had experienced limited success. This could fit within a wider critique of bureaucratic initiatives of isolated personnel departments. Instead, an approach which seeks to align human resource interventions with wider business strategy has gained currency beyond equality issues.

While understanding the reasons for this development it is important also to draw attention to its negative consequences. Once social justice and efficiency arguments are counterposed then the logical consequence would seem to be that an intervention cannot be both ethical and acting in the interests of business. This perhaps explains the initially odd absence of writing on equality as part of recent interest in business ethics. By polarising business and social justice concerns there is also the tendency to narrow down the meanings of 'business concerns' to the financial and little else. The danger, as has already been alluded to, is that if an employer can show that something they are being asked to do in the pursuit of equality is not an efficient use of resources on a quantifiable cost–benefit analysis then there is no responsibility to pursue it. Even if 'business interests' are perceived as broader than the narrowly financial, action is still contingent. Treating people fairly can be part of a management approach based on engendering high trust and high commitment but not all organisations will wish to adopt this particular management style. Selective equality action is inherent in the business case approach since it will occur only where organisational needs dictate. This can be seen in the way various equality measures are targeted on particular groups of women rather than made universally available (Holtermann and Clarke, 1992). Thus business case arguments are more likely to generate equality initiatives for women at senior levels and in areas of skill shortage (Cockburn, 1991; Coyle, 1995; Dickens, 1994a). While they may benefit a female IT manager they may offer less to women working as part-time check-out operators.

Although contrasted with a social justice approach this emphasis on business interests is not unethical according to a teleological perspective in that this allows people to be treated as a means to an end if it is in the interests of the majority to do so. On the assumption that competitive success of the individual firm is to the advantage of the majority then this ethical framework permits 'unfair' treatment, for example treating women as a cheap, disposable, peripheral labour force, if it serves this end. By the same token, equality action is likely in circumstances where this can be seen to aid competitive success, for example measures to ensure a representative workforce where this is important to secure a particular customer base. The fact that the business case centres on the individual organisation may narrow the scope for demonstrating benefits since the costs of inequality and wasted human resources may only be evident at a more aggregate societal level.

Questions also can be raised about the underlying basis for change in this approach. While it appears superficially plausible that managers will do something for business reasons that they would not do for social justice reasons, there are missing stages to the argument. The main one is the assumption that organisational decision makers will be persuaded by the argument that women have the same skills as men and are potentially the best person for the job. In practice, the evidence ranging from even extreme labour/skill shortage situations, world wars for example, to studies of modern selection interviews (Curran, 1988; Jenkins, 1986; Summerfield, 1989) suggest there is still considerable connection in many managers' minds between the criteria listed on job descriptions and people specifications and what are believed to be sex- or race-linked characteristics. Jobs are gendered and thus it is difficult for many managers to assess a woman as the best candidate for a particular post, for example, a financial products salesperson (Collinson *et al.*, 1990). In this context, business case arguments to the effect that equality approaches allow organisations to tap into a wider labour pool become less persuasive. At a more basic level questions can be raised about whether the rational model of decision making portrayed in business case arguments reflects the reality of how managers process information.

So a further dilemma, or vicious circle, seems to be that the apparently rational, if ethically suspect, approach of abandoning social justice arguments in favour of business-focused ones not only risks abandoning equality goals for a significant part of the workforce, but may also fail to persuade those managers who do not share the underpinning values such as a belief that men and women are interchangeable as human resources.

Diversity-based equality: issues raised by taking account of difference

The second dimension on Billing and Alvesson's (1989) matrix is based on whether men and women are seen as fundamentally similar or fundamentally dissimilar. While there is a long-standing theoretical debate about the merits of adopting 'sameness' or 'difference' approaches most practical equality interventions have been firmly premised on the view that the case on which equality claims should be based is that men and women are fundamentally the same.

The reasons for emphasising the similarity between men and women are varied. At a pragmatic level there is the argument that historical experience has been that whenever attention is drawn to the differences between men and women this has been used as a basis for not just different treatment, but worse treatment. Examples range from skill issues such as 'nimble fingers' through to responsibility for childcare. In both cases women are seen to have particular attributes but these are not rewarded. It is worth noting that at this pragmatic level there are no particular claims being made about whether men and women are really fundamentally the same or not. Rather, the argument is that it would be best to keep quiet about any areas of difference and base claims for equality on the assumption of sameness, or on those areas where sameness exists, or on trying to ensure other developments which will make sameness claims more plausible (e.g. increased availability of childcare).

At a theoretical level, two rather different arguments are pursued. The first argues that difference approaches cannot be pursued, or are at least very difficult to pursue, without accepting some element of essentialism. That is, one needs to say what the difference consists of, and in doing so one inevitably provides an over-homogenised view of members of each group (women, black people and so on) and an overly polarised view of the difference between groups (for example, women and men). Furthermore these perceptions present an overly determinist account of what it means to be, say, a man or a woman.

A distinctive theoretical position does not take issue with claims to difference per se but rather challenges the ways in which 'difference' is utilised within equality debates. So, for example, MacKinnon (1987) makes the telling remark that men and women are equally different but not equally powerful. From this perspective the equality problem is disadvantage, and the maintenance of, or emphasis on, difference is one of the ways in which this oppression is maintained. (In support of this one might note that there are lots of differences between people that are not used as the basis for social or workplace organisation.)

Powerful as these arguments are, they are being challenged by the recent interest in diversity approaches to equality that see value in developing equality initiatives which acknowledge differences between people. This perspective is attractive at least in part because it addresses critiques of traditional equality approaches which in relation to race, for example, demand assimilation in the dominant culture as the price of equality. As, for example, in the infamous 'Tebbit test' whereby a Conservative peer suggested that you were only entitled to claim the rights and benefits of being English if you cheered the English cricket team. More broadly, this approach suggests that if ethnic minorities want to be treated equally then they must be prepared to adopt the dominant language and culture. In gender terms this is usually discussed in terms of the 'male standard' whereby equality is granted to those women who are willing and able to work in the same way as men, involving, for example, long hours, continuous careers, commitment to work over family. Instead of demanding that individuals adapt to the dominant modes of organisations, the diversity approach suggests that organisations should accept people's differences and adapt to them. In pragmatic terms it also addresses the disillusionment felt by those whose attempts to convince managers that women can bring exactly the same skills to management as men, have fallen on deaf ears. Furthermore, it is not necessarily as contradictory to the theoretical positions outlined earlier as at first it seems since we can argue that the response to having difference used against us is not to pretend it does not exist but rather confront it head on as an issue which demands a different type of response.

There are different versions of what diversity is – in particular whether differences are distributed on an individual or social group basis (Liff, 1997). Those diversity approaches which stress differences based on social group membership (for example, ethnicity, gender or religion) come closest to the concerns of existing equality policies. Other versions stress sources of difference as varied as learning styles, personality and appearance which might affect experience in the workplace. They have focused on ways in which policies can help people realise their full potential within the organisation rather than simply to ensure they are not being discriminated against.

The key aspect of diversity approaches that raises ethical issues is the move away from universalistic HR policies. The problem this raises is best exemplified by the positioning of 'meritocracy' on the matrix. Billing and Alvesson (1989) show meritocracy as an approach based on an underlying belief in the similarity of men and women and one rooted in business case-type arguments about efficiency. This is an accurate representation of the way in which meritocracy is commonly understood – people should be assessed against the same job and organisation-based criteria, and the best person should be given the job or promotion. Since meritocracy is a core value in western societies it is very difficult to question. Yet recognising difference appears to require this since our views of how to determine merit are almost all based on comparison against a common standard. Attempts to deviate from 'meritocratic' approaches invariably invoke claims of special or preferential treatment which have been damaging for all equality claims. This has been particularly apparent in relation to affirmative action initiatives in the USA. Having identified the dominant approaches and the problems which arise from counterposing different bases for action we conclude by considering the ways in which these dilemmas might be reconciled.

Reconciling dilemmas

Integrating social justice and business case approaches

Counterposing efficiency and social justice concerns creates a serious problem for equality strategies but it is one that may be more apparent than real. This separation of rationales for equality action can be challenged at both an empirical and theoretical level. At an empirical level there is evidence that organisations do not necessarily experience social justice and business case arguments in as polarised a way as our analysis suggested. For example the third annual report for Opportunity 2000 (Business in the Community, 1994) suggests that while the language of the business case is ubiquitous this is not constructed in a narrowly economistic way, it is not simplistically counter-posed with social justice claims. So, for example, companies were able to articulate a wide range of business cases which included things like improvements in workplace morale and the motivation of women employees (arguably an *equal opportunities perspective* on Billing and Alvesson's matrix), and to change the perceptions of the organisation or the nature of the service provided towards a more 'feminine' approach (arguably an *alternative values approach* on Billing and Alvesson's matrix). Since these approaches draw on arguments which appear to derive from the social justice side of the business case/social justice divide in the matrix in defence of 'business' rationales, it suggests the discourses can co-exist in managerial thinking.

Similar practical evidence comes from a Department of Employment (Welsh *et al.*, 1994) survey of a group of organisations which were leaders in pursuing initiatives in the race equality field. When these 75 organisations were asked why they had decided to pursue positive action initiatives 88 per cent said it was to demonstrate a commitment to social justice and 87 per cent said it was to make better use of human resources. This again demonstrates that for many managers there is no contradiction between simultaneously pursuing business case and social justice arguments for equality interventions (Liff, 1995).

Are there ways in which these integrative tendencies can be reinforced? The most obvious way might seem to be to manipulate the context in which businesses operate to change the costs and benefits of ignoring equal opportunities. This has been a traditional role for the legal framework where costs can be imposed on those acting 'immorally' sufficient to undermine any economic benefits that might accrue from so doing. In practice UK legislation has largely failed to act in this way as a result of difficulties in bringing cases, low levels of applicant success and, until recently at least, low levels of compensation where discrimination was found. Furthermore, anti-discrimination legislation is actually framed in such a way that business reasons can be used explicitly as a justification for differential treatment (Dickens, 1992).

Consumer boycotts, or ethical investment, and trade union action are ways in which activists have tried to change employers' perceptions about the business significance of social justice issues. There are practical problems with this approach in relation to workplace gender and ethnic equality in that these have not figured highly in either trade union bargaining (where a focus on class concerns tends to play down diversity among workers) or in consumer campaigns. Consumer concerns for animal welfare and the environment have arguably had a much greater influence on business practice than any human welfare issues. This is true even in relation to Third World producers – despite some evidence of increasing pressure around the issue of child labour. The situation is particularly problematic in the UK where part of the attack on the public sector has been to set workers and 'consumers' against each other by arguing that, for example, local councils are being run for the benefit of their employees rather than local residents. This has undermined equality action as part of 'good employer' practice, leaving it to be justified in terms of delivering better quality service and to be abandoned when the emphasis is on the cost of service provision as under compulsory competitive tendering (Escott and Whitfield, 1995).

In addition to the practical difficulties with these ways of changing the business context there is a further concern that if they operate in an environment where a social justice/business split in motivations for action is the dominant discourse they risk reinforcing such thinking rather than challenging it. Trade union action mobilising around equality provides a potential mechanism for arguments based on fairness to be asserted although perhaps more commonly it operates with the business case logic, affecting the employer's cost–benefit analysis by increasing the costs of not taking equality action. Rather than changing the understanding of what is a business issue such interventions appear to accept uncritically that organisations are only interested in the economic sphere and simply try to broaden what falls within this sphere.

In contrast, stakeholder theory provides a more radical basis for underpinning what appears clear from the empirical data – that many organisations do act in pursuance of social as well as economic goals. By legitimating the interests of actors in addition to shareholders, stakeholder approaches provide a basis for seeing that organisations also have a responsibility towards groups such as their employees. Organisations, in this view, have certain moral responsibilities towards stakeholders (over and above those they have to all human beings) and have an obligation to consider the interests of stakeholders alongside the duty to pursue more conventional organisation goals (Nijhof and Fisscher, 1998). Internal levers could be used to promote a reconciliation between the rights of various stakeholders in relation to equality issues. Currently this is rare, as few line managers are appraised and rewarded on the basis of their contribution to furthering equality in the enterprise in addition to more traditional business performance measures.

The application of stakeholder theory to workplace social group equality issues is far from straightforward. If employees are considered to have particular rights over non-employees (as would appear to be implied by tighter definitions of who constitutes a stakeholder), then this could legitimate indirectly discriminatory HR practices such as internal and word-of-mouth recruitment, and last-in-first-out redundancy selection which often perpetuate a non-representative workforce. If current employees are seen as a group of stakeholders with common interests then this could legitimate trade unions prioritising, say, protection of overtime over shorter working hours with the possibility of increased employment overall. As this example makes clear such a development not only gives priority to employees over non-employees but, by presenting the workforce as an homogeneous group, may also embody the needs and priorities of one group of employees (in this case, men) over another (in this case, women with domestic commitments). If a utilitarian position is adopted which allows the rights of some stakeholders to be traded off in favour of the greater good of all then this again raises problematic equality issues particularly in a context where some groups have been more successful than others in establishing their needs as central.

Nijhof and Fisscher's (1998) development of a stakeholder approach founded on an ethics of care (Gilligan, 1982) does provide some ways of addressing these concerns. They suggest that among other things such an approach implies the need to take account of individuals' particular needs and circumstances and, importantly, to involve them in moral deliberations. In equality terms this seems compatible with a diversity approach, although perhaps with the more strongly individualistic approach to diversity already identified. It would also suggest the need to move away from an HR approach based solely on the top-down procedural model favoured by codes of practice.

Developments away from the top-down approach are already apparent in the decision to give more attention to issues of organisational culture change within Opportunity 2000's latest round of annual awards (Business in the Community, 1998). One of the key dimensions of such culture change is said to be *sharing ownership*. An example of how an existing HR policy might by changed by such a perspective is that the mentoring of female or ethnic minority employees could be seen as a two-way process, with management learning about their experience and the issues that are important to them, as well as supporting their advancement in the organisation (Kram and Hall, 1996).

Integrating valuing diversity and meritocracy approaches

HR policies based on meritocracy, such as well-defined job specifications against which applicants can be measured using selection techniques with high validity, have been the backbone of workplace equality policies. Yet there is widespread recognition that they have not achieved what most people expect to be the outcome of equality policies – a more equitable (proportional) distribution of jobs between men and women and between people from different ethnic groups. Policies which attempt to address this problem by treating people differently and responding to their different needs through positive action give rise to concern that people are being given jobs because of who they are rather than on the basis of what they can do. This has created ethical issues not simply because people are attached to meritocracy as an ethical value but also because it appears to be violating the rights of those individuals from dominant groups who are denied, say, a job even although they are not personally guilty of discrimination (Edwards, 1995).

As with the earlier dilemma there are both practical and theoretical developments and arguments that can be used to rethink this problem. At a practical level it is important to recognise that in many cases the problem is more apparent than real. Where there has been no effective rethinking of the white male standard against which individuals are assessed then the merit principle is not being applied in a neutral way and no ethical good is being served by its maintenance. Thus HR policies which prevent selectors insisting that a particular job must be worked on a full-time basis, or on the appointee having a degree when what is being sought is a particular level of intellectual ability rather than a specific set of knowledge, are not breaching the merit principle so much as trying to ensure that it operates equitably.

Research evidence suggests members of dominant groups find it very hard to understand such interventions in these terms (Cockburn, 1991; Salaman, 1986). White men's feeling that *they* are being treated unfairly by equality initiatives stem here less from a genuine granting of rights to some at the cost of removing them from others, than from a failure to see how they were advantaged by the way HR policies previously operated. Dominant notions of equality based on sameness discourage white males from thinking about the ways in which they work as specific to their circumstances. Neither do they encourage them to understand job requirements as anything other than inherent in the job or the efficient running of the business. Attempts to change the ways in which work is carried out are therefore seen as changing the rules of the game in favour of members of less adequate groups rather than redressing the ways in which white men were previously advantaged. Similarly, excluded groups have felt that if they want equality, it is up to them to comply with the way things are currently done, and may see attempts to facilitate their entry as implying they are not able to make it on their own merits (Young, 1990).

Liff and Cameron (1997) suggest some HR interventions which might help to change understandings of the ways in which organisations currently advantage and disadvantage different groups. This in turn could help build a consensus in favour of equality measures which are currently opposed as special treatment. Such initiatives could include audits which show not simply where men, women and members of different ethnic groups are within the organisation but also what experience and expertise they have and their level of performance. This can highlight the ways in which the organisation is currently under-utilising the skills and abilities of those who are currently excluded from higher level posts within the organisation. Assessments of the costs of current ways of organising, such as long hours, could highlight high levels of stress-related sickness, personal problems and turnover which might make organisations reassess their assumptions about the efficiency of ways of working that have traditionally been problematic for many women. In these and other ways it may be possible to at least reduce the extent to which an attention to employees' differences is seen as an abuse of meritocratic or efficiency principles.

Conclusion

This chapter has drawn on a matrix which offers explanations for women's exclusion to demonstrate the apparent choices that underlie HR intervention to promote equality in employment. We considered the choices posed between the *rationale* for equality action – a concern with social justice or efficiency – and the *bases* on which action is taken – that men and women are fundamentally similar or dissimilar.

Different ethical frameworks connect with the contrasted positions. Thus social justice versus business case dilemmas connect to the Kantian/deontological versus teleological or utilitarian frameworks. Our contention is that this counterposing of approaches and positing of ethical dilemmas compromises equality interventions and is unnecessary. The potential for reconciling social justice and business efficiency rationales and of marrying diversity approaches with merit was explored. Although the particular political and economic context of the 1980s and 90s saw the ascendancy of business case over social justice rationales the two approaches could be integrated in a way suggested by some stakeholder theories. Similarly we exposed the falsity of the apparent dilemma between merit and diversity showing it to be based on a problematic understanding of merit.

At a more theoretical level a problem does remain but it is one that is less an ethical dilemma and rather a dilemma of dominant perspectives on ethics. It arises from the way in which writers about social justice work almost exclusively within a distributive framework. Thus the 'equality problem' becomes how jobs, benefits and opportunities can be equitably shared between members of different social groups. In a context of scarce resources we have seen how this turns into concerns about how to determine who is most deserving of success and about protection of the rights of those who might be displaced in favour of greater equality. Yet, as Young (1990) points out, these issues are in part at least problems created by the distributive paradigm failing to raise certain questions. Most importantly, the dominant approach does not question what is to be distributed. In the workplace context this means that the hierarchical organisation of work and a division of labour that creates large numbers of mundane, repetitive jobs and few where the occupant has the opportunity to use skill and discretion are taken for granted. At the societal level it does not question the ways in which some people end up with too much work, working long hours and suffering from stress and burnout, while others are unable to gain employment. From this perspective the challenge for equality initiatives is less to ensure that a small number of women or ethnic minority men make it to the top of organisations but rather to create a context in which everyone has access to meaningful and rewarding work compatible with their other responsibilities and interests.

References

Billing, Y. and Alvesson, M. (1989) 'Four Ways of Looking at Women and Leadership' *Scandinavian Journal of Management* **5**(1): 63–80

Business in the Community (1994) *Opportunity 2000: Towards a balanced workforce*, 3rd year report, London: Business in the Community

Business in the Community (1998) *Towards Culture Change: Examples of Best Practice*, London: Business in the Community

Cockburn, C. (1991) *In the Way of Women: Men's resistance to sex equality in organisations*, London: Macmillan

Collinson, D., Knights, D. and Collinson, M. (1990) *Managing to Discriminate*, London: Routledge

Commission for Racial Equality (1995) *Racial Equality Means Business – A Standard for Racial Equality for Employers*, London: Commission for Racial Equality

Coyle, A. (1995) *Women and Organisational Change*, Research Discussion Series no.14, Manchester: Equal Opportunities Commission

Curran, M. (1988) 'Gender and recruitment: people and places in the labour market' *Work, Employment and Society* **2**(3): 335–51

Dickens, L. (1992) 'Anti-discrimination legislation: Exploring and explaining the impact on women's employment' in McCarthy, W. (ed.) *Legal Intervention in Industrial Relations: Gains and Losses* Oxford: Blackwell

Dickens, L. (1994a) 'The business case for equal opportunities: is the carrot better than the stick?' *Employee Relations* **16**(8): 5–18

Dickens, L. (1994b) 'Wasted Resources? Equal opportunities in employment' in Sisson, K. (ed.) *Personnel Management: A Comprehensive Guide to Theory and Practice in Britain*, Oxford: Blackwell

Dickens, L. (1998) 'What HRM means for gender equality' *Human Resource Management Journal* **8**(1): 23–40

Edwards, J. (1995) *When Race Counts: The Morality of Racial Preference in Britain and America*, London: Routledge

Escott, K. and Whitfield, D. (1995) *The Gender Impact of CCT in Local Government*, Research Discussion Series No. 12, Manchester: Equal Opportunities Commission

Forbes, I. (1996) 'The privatisation of sex equality policy' in Lovenduski, J. and Norris, P. (eds) *Women in Politics*, Oxford: Oxford University Press

Gilligan, C. (1982) *In a Different Voice*, Cambridge, MA and London: Harvard University Press

Holtermann, S. and Clarke, K. (1992) *Parents, Employment Rights and Childcare*, Research Discussion Series No. 4, Manchester: Equal Opportunities Commission

Humphries, J. and Rubery, J. (eds) (1995) *The Economics of Equal Opportunities*, Manchester: Equal Opportunities Commission

IPD (1996) *Managing Diversity: An IPD Position Paper*, London: IPD

Jenkins, R. (1986) *Racism and Recruitment: Managers, Organisations and Equal Opportunity in the Labour Market*, Cambridge: Cambridge University Press

Kram, K. and Hall, D. (1996) 'Mentoring in a context of diversity and turbulence' in Kossek, E. and Lobel, S. (eds) *Managing Diversity: Human Strategies for Transforming the Workplace*, Oxford: Blackwell

Liff, S. (1995) 'The Reality of Positive Action' *Industrial Law Journal* 24(3): 291–5

Liff, S. (1997) 'Two routes to managing diversity: Individual differences versus social group characteristics' *Employee Relations* 19(1): 11–26

Liff, S. and Cameron, I. (1997) 'Changing equality cultures to move beyond "women's problems"' *Gender, Work and Organisation* 4(1): 35–46

Lodge, D. (1987) 'Working equality into manual job evaluation' *Personnel Management* 19(9): 27–31

MacKinnon, C. (1987) *Feminism Unmodified: Discourses on Life and Law*, Cambridge, MA and London: Harvard University Press

Nijhof, A. and Fisscher, O. (1998) 'From stakeholder theory to acting in a responsible way: Implications for human resource management'. Paper to the 2nd UK conference on 'ethical issues in contemporary HRM', Kingston University, January

Salaman, G. (1986) *Working*, Chichester: Ellis Harwood

Summerfield, P. (1989) *Women Workers in the Second World War*, London: Routledge

Welsh, C., Knox, J. and Brett, M. (1994) *Acting Positively: Positive Action under the Race Relations Act 1976*, Research Series No. 36, Sheffield: Employment Department

Woodall, J. (1996) 'Human resource management: the vision of the gender blind' in Towers, B. (ed.) *The Handbook of Human Resource Management* (2nd edn), Oxford: Blackwell

Young, I.M. (1990) *Justice and the Politics of Difference*, Princeton, NJ: Princeton University Press

CHAPTER 6

HRM and employee well-being: raising the ethical stakes

Noeleen Doherty and Shaun Tyson

Introduction

For many years, employers have been urged to take care of the physical health of their workforce, both through the pressure of legislation and through the pressure of higher expectations, which have increased the social desirability of avoiding hazards and accidents at work. Often the appeal to provide good physical working conditions has been through addressing the enlightened self-interest of employers, by, for example, reducing lost time from accidents. Now that we have moved to the age of the knowledge worker, there is a growing interest in employee mental well-being in the work context, which has similar potential for mixed motives, but a far greater impact on the person and on his or her relationships.

The concern for mental well-being may be seen not necessarily as a sign that senior management has moved to a more normative stance, with the interests of employees as central to management concerns, but more as avoidance of the loss of potential creativity and commitment and the threats of litigation. We see little evidence so far of employee mental health being considered a matter for proactive managerial initiative. Instead, management often sideline questions of mental ill health. We believe this is in part because of the confused ethical position in which they find themselves. The lack of employment security and the use of management practices which are designed to manipulate employee attitudes and behaviour in order to deliver high-quality performance, generate many pressures on individual well-being. If employers are now claiming the high moral ground with statements that they believe in employee well-being, the position that they take up would require them to place the mental well-being of employees as a keystone for human resource (HR) policies and practices, raising the ethical stakes.

Despite an extensive and growing body of literature and research evidence to support the proactive management of mental well-being in the workplace, the development of a convincing business case still appears to be the driving force for the majority of organisations to give serious consideration to this issue. The business case relies on cost statistics and the growing risk of litigation such as that evidenced by the legal precedent of the *Walker* v. *Northumberland County Council* case which we describe later. In addition, a preoccupation with the concept of stress and the proliferation of approaches and packages which are essentially crisis management after mental illness has occurred, appear to be somewhat detrimental to the more positive, proactive approach to mental well-being which is embodied in the definition of health as *more than the absence of disease or infirmity* proffered by the World Health Organisation. Is the ethical case for promoting well-being, integrity of individual functioning and the facilitation of mental well-being at odds with human resource management policies? Human resource management (HRM) policies and practices are often seen as a form of social engineering, in essence designed to mould, direct, control and shape behaviour to achieve optimal performance, based on the premise that particular management actions will generate specific sets of behaviours at the level of the individual employee. One argument for addressing issues of employee well-being is that there is a relationship between mental and 'organisation health', based on the assumption that mentally and physically fit employees are productive workers. However, in the current context of organisational insecurity, greater work pressure on employees, the use of strategies such as organisational downsizing and the decline in job security and organisational commitment to providing continuity in career, the rather convenient belief in an identity of the interests between employers and employees could be challenged. These pressures and changes render untenable the unitary frame of reference that employer and employee interests are identical.

Behaviour within organisations is contingent upon an array of factors. The management of mental well-being spans a wide array of policy issues in addition to the development of skills, knowledge, attitudes and behaviours among employees. The impact of organisational change as well as external factors such as the interaction between home and work life all place an added layer of unpredictability on the potential effect of HR policies. At a time when management appears to engineer mental states socially to meet business and financial objectives, the challenge to those responsible for managing people at work is seen as one of ensuring that employee mental well-being is safeguarded.

Work and change – the effects on mental well-being

The workplace is where a considerable number of people, over 25 million in the UK, spend a large proportion of their time. Increasingly the world of work is undergoing major changes and employees are facing many challenges. In addition to the daily demands of work and routine practices and processes, there are internal and external forces driving changes in the nature of work. Rapid and accelerating changes in work structures and processes are occurring worldwide. Economic and market pressures, technological innovation and global competition are on the increase, promoting the use of business process re-engineering, flexible working practices, outsourcing and restructuring through downsizing, rightsizing and delayering. This has resulted in flatter organisational structures, new work patterns and changed contractual arrangements, with increased performance expectations and changes in career patterns and opportunities for many employees. There is the suggestion that these changes amount to work intensification and the alienation of working people, in the classic Marxist sense.

Levi (1994) argued that while many of these changes are being instituted with good intent, there are still negative side effects. Some change is planned and intentional and the negative impact can be foreseen, such as in the potential exploitation of workers through excessive work demands. Other changes, such as the longer term impact of continual downsizing, may have unintentional effects. For example, Jenkins *et al.* (1982) examined the relationship between the threat of redundancy and mental health. They found that there were links between increases in minor psychiatric disorders (such as poor sleep, depression, fatigue, anxiety and irritability) and the threat of redundancy. Lack of interesting work, too, can cause problems, for example, if underemployment is allowed to persist or if working conditions which are harmful are not addressed, employees may be adversely affected. Change is often discontinuous and sometimes uncontrolled and it is argued, any change has the potential to impact on mental health and well-being negatively. For example, a recent study showed that the most highly rated causes of stress in the workplace are: 60 per cent time pressures and deadlines, 54 per cent work overload, 52 per cent threat of job losses, 51 per cent lack of communication and consultation and 46 per cent under-staffing (Cooper/TUC, 1997).

The cost of mental ill health and the business case

The consequences at the individual level of the pressures we have outlined may include poor performance, high labour turnover (including ill health retirements) and increased sickness absence (due both to physical and mental causes). There are a wide variety of statistical estimates of the extent of ill health and mental ill health within the work context. These are published from different sources and report different financial costs to industry which can be confusing. For example, in the *Financial Times* (Taylor, 1995) it was reported that 2.2 million people suffer from ill health (physical and mental) at any one time, due to or made worse by work, and it was estimated that the resulting cost to industry is between £4 and £9 billion per annum. This is equivalent to 2–3 per cent of UK gross domestic product. It has been suggested that mental illness is one of the top three causes of certified sickness absence. Muir (1994) reported a range of statistics including findings from the Department of Social Security's survey of doctors certificates which showed that absence from work exceeded half a billion days in 1991. The CBI (1993 and quoted in Kogan, 1997 p. 142) found that 30 per cent and Muir (1994) quoted that 35 per cent of employee sick leave in the UK is related to stress, anxiety or depression. The Department of Health (quoted in IPD, 1995) estimated that 91 million work days are lost each year due to stress-related illness at a cost of £3.7 billion. The Health and Safety Executive added questions to the 1990 Labour Force Survey to gather data on self-reported work-related illness, and estimated as a result that approximately 17 million days lost as a result of stress/anxiety/depression caused or made worse by work (Hodgson *et al.*, 1993). The estimated cost of these days lost is £100 million. The 1990 Labour Force Survey indicated that there were 105,000 cases of stress and depression caused by work (Hodgson *et al.*, 1993) and 76,000 cases made worse by work. It has also been estimated that thirty times as many days are lost from mental illness as are lost from industrial disputes (O'Leary, 1993).

In addition, mental illness has been quoted as a primary cause of reduced productivity and high staff turnover, accounting for the loss of 91.5 million working days in 1991 alone. It is estimated that annually, nearly 3 in 10 employees will have a mental health problem and an estimated 80 million working days are lost annually, for example, from sickness absence arising from problems such as anxiety and depression, as well as labour turnover, poor performance and accidents at work. The cost to industry has been estimated at £5.3 billion annually (Banham, 1992). The financial case for taking mental well-being seriously appears compelling and despite the array of different estimates in financial cost and a lack of coherent methods for calculating the cost benefits of addressing mental well-being, these statistics often form the basis of the business case.

The growing risk of litigation for both physical and mental ill health caused by work is increasingly apparent in the UK and has put further pressure on companies. For example, a recent survey (UNUM, 1997) indicated that changes in UK work patterns have resulted in a 90 per cent increase in claims for compensation arising from mental and psychological problems over the last five years. The TUC calculated that in 1994, members of affiliated trade unions were awarded a total of £355 million in legal damages after having suffered injury or ill health as a result of their work (Institute of Personnel and Development, 1995). In addition to the litigation element, the responsibility of the employer, for mental well-being, is also emphasised by recent events such as the *Walker* v. *Northumberland County Council* case (November 1994 High Court ruling). Here the failure of the employer to deal with the organisational causes underlying and leading to the mental ill health of their employee was highlighted. This case emphasised the potential for litigation and contingent liability specifically relating to mental ill health caused by work as John Walker was awarded £175,000 for stress and legal fees (Welch, 1996). This has caused employers concern. Given the precedent set by the Walker case, the potential effects of the growing pressure on people in work which gives rise to stress, depression and anxiety may result not only in costs due to poor performance among knowledge workers, accidents, public risk and business costs such as reduced sales and productivity, but may also pave the way for further litigation. The introduction of the Disability Discrimination Act 1996, has further contributed to the need to address mental well-being as an integral aspect of work life (James, 1996).

Health and mental well-being

Health is a difficult concept to define as it has a range of different meanings. The World Health Organisation (1986) defines health as not merely the absence of disease or infirmity but as a state of physical, mental and social well-being. Thus, health is the state which allows the individual to enjoy life and to be able to cope with the inevitable problems of living, without prolonged or significant change of mood. Mental well-being is one key element of health, well-being and fulfillment, which are all conducive to growth and development.

In a number of publications the promotion, development and maintenance of an environment which is sympathetic, supportive and conducive to mental well-being is said to be underpinned by good management practices. The Health and Safety Executive (1995, p. 10) states that 'Ordinary plain good management and regard for people may well be as effective a way of dealing with stress and reducing its effects as a high profile approach.' This notion that 'good management' underpins not only good practice but is also fundamental to well-being and good performance has fuelled the search for 'golden rules' which will provide a comprehensive list of criteria for organisational success. Good management practice is supposed to be associated with higher output, better quality products and services and hence financial success. It also implies a better sense of satisfaction and well-being for employees. There has always been a notion that 'good employers' are those who are concerned with the well-being of their employees since the days of the Quaker companies (Child, 1964). The link between good practice in management and mental well-being has been made explicit in the reported positive impacts of such practices as coherent job design, employee involvement and a proactive approach to well-being which acknowledges the importance of the human resource. The underlying assumption is that certain management practices lead to a better working environment and a more fulfilling and rewarding employment relationship.

In addition, it is suggested that organisations which follow such good practices are recognised as satisfying a social and moral responsibility towards people. Newell (1995) suggested that it is essential for organisations to implement a policy of good human relations, which treats all employees with respect and trust and supports their individual development needs, to generate the reciprocal commitment needed for organisational success and excellent performance. Thus, it is argued, the factors which contribute to the creation of a 'healthy organisation' are also considered essential in order to secure employees' commitment as valuable assets, generating a sense of well-being and ultimately guaranteeing organisational success. However, the debate on what constitutes 'best practice' continues and is subject to much controversy.

The belief that there are 'best practices', which organisations should pursue in order to achieve both organisational success and employee well-being is a central tenet of one school of thought in HRM, which relies upon a unitary frame of reference (an area discussed also in Chapter 2). This views the role of HRM as an instrument to bring about 'transformational change' and requires subtle work on the values and attitudes of employees to convince them that the changes proposed are in their own best interests, and embedding 'HR best practice' as part of line management activity. The HRM mission is found in the individualisation of the employment contract, which provides the ideology that underpins the employee development and flexible workforce managerial strategies. This is a convincing ideology because it is entirely consistent with the unitary frame of reference.

'Best practice' is best understood as those HR practices and policies which, taken as a 'bundle', are inherent within the technical systems for delivering a service to customers, or in manufacturing the product at specified cost and quality levels. This is supported empirically (Huselid, 1995; MacDuffie and Krafcik, 1989). There is also evidence that notions of 'job satisfaction' and organisational performance are related (Patterson *et al.*, 1996), and that the idea of the 'mutual gains' enterprise is a way to bridge the gap between potentially competing interest groups as a 'best practice' (Kochan and Osterman, 1994; Kochan *et al.*, 1986).

However, Legge (1995) challenges the assumptions of the unitary frame of reference and questions the mechanisms used to encourage, direct and reinforce behaviours such as commitment and motivation which are considered conducive to organisational success. Purcell (1997) also questioned the notion that a best practice model of HRM is universally applicable and indicated that many powerful, significant changes to work, employment and society, exert a fundamental impact on whether or not companies apply what are considered to be best practice policies and practices. Guest (1996) suggested that the problems inherent in trying to make explicit the links between best practice and performance could be addressed by considering a behavioural model which explores employees' expectations, challenging the notion that the proposed best practices always result in particular behaviours which result in superior performance. Tyson (1997) further highlighted the interpretational character of organisational life and suggested that implementing the policies and practices of HRM requires a re-interpretation of social realities. There may be many different perceptions of what constitutes 'appropriate behaviour' and doubts as to whether or not 'good practices' actually result in 'organisational success'.

What is significant is that employers now believe there is a commercial benefit to shaping the attitudes and values of employees, and that there are 'best practices' in doing so. Furthermore, employers see these best practices as the means to shape employee behaviours, and their role as reinterpreters of the employment relationship as the opportunity to install the attitudes and values consistent with their organisational goals.

We can summarise the HRM argument here. HRM now seeks to work directly on the values and attitudes of individual employees, for example, by marketing the company philosophy and values and by using competency frameworks to give coherence to the various policies in recruitment, induction, training, reward and development. Performance management systems are also a part of the package of measures used to reinforce the need for individual objectives and performance measures. A further powerful argument is also deployed, which proposes that improved customer care and higher quality work are more satisfying than the opposite, whatever the level of the employee, and that job satisfaction for employees improves organisational performance. By this means an ideology supportive of customer care, responsiveness and total quality management is believed to be sustained by HRM initiatives which work on employee attitudes and beliefs. The question of what are 'best practices' leads to the question 'best for whom?' The underlying purpose of job satisfaction, according to this view, is ultimately to serve the employer's need, resting on a utilitarian ethical position.

The basis for an ethical dilemma

Given the importance of mental well-being to managers, it is difficult to understand why they pay little attention to this area. Although the workplace can be a source of mental ill health, it can also provide the opportunity to address mental well-being issues. This can be achieved through the use of health education, health screening and preventative measures, and the provision of support and intervention when problems do arise. These opportunities are supported and legitimised by legislation such as the Health and Safety at Work Act 1974 and the Management of Health and Safety at Work Regulations 1992 which require employers to do whatever is reasonably practicable to prevent their employees becoming ill because of their work.

There are prescribed 'best' practices, in the management of mental well-being within the organisational context. These activities are broadly categorised as prevention, promotion, and intervention, and it has been suggested that an overall coherent strategy for good mental health combines education, treatment and an emotionally supportive environment (Jenkins and Warman, 1993). There are three common types of intervention identified in the literature (for example see Cox, 1993; Keita and Sauter, 1992; Quick *et al.*, 1992). Prevention strategies focus on the removal or reduction in the sources of problems and include work design and ergonomics. Promotion is concerned with improving the ability of organisations and managers to recognise and deal with problems as they arise. It also focuses on altering the ways in which the individual responds to risks and includes training and the development of psychological skills. Rehabilitation involves helping employees to cope with and recover from problems which exist at work, and at the individual level aims to heal those who have been traumatised or distressed.

Despite the availability of interventions to address mental well-being across a number of levels, the majority of workplace initiatives have focused on symptom recognition and treatment, with little input at the prevention level. Many organisations have adopted programmes providing counselling in the form of employee assistance programmes (EAPs). The EAP philosophy means that the organisation recognises and acknowledges that work can at times cause pressures even among the most capable and resilient of employees. Typically EAP-type provision consists of telephone hotlines and on-site counsellors. Among the most popular types of programme currently available are those which focus on stress management. However, these tend to concentrate on recognising and treating the symptoms rather than tackling the causes. They often arise as crisis management and few appear to be evaluated rigorously.

'Wellness programmes' are on the increase and offer a more diverse range of intervention such as education programmes and a range of facilities to include health screening and fitness. Corporate health strategies are the most comprehensive interventions. These usually take a holistic approach to the individual and the organisation and are often proposed as part of the culture of the company. They involve a coherent strategy for well-being which recognises the reciprocal impact of work and well-being and an organisational obligation to manage well-being as an integral part of company life. However, this type of approach is much less commonly found.

Producing a cost–benefit analysis to support the use of interventions faces many difficulties, in particular, the difficulty in showing direct correlations between programmes or interventions and bottom-line results for the organisation since individual health behaviour is affected by a complicated mix of social and economic factors. Thus, rather than adopting a holistic, proactive approach, many organisations appear to be moved to action by the potential cost of lost productivity, sickness absence and potential litigation as the most influential elements in creating an impetus to address mental well-being at work.

Having taken the tack of individualising the employment contract and having attempted to shape the values and attitudes of employees, managers face a dilemma when asked to promote mental well-being. The depth of the interventions necessary are such that their actions would cross the boundaries beyond a purely economic relationship with employees, and could be said to violate the psychological contract in a number of ways. First, interventions which explicitly seek to influence mental well-being would openly suggest that the alteration of mental states is a legitimate use of managerial power and, second such interventions would imply a relationship which goes beyond everyday work interactions.

The dilemma arises from the fact that management have long ago crossed this Rubicon. Communication and internal marketing policies, 'brain washing' development programmes and workshops which seek to create very specific responses to marketing and sales initiatives are examples of attempts to alter mental states. The responsibility for creating and sustaining the psychological state of the employee is now *de facto* a part of human resource management, if we take the unitary view. This is also the implication of the Walker case.

With the expansion of service industries has come the demand for emotional labour (Hochschild, 1983), where a genuine and personal response to customers is expected of employees. Such occupations as airline cabin crew, sales staff, and shop assistants are expected by their employers to act towards *their* customer (that is, there is a personalised relationship) from a set of activities and values which go beyond the range of conscious decisions and control. Emotional labour may produce a 'false consciousness' but what it does require is a forced emotional attachment to work and to customer relationships which requires employees to give of themselves, to receive employment and rewards in return for their personal commitment to customers whom they do not know, and whose only requirement of the relationship is to achieve a service in return for payment. This Faustian pact can only be achieved by changing the way the employee thinks about him or herself and his or her relationships. Employers are in the dilemma of wanting to dip in and out of a closer relationship with employees, and consequently find themselves wishing to influence the mental state of employees, without fully accepting all the responsibilities.

The legal and moral basis for mental health interventions derive from a deontological, Kantian ethical position. Employers may feel there is a duty to treat people in a way which is consistent with maintaining their sense of self and their identity. The mental well-being of employees is a moral duty according to this view. This is in accordance with ethics of care and virtue ethics perspectives. In practice, however, the main appeal to employers by Government agencies and the appeal which is easier in persuasion, is the utilitarian position: arguing the need to maintain employee mental health in the interests of the employees as a whole. The problem with this confusion over the ethical position of HRM in relation to mental well-being is encountered when we need to seek reasons for interventions which by their nature are of a very personal and influential nature. The danger is that managers might come to regard these interventions as entirely appropriate in order to service their own interests, or the economic interests they represent. To quote Legge (1998, p. 24) 'what must be avoided is to disregard someone's personhood by exploiting or otherwise using them without regard to their own interests, needs and conscientious concerns'. The confusion over the reasons for intervention designed to influence the mental states of employees is summarised in the following paragraphs.

Work intensification including many of the highly routinised practices now in the service sector and the inherent uncertainties of working life with downsizing and redundancy are one source of mental ill health (Kettley, 1995; Parker *et al.*, 1997). In addition, organisations now require the creativity, innovation and commitment of knowledge workers, who work with their minds rather than their physical strength. Paradoxically, just at a time when organisations are able to appreciate the intellectual contribution of their employees, this is threatened by the demands made upon employees, who must now cope with continuous change and pressure to meet ever higher targets. The potential for litigation raises awareness of these pressures.

The ethical viewpoint on the problems of stress caused by overwork and the resultant physical disorders which also influence the mental state (for example, high blood pressure, eating disorders, damage to the immune system and so on) is a form of consequentialism on the part of employers, who wish to avoid litigation and who wish to convince their other employees that they are a good employer. However, the stance taken on the legitimacy of interventions to improve productivity of employees must be considered to be utilitarian, although often cloaked in a form of virtue ethics, that what is done here is for society as a whole.

The final issue here is the desire to present the organisation as a 'family friendly' concern, with all the policies directed at enabling employees to have healthy, happy family lives. In the nineteenth century this case was argued by the old welfare workers from a perspective of universalism, or on the grounds of virtue ethics (Niven, 1967). A genuine belief in the employer's role in creating a good society may well prevail in some organisations. Employers were concerned even in the nineteenth century to ensure a respect for the person, and Child (1964) suggests this might have been prompted by a sense of guilt by those with a strong Christian faith. Nowadays, it is the court of public opinion which holds more sway. The dilemma is between acting to satisfy stakeholder interests or those of employees and the dilemma is resolved by presenting these as identical. The reason a business case is necessary before managers will be allowed to spend money on creating a sense of well-being is because the influence on the mental state of employees has to be brought into the realm of rational, economic action in order to legitimate the activity formally (see, for example, Johanson, 1997). There is a need to legitimate the activity to society as a whole also, and here the ethical threshold is reached. As Parsons (1965, p. 58) reminds us:

> Institutional patterns depend for their maintenance in force on the support of the moral sentiments of the majority of the members of society.

As we have pointed out, there may be some hypocrisy in the demand for a business case given that mental well-being is affected by work situations and management actions, such as extra work hours, conflicting demands and by the explicit attempts to change the values and attitudes of employees. Management may have been drawn into this situation willy-nilly, but managers are now faced with the wider responsibilities implied by taking on the unitary frame of reference, and by seeking to deal only with employees as individuals rather than as collectivities. The ethical threshold which has been reached is whether or not having already gone down the path of seeking to create specific psychological states of mind, organisations can stop short of addressing the broader, holistic mental well-being issue.

Conclusions

In this chapter we have examined how a heightened awareness of mental ill health at work has brought managers into an ethical dilemma. The various interventions which are commonly made, for example employee assistance programmes, or stress reducing workshops are not based upon a clear, unambiguous rationale. Stress management programmes are often justified by a form of utilitarian consequentialism, to avoid the potential litigation or the adverse effects of other HR policies such as performance-based pay which have also been sponsored by the HR function. By the same token, corporate health strategies and policies aimed at screening employees, for example, are often prompted by a universalistic concern for all employees' health. Similarly, family friendly policies which are put together, no doubt for marketing reasons, are sold to employees on the back of a virtue ethics message. Even the latter may be occasioned by the ulterior motive to present a good employer image in the marketplace, and thus to strengthen the vision of a good company in which to invest among shareholders and to impress the other stakeholders.

We have argued that these issues are important because now organisations have reached the position where they are acknowledged to be responsible for the mental states of their employees, the unitary frame of reference requires a response from organisational managers. The ethical basis for such a response is not clear and mixed responses result. Human resource management has raised the ethical stakes over mental well-being: this produces a series of ethical dilemmas and a confusion over the reasons for action.

References

Banham, J. (1992) 'The costs of mental ill health to business' in Jenkins, R. and Coney, N. (eds) *Prevention of Mental Ill-health at Work: A Conference*, London: HMSO, pp. 24–9

CBI (1993) in Kogan, H. (ed.) (1997) *The Corporate Healthcare Handbook*, London: Kogan Page, p. 142

Child, J. (1964) 'Quaker employees and industrial relations', *Sociological Review*, **12**(3): 293–315

Cooper, C./TUC (1997) 'Crisis talks', *Personnel Today*, October, pp. 29–32

Cox, T. (1993) *Stress Research and Stress Management: Putting Theory to Work*, Health and Safety Executive Contract Research Report No.61, Sudbury

Department of Health (1995) quoted in Institute of Personnel and Development *IPD Guides on Occupational Health and Organisational Effectiveness*, London: IPD

Employment Trends (1994) 'The centre cannot hold: devolving personnel duties', *Industrial Relations Review*, 6–12 August

Guest, D.E. (1996) Human Resource Management, Fit and Performance p. 13. Unpublished paper prepared for the ESRC Seminar on 'Strategic Human Resource Management', 1 February

Health and Safety Executive (1995) *Stress at Work: A Guide for Employers*, Health and Safety Executive, (G) Vol.116, Sudbury: HSE Books

HMSO (1974) *Health and Safety at Work Regulations*, London: HMSO

Hochschild, A.R. (1983) *The Managed Heart: Commercialization of Human Feeling*, Berkeley, London: University of California Press

Hodgson, J.T., Jones, J.R., Elliott, R.C. and Osman, R. (1993) *Self-reported Work Related Illness: Results from a trailer questionnaire on the 1990 Labour Force Survey in England and Wales*, Research paper 33, Sudbury: HSE Books

Huselid, M.A. (1995) 'The impact of human resource management practices on turnover, productivity and corporate financial performance', *Academy of Management Journal*, **38**: 635–72

Institute of Personnel and Development (1995) *The IPD Guide on Occupational Health and Organisational Effectiveness*, London: Institute of Personnel and Development

James, P (1996) 'Disability bill receives Royal Assent', *Occupational Health Review*, January/February, p. 17

Jenkins, R. and Warman, D. (eds) (1993) *Promoting Mental Health Policies in the Workplace*, London: HMSO

Jenkins, R., MacDonald, A., Murray, J. and Strathdee, G. (1982) 'Minor psychiatric morbidity and the threat of redundancy in a professional group', *Psychological Medicine*, **12**: 799–807

Johanson, U. (1997) 'The profitability of investments in work life rehabilitation', *Personnel Review*, **26**(5): 395– 415

Keita, G.P. and Sauter, S.L. (eds) (1992) *Work and Well-being: an agenda for the 1990s*, Washington: American Psychological Association

Kettley, P. (1995) 'Employee morale during downsizing', *Institute of Employment Studies Brief*, Brighton: IES, p. 39

Kochan, T. and Osterman, P. (1994) *The Mutual Gains Enterprise*, Boston MA: Harvard Business School Press

Kochan, T., Katz, H. and McKersie, R. (1986) *The Transformation of American Industrial Relations*, New York: Basic Books

Kogan, H. (ed.) (1997) *The Corporate Healthcare Handbook*, London: Kogan Page

Legge, K. (1995) *Human Resource Management, Rhetorics and Realities*, London: Macmillan

Legge, K. (1998) 'The morality of HRM' in Mabey, C., Skinner, D. and Clark, T. (eds) *Experiencing Human Resource Management*, London: Sage

Levi, L. (1994) 'Work, worker and well-being: an overview', *Work and Stress*, 8(2): 80

Macduffie, J.P. and Krafcik, J.F. (1989) Flexible Production Systems and Manufacturing Performance: the role of HR and technology, Annual Academy of Management Conference, Washington DC

Management of Health and Safety at Work Regulations (1992) London: HMSO

Muir, J. (1994) 'Dealing with sickness absence', *Work Study*, **43**(5): 13–14

Newell, S. (1995) *The Healthy Organisation: Fairness, Ethics and Effective Management*, London: Routledge

Niven, M. (1967) *Personnel Management 1913–1963*, London: IPM (now IPD)

O'Leary, L. (1993) 'Mental health at work', *Occupational Health Review*, **45**: 23–6

Parker, S.K., Chmiel, N. and Wall, T.D. (1997) 'Work characteristics and employee well-being within a context of strategic downsizing', *Journal of Occupational Health Psychology*, **2**(4): 289–303

Parsons, T. (1965) 'The motivation of economic activities' in Smelser, N. (ed.) *Readings on Economic Sociology*, Englewood Cliffs, NJ: Prentice Hall, pp. 53–66

Patterson, M., Lawthom, R., Maitlis, S., Nicolitisas, D., Nickell, S., Staniforth, D. and West, M. (1996) Organisational Characteristics and Practices, Employee Attitudes and Effectiveness in UK Manufacturing. ESRC Seminar Paper, London School of Economics, 20 June

Purcell, J. (1997) 'Human resource bundles of best practice: a utopian cul-de-sac?' Draft paper for ESRC/BUIRA Seminar Series: 'Contribution of HR Strategy to Business Performance', 1 February

Quick, J.L., Murphy, L.R. and Hurrell, J.J. (eds) (1992) *Stress and Well-being at Work* (2nd edn), Washington DC: American Psychological Association

Storey, J. (1992) *Developments in the Management of Human Resources*, Oxford: Blackwell

Taylor, R. (1995) 'FT guide to health in the workplace (3): Healthy, wealthy and wise – a well workforce makes sound financial sense', *Financial Times*, 1 December, pp. III

Tyson, S. (1995) *Human Resource Strategy: Towards a General Theory of HRM*, London: Pitman

Tyson, S. (1997) 'HR knowledge base and contribution to the management process'. Unpublished paper prepared for the ESRC Seminar Series: 'Contribution of HR Strategy to Business Performance', Cranfield School of Management, 17 June

UNUM (1997) General press release, 4 March

Welch, J. (1996) 'Stress ruling ups the stakes for employers', *People Management*, 2(10): 13–15

World Health Organisation (1986) Constitution of the World Health Organization in *Basic Documents* (36th edn), WHO: Geneva, p. 1

CHAPTER 7

Winning hearts and minds: ethical issues in human resource development

Jean Woodall and Danielle Douglas

Introduction

Training and development activities are perhaps the area of human resource policy and practice that is least likely to come under ethical scrutiny, invariably being presented as intrinsically 'good' activities. Only perhaps within the realm of critical management theory (Alvesson and Willmott, 1996; Burgoyne and Reynolds, 1997; French and Grey, 1996) and labour process theory have training and development been presented as vulnerable to the social and contextual processes of power and control and as an instrument of deskilling. Yet, in comparison, recruitment and selection, assessment, performance and reward management as well as employee relations procedure are all more readily held to account on ethical grounds such as fairness, equal treatment and confidentiality.

Training and development have connotations of an ethically positive orientation towards the treatment of human beings. 'Learning' is an intrinsically good or virtuous activity and so it is often inferred that organisations which provide the means of training and development to pursue this are acting virtuously. Unfortunately, there are several issues of ethical concern in the general field of human resource development, especially around culture and attitude change. This chapter will provide an outline of why the tradition of ethical humanism present in earlier work on adult learning and organisational development can be undermined by developmental interventions to change culture and personal values.

The changing organisational context within which HRD interventions take place will be examined, drawing particular attention to the implications of competence-based development, career management and culture management. It will end with a brief overview of three HRD interventions that are increasingly used to bring about culture and attitude change: outdoor management development, neuro-linguistic programming (NLP) and Gestalt in organisations. The aim is to identify the ethical implications of such interventions: with particular reference to the concept of individual psychological safety as it is observed in the behaviour of HRD professionals.

The traditions of ethical humanism and professional standards of practice in adult and organisational development

The tradition of humanistic adult learning theory infuses most organisational training and development practice The key exponents, Carl Rogers (1969) and Malcolm Knowles (1989), adopted a positive ethical stance towards adult learning infused with the principles of virtue ethics and respect for individual rights. The emphasis was upon developing the whole person through participative and experiential methods. There was an explicit commitment to upholding individual dignity and self-worth and to adopting an appropriate intervention style. Rogers (1969) argued that in an ever changing environment teachers and trainers should become 'facilitators of learning', that they should create a climate of trust and elicit individual and group aims. The learning should be 'student-centred' and teachers and trainers should provide access to resources, accept and share emotional as well as intellectual contributions and, above all, accept their own limitations. Knowles' (1989) synthesis of the distinctive principles of adult learning also takes a very individual-centred stance. He affirms the importance of the individual's 'need to know', acknowledging their self-concept, their 'readiness' to learn and their specific internal and intrinsic motivators. In addition, the specific past experiences of adults (negative as well as positive) is recognised and the training and development agenda starts with their problems and objectives rather than those of the organisation or the knowledge, skills, behaviours and values to be learnt. Rogers' and Knowles' humanistic approach has been criticised for decontextualising the learning process by undue focus upon the individual relative to the social and cultural context (Reynolds, 1997), but there is an undeniably strong respect for individual human agency in the learning process.

The other main influence upon contemporary training and development is the concept of 'learning style', originally developed by Kolb and Fry (1975) from the tradition of cognitive psychology and later modified by Honey and Mumford (1992). Kolb and Fry identified four stages in a linked cycle: 'concrete experience', 'reflective observation', 'abstract conceptualisation' and 'active experimentation'. Their main argument was that, to be effective, a learner needed to pass through all four stages, but that individuals had a learning style preference which usually corresponded to one single stage in the learning cycle. If individuals were unconscious of their learning style preference, this could lead to ineffective learning. Consequently, the role of the trainer should be to identify the preference and provide appropriate learning activities and teaching methods to support individuals through each stage of the learning cycle. The identification of individual learning styles preferences and remedial support for individuals with an unbalanced style have become the dominant design principles for the majority of HRD practitioners. Although to a lesser extent than Rogers' and Knowles' ideas, it is still a student-centred approach. The ethical basis of the model also incorporates a utilitarian dimension, in that choice of intervention is determined not so much by what the individual wishes, as what the HRD professional perceives is needed or useful.

Respect for individuals has also been a feature of the organisation development (OD) movement. The ethical basis of change agent behaviour has been a major preoccupation ever since the inception of organisation development in the 1940s. It is worth recalling Kurt Lewin's (1952) insistence that the consent and co-operation of all stakeholders in the client organisation should be sought prior to an OD intervention. In particular there was a great deal of discussion during the early 1980s about ethical standards for the OD profession (Walter, 1984; White and Whooten, 1983). Many practitioners were concerned at a tendency to disregard freedom, privacy and self-esteem in the process of focusing upon task accomplishment and commitment to organisational objectives. These ethical concerns were summarised in one of the major textbooks (French and Bell, 1990, pp. 219–33) which outlined the minimum ethical standards for OD:

- interventions must be selected that have a high probability of being helpful in the particular situation
- the consultant should not use interventions that exceed his or her expertise
- the 'client system' should be kept as informed as is practicable about the nature of the process
- the consultant must not be working on any personal, hidden agendas that might obtrude into high quality service for the client
- commitments to confidentiality must be kept
- individuals must not be coerced into divulging information about themselves or others.

OD codes of professional conduct emphasise practitioner integrity in behaviour. While these codes focus upon the ethics of the intervention process, the choice of specific interventions is left to the discretion of the OD professional. However, from the ethical perspective, to make this choice dependent upon the individual professional's level of expertise and perception of the probable 'helpfulness' of the intervention is to resort to a utilitarian ethic with all the limitations of contingency and consequentialism. That certain OD interventions themselves might raise ethical concerns as opposed to the manner in which they are applied is overlooked.

Thus training and development theory does contain strong implicit ethical assumptions. These are centred around a humanistic respect for individual rights such as dignity, self-esteem, privacy and autonomy; and a professional ethic which is a combination of three elements. These are the development of professional training and development 'virtues'; an ethic of care that recognises that judgement of what is appropriate is situationally attuned and that empathy and concern are essential; and a rather weaker utilitarian justification of interventions in terms of their anticipated consequences or 'helpfulness' (see Table 7.1). However, in many areas of training and development activity there are grounds to believe that this ethical foundation may be disregarded or under threat. Training and development professionals, although on balance not inclined to reflect upon ethical issues, occasionally voice anxiety about the ethics of professional behaviour, often masked by bold statements of principle such as the following:

> For me, such choices have to be based on fundamental personal values about the autonomy of the learner, and the right that people have to choose what they do and don't learn; on the principle of clear and open contracting with people; on erring on the side of confidentiality when in doubt; and on never abusing a position of power. (Hardingham, 1997)

However, how easy is it to uphold these principles in practice? In many areas of training and development activity there are grounds to believe that this ethical foundation may be disregarded or undermined. A major contributory factor has been the 'repackaging' of training and development as a component of human resource development.

TABLE 7.1   Ethical positions around development

Learning theory	Ethical assumptions
Adult Learning Theory	Strongly deontological – absolute rights of the learner; strong ethic of care to be observed by the trainer
Learning Style Theory	Consequentialist/utilitarian justification for interventions; and ethic of care to be observed by trainer
Organisation Development	Strong ethic of care to be observed by trainer; and consequentialist justification for interventions

Human resource development – ethical development at risk?

The idea that development activity could be essential to corporate success has been given support by the emergence of human resource management (HRM). This has shifted the emphasis away from development of individuals to organisational interests. While there is a continuing debate around what HRM involves ('hard' v. 'soft'; 'best practice' v. 'best fit') which has continued for over ten years (Mabey *et al.*, 1998), the debate around HRD has achieved greater consensus. The only apparent area of dispute is whether it is indeed a separate area of concern or a sub-set of HRM activity. In some formulations (Gilley and Eggland, 1989; McLagan and Suhadolnik, 1989; Rothwell and Kazanas, 1989) HRD is presented as achieving a synthesis of individual and organisational development and even group objectives. Others emphasise the importance of culture leadership and commitment in making the connection between the strategic direction of the organisation and individual behaviour and practice (Stewart and McGoldrick, 1996). Yet the principal tools of developing individual competence, organisational career management and culture management tend to be driven principally by organisational agendas and the existence of a mutually shared interest between organisation and employee can be challenged (Woodall and Winstanley, 1998). This is not surprising, because business environmental influences are forcing organisations to justify the cost of training and development expenditure and to design and deliver interventions in a manner that enhances competitiveness and responds to organisational change. If we start with an examination of competence-based development, career management and culture management, it is immediately apparent that ethical issues arise.

Since the mid-1980s, competence-based development has displaced the conventions of traditional instructional systems design which compartmentalised knowledge, skills and attitudes as discreet targets for off-the-job training interventions and separated the stages of 'learning' and 'transfer of learning' in a rather mechanistic fashion. Competence re-integrated knowledge, skills and attitude development and brought learning immediately into the workplace, focusing upon the behaviour and practice required for effective performance, thereby overcoming the learning transfer problem. While there are differences in the definition of 'competence' (Sparrow, 1994; Woodall and Winstanley, 1998, Chapter 4), in managerial usage the most frequently used definition relates to the behavioural repertoires which people put into a job, role or organisational context (Sparrow, 1994). Yet, it should not be forgotten that the main driving force behind the usage of competence as a component of HRD strategy was to ensure that development interventions and learning were closely linked to improved performance. The 'irresistible rise' of competence (Holmes, 1995) is linked to the contemporary obsession in HRM with grading, classification and surveillance of individuals (Townley,

1994). Thus the identification of training needs, the setting of competence thresholds and the assessment of performance become vulnerable to the same technical and perceptual problems that bedevil assessment for selection and performance management (see Alimo-Metcalfe, 1995; Bevan and Thomson, 1992; Winstanley and Stuart-Smith, 1996). Individuals become treated in an instrumental and often unjust manner and the purpose of development activity becomes the achievement of organisationally fixed competencies, rather than authentic individually determined needs.

The concern with competence has also been followed by a reconsideration of career expectations. Indeed, the two issues are linked, as the focus upon competence raises the issue of the basis upon which individuals may expect the organisation's commitment to their careers. Debate has centred around the notion of the 'psychological contract' (Rousseau, 1995), referring to the set of expectations held by individuals over what the individual and the organisation give and receive in the working relationship. Herriot and Pemberton (1995) and Sparrow (1996) outline differences between 'old' and 'new' psychological contracts. 'New' contracts rest upon the expectation of high performance, responsiveness to change in return for horizontal career paths, with less job security and the individual taking responsibility to improve employability. Talk of the so-called 'new' psychological contract, replacing the 'old' career for life model with development for 'employability' has, in most cases, been associated with a retreat from career development and promotion. Yet recent research (Ebadan and Winstanley, 1997; Guest and Davey, 1996) has shown that employability is often little more than an invitation to individuals to develop themselves for *external* as opposed to *internal* labour market mobility and that organisations which withdraw from career management in the face of downsizing and delayering can face an even bigger drain on the organisational commitment of their employees. Despite recent research indicating more rhetoric than practical reality around this (Guest and Conway, 1997), current debate about the 'new realism' in career management masks an ethical concern around sanctioning greater insecurity.

Over the same period culture management has become a major preoccupation and central platform for HRD. The 'excellence' movement of the mid-1980s fuelled the belief that effective corporate performance depended upon the alignment of individual employee values with those espoused by the organisation. Culture management is therefore based upon a number of assumptions:

- effective management involves the alignment of values
- values can be easily changed
- only management can change these values
- successful organisations have 'strong' cultures.

Despite evidence that all these are questionable (Woodall, 1996) and that there are different perspectives of what culture is (Martin, 1992), organisations have nonetheless become preoccupied with the management of values. Very often this arises out of a concern with achieving uniform standardised customer service, as in retail financial services or fast food or in ensuring a commercial focus on the part of knowledge workers, such as engineers or R&D scientists. Yet organisations will often pursue such culture management initiatives, in the face of evidence that they are having a deleterious effect upon staff motivation and performance. The strictures of stockmarkets, which increasingly do not permit a company's performance to be 'turned around' over a period of any longer than a year, may override more cautious approaches to culture management.

The potential for ethical principles to be violated in relation to culture change, and change management in general has been outlined in detail elsewhere (Mayon-White, 1994; McKendall, 1993; Woodall, 1996). This concerns the process by which the change is managed as well as the outcomes. The principles of individual autonomy, dignity, self-esteem and privacy, as well as organisational justice and integrity, can be violated in the operation of the 'ice-cube' model (unfreeze-change-refreeze) of change management. Culture change experts face an ethical dilemma. This is illustrated by Schein (1993), who concedes that change management does require 'disconfirming' activities to shock and raise anxiety levels to create an awareness that change is needed, but feels that for change to happen, people need to feel 'psychologically safe':

> To make people feel safe in learning, they must have a motive, a sense of direction, and the opportunity to try out new things without fear of punishment. (Schein, 1993, p. 91)

The case of 'ServiceCo' (Woodall 1996) provides an (albeit extreme, but also not isolated) illustration of how such irresponsible manipulative culture change can generate cynicism, stress, anxiety and apprehension in the face of uncertainty. Culture change and management is a good example of how development interventions can offer employees injustice, uncertainty, insecurity, loss of dignity and lowered self-esteem.

Thus we would argue that far from being intrinsically virtuous and despite an espousal of ethical humanism and professional standards, training and development activities can be vulnerable to unethical practice. This can arise both around the process by which training and development interventions are managed and around the substance of the intervention itself – especially where this involves value change. There has been some formal recognition of this within the American Society for Training and Development, but with much uncertainty about how to proceed (Marsick, 1997). The rest of this chapter proceeds to illustrate this point with reference to three different approaches to value change: outdoor management development, neuro-linguistic programming and Gestalt in organisations. It will examine the way in which these interventions acknowledge the importance of psychological safety for the individual involving a respect for individual autonomy, dignity, self-esteem and privacy and the exhibition of professional integrity on the part of the relevant development professionals. In addition to a review of the secondary literature, the analysis is based upon professional publications and in-depth interviews with two or three leading commercial providers of each approach. A semi-structured interview schedule was used examining the ethical basis of forming contractual relations with commercial clients; espoused values; the use of psychological change tools; and awareness and management of issues around participant 'psychological safety' and professional integrity. The chapter concludes by arguing that virtue ethics and the ethics of care have an important place within HRD.

Outdoor management development: ethical issues

Outdoor management development (OMD) is one of a number of definitions used to describe developmental activities that take place outside the normal work environment, but also in a 'natural' setting. It has its origins in the work of Kurt Hahn (the German founder of Gordonstoun School), and subsequent 'survival' training for military recruits (Burletson and Grint, 1996; Irvine and Wilson, 1994). The Outward Bound Movement and the Duke of Edinburgh's Award Scheme were early applications of this. Other related outdoor management development models include those developed by the leadership trust and Ralph Coverdale (Taylor, 1992). OMD is based upon the assumption that the outdoors 'provides activities and/or environments devoid of traditional organisational and educational norms' (Irvine and Wilson, 1994, p. 26). The assumption is that placing individuals in a novel environment allows them to focus upon management processes rather than substantive tasks. While there is no full agreement on the process skills to be developed, these tend to centre around either leadership or team development and include, among others, interpersonal skills such as communication, managing change, managing time, problem solving and creative thinking. They are commonly delivered around the Kolb and Fry 'learning cycle' (see earlier). OMD became extremely popular in the early 1980s and, after a decline in demand during the early 1990s, is popular once again. Yet there is a great deal of confusion over what is involved. OMD can in fact take a variety of formats, summarised in Table 7.2.

TABLE 7.2   Holman's categories of outdoor training

	1 *Endurance training*	2 *Challenge training*	3 *Outward bound-type training*	4 *Outdoor management courses*	5 *Management development training*
Characteristics	Pain Stress Fear Appreciation Shock Minimum debrief Low analysis	Activity based training Task-oriented Achievement based Task review and debrief, though superficial	Character building training Variety of novel activities Ethics and example Stretching activities Physically oriented Some informal debrief	Outdoor activities with debrief Analysis and learning	Uses the learning cycle Experientially based With objectives Debriefed Using the outdoors as the learning vehicle Often uses psychometric analysis
Venue	Bunk house (spartan)	Bunk house	Bunk house with comfort	Hotels and bunk houses	Hotels with seminar facilities
Aims	None set	Venue challenges	Taken as supplied by provider	Broadly discussed with customers	Behavioural objectives agreed and determined
Staff	'Macho' perhaps ex-military, minimum outdoor qualifications, but high outdoor experience	Outdoor pursuits experience	Outdoor pursuits qualified	Outdoor qualified at least to MLC standard, with business professional trainers	Outdoor qualified at least to MLC standard, chartered psychologists and professional trainers
Debrief	Vague value judgements on performance	Informal task discussions	Informal task and some process discussion	Formal structured debrief built into time plan	In-depth transfer to workplace, structured with objectives

(Adapted from Holman, 1993)

Table 7.2 shows that by this definition outdoor management development is in fact a discrete category that is distinguishable from wider 'adventure training' in that it is based on behavioural objectives negotiated in advance and is facilitated by occupational psychologists and training professionals as well as outdoor pursuits instructors. That is not to say that many organisations contract exclusively with the providers of 'outdoor management development', which can complicate evaluation of this intervention.

As outdoor development in general has been the butt of much adverse media criticism, it is not surprising that OMD suffers from the same image problem. Television programmes depicting 'macho' instructors forcing non-swimmers to jump off a boat and swim underneath it, plus media reports of tragedies such as the Lyme Bay disaster in the early 1990s (when several children's lives were lost in a canoeing accident) or the sensationalised toll of accident and death in the mountains, have contributed to the persistence of a poor media image and pressure for attention to health and safety. Like all other training providers, OMD providers are covered by Health and Safety at Work legislation, and specifically the Health and Safety at Work Regulations 1992 relating to risk assessment, safety records, standard operating procedures and safety management (IPD, 1998). However, the emphasis upon physical safety masks the additional ethical dimension of psychological safety.

In many ways the psychological safety of participants on OMD programmes is as important, if not more important, than the physical safety. This is particularly problematic where corporate organisations intend to use OMD for change management and there might be strong pressure on individuals to attend or even to 'prove' their worth on development activities. This has been acknowledged by a number of not-for-profit providers of OMD which formed the Development Training Advisory Group (DTAG, 1994), and approved a Statement of Principles in 1991 that incorporated considerations of psychological as well as physical safety. All three providers of OMD interviewed in this study were founder members of DTAG and had a very clear view of what psychological safety involved. Without exception they cited maintaining confidentiality about individual participant progress: ensuring that peer pressure on individual participants to go beyond their 'comfort zones' is directly confronted, while endeavouring to maintain a balance between challenge, support and respect for individuals. When asked about their values, again all three providers were able to recall them immediately, even although only one had an explicit values statement. In the interviews with providers, phrases such as 'respect for the uniqueness, dignity and potential of each individual', an aim for 'mutual trust... [involving] both sides being open honest, truthful and reliable', the provider's assumption of 'full responsibility for physical and emotional safety' and professionalism in terms of skills, experience and knowledge' illustrate this.

This is backed up by the DTAG Statement of Principles (1991) which refers to up-holding certain values and beliefs:

Political and religious tolerance, mutual respect, a belief in the dignity and importance of every person irrespective of status, age, sex, origin or preconceived contribution to society; a belief in every individual's capability to learn and to go on
learning; respect and care for the environment.

The implications of this for the psychological safety of participants were
further elaborated upon in the DTAG *Guidelines on Health Aspects of
Development Training* (1994) with respect to identifying, handling and
preventing mental and emotional disturbance at all stages of trainee selection,
preparation, design and course delivery. There is an acknowledgement that
'evangelical', aggressive, confrontational, high-energising leadership styles in
trainers were more likely to incur psychological injury. The emotional component of development was fully accepted.

However, in addition, it was evident from the interview data that this was
built into the process of negotiating client contracts from a very early stage.
Learning contracts based on strong diagnosis and regular evaluation and
feedback provided the opportunity to identify problems with the client. All
three providers interviewed were concerned about client probity and openness, and felt that although they had seldom turned down work with a client,
their processes of contracting would screen out undesirable clients or would
bring to the surface unethical intentions. All three stressed the importance of
openness and transparency and handling issues of power. They were all
committed to staff training, both of developers and outdoor instructors. Most
developers were qualified to at least IPD standard and some had qualifications in psychology or counselling. Lengthy processes of screening were used
for the selection of staff, usually involving work sampling such as offering
freelance contracts prior to engagement. However, there were few formal
opportunities for collective reflection and review, with this most often tending
to occur on an ad hoc basis.

So, despite much criticism from the media, and other academic research of
the efficacy and ethics of this area of training, it could be argued that high
standards of both professional practice and ethical behaviour are endorsed by
at least some of the leading providers of OMD who subscribe to the DTAG
code of practice.

Neuro-linguistic programming – a technique rather than an ethical practice?

This curiously named development tool emerged in the 1970s and has
assumed increasing popularity within the UK since 1990. The now legendary
status of its origins can be traced to when John Grinder, a lecturer in linguis-

tics and Richard Bandler, a mathematics graduate interested in psychology at the University of Santa Cruz in California, conducted research through observation and modelling of excellent communicators in an attempt to determine what makes the difference between basic competence and excellence in a skill. Bandler was interested in the fact that some personal development therapists were more successful than others who followed their teaching. In particular, he examined the work of Gestalt therapist Fritz Perls, the family therapist Virginia Satir, and the hypnotherapist Milton Erickson. With Grinder, Bandler studied the language patterns, physiology and mental processing used by Perls and Satir and later Erickson to produce books: *The Structure of Magic I and II* (Bandler and Grinder, 1976; Grinder and Bandler, 1976). Their focus upon thinking patterns and ways in which communication is filtered, the use of language patterns and metaphors and modelling, enabled them to develop a model for behavioural excellence: neuro-linguistic programming (NLP).

While it is claimed that NLP has a use in almost any area of human activity which involves communication and concern with high performance, in business it has proved very popular as a means to improve and enhance communication, to build rapport and set goals and for dealing with 'difficult' people. Initially, NLP training was very popular among sales staff and acquired a reputation for helping them to close deals. Similarly it has been used with information technology trainers and has subsequently spread among HRD professionals and line and project managers as a useful instrument in the repertoire of influencing skills. It has been particularly popular with large organisations engaged in culture and value change.

The arcane secrets of NLP are shrouded in considerable mystique and it is usually presented as unfathomable to those who have not been initiated via 'practitioner' and 'master practitioner' level training courses. Several introductory texts have been written (Dilts 1990; Knights, 1995; Laborde, 1995; O'Connor and Seymour, 1990). The basic tenets have been summarised for the HRD community by Lyon (1996) in terms of 'elements', 'presuppositions' and 'techniques'. Lyon (1996) summarises the four basic elements of NLP as:

1. Having a *goal or outcome* – knowing what you want in specific terms.
2. Having the *behavioural flexibility* to attain an outcome.
3. Having the *sensory acuity* to notice the effect of your behaviour on others.
4. *Self-maintenance* – having the ability to stay resourceful and on target.

Many of the 'presuppositions' are expressed as aphorisms which have a comforting indisputable quality (ANLP, 1998, pp. 9–10), such as:

> 'we are all unique and experience the world in different ways'
> 'people respond to their map of reality; not to reality'
> 'mind and body form a linked system'

'if what you are doing isn't working, do something else'
'the meaning of your communication is the response you get'
'there is no failure, only feedback'.

These are injunctions that would be equally at home with a variety of other 'New Age' and holistic therapies, and their psychological validity is questionable. The basic NLP techniques are listed in Table 7.3.

TABLE 7.3   The basic NLP techniques

Establishing rapport	This can be built by matching ('pacing and leading') through the following: • Body posture, facial expressions, hand gestures, weight shifts, breathing patterns, movement of feet, eye movement • Vocal and verbal mirroring, tempo of speech and auditory tone
Accessing representational systems	Recognising that individuals approach the world in different ways, through visual or auditory or kinaesthetic (sensory) processes. By watching a person's eye movements and listening to their language, better rapport can be built
Anchoring	This is the process of eliciting a desired response in the self by linking it with sight, sound or feeling, and then using this to trigger the desired outcome
Setting well-formed outcomes	This is a process for goal setting and clarification in specific, positive terms that can be visualised, heard or sensed
Meta-model	This is a process of gathering information about someone else's experience in order to acquire a full representation of that experience, by means of skilful questioning techniques
Perceptual positions	This is developing the ability to look at a subject from different perspectives: the self, the other person and an independent observer

To the non-initiate, the impression is gained of a very eclectic method of intervention with a strong cognitive orientation. It echoes the some of the insights and techniques of a number of psychological perspectives such as Gestalt (see later), transactional analysis and behaviour modification. Providers of NLP training would argue that true understanding can only be acquired by full participation in accredited NLP training. However, the US trademarking of the concept by Bandler in an attempt to license the practice of NLP, and subsequent litigation around alleged unauthorised practice, has engendered a great deal of controversy (Pickard, 1998; *Rapport*, 1998; Welch, 1997), while US research (Druckman and Bjork, 1991; von Bergen *et al.*, 1997) cast doubt upon the validity of its assumptions and the efficacy of its claims.

It is also at this point that the ethical basis of NLP interventions comes into question. Like outdoor management development, it has proven very controversial. For instance the use of instrumental techniques to build rapport does raise the question of integrity (in the sense that recipients may be totally unaware of what the NLP practitioner is doing) and the purpose of building that rapport (which might involve achieving something at the expense of the recipients – from closing a sale, to getting them to agree to do something they might otherwise not wish to). However, the question of what is integrity is left to the individual practitioner employing NLP techniques: 'It is the user who dictates whether a process is manipulative or not' (Yemm, 1997). Others are not happy with this (Hague, 1997; Hardiman, 1994). Hardiman is concerned at both the absence of ethical concern and any grounding of the practice at a feeling level, as opposed to an intellectual and sensory level. It thus becomes :

> a powerful conceptual tool which can be used by both those with integrity, and those whose only intention is to manipulate others. (Hardiman, 1994)

Unlike OMD, the professional association (in this case the Association of NLP in the UK) has not provided a statement of principles or code of practice to be adhered to by all its members. Only those ANLP members who are also professionally trained psychotherapists and counsellors (for whom NLP is one of many techniques in their professional repertoire) have adopted a code of professional ethics as promulgated by ANLP Psychotherapy and Counselling Ltd. These are very similar to the various codes of professional ethics adopted by the orthodox professional bodies for psychotherapy and counselling. Further investigation for this chapter, through interviews with leading NLP practitioners, proved difficult. There was a marked reluctance to participate. Possibly this was overshadowed by litigation over the trademarking of NLP, but only two leading practitioners were willing to talk at length. They were both sole practitioners but had very different backgrounds: one in Gestalt and humanistic psychology and the other in information technology management. While the former specialised on working with individuals experiencing personal and work relationship difficulties for a number of blue chip companies, the other focused more upon delivering programmes open to the public in NLP training plus executive coaching. These different backgrounds were reflected in the sophistication of their ethical awareness, in terms of the values they espoused, their awareness of psychological safety and what was involved in professional integrity. A very conscious concern with 'boundaries' in relation to clients, recognition of the limits of their professional expertise and acknowledgement of the presence of transference-counter-transference processes in client relations, could be contrasted in one case with an instrumental naïveté around values, emotions and relationships with clients: 'NLP is a means to an end – ultimately it's about what works!' in the other.

This becomes extremely problematic where NLP is used by HRD professionals to enhance activities such as personal interactions and communication, presentations and working with groups or coaching and facilitating. While the 'technical' justification of NLP for developing training materials and planning and delivering them appears acceptable on grounds of utilitarianism, its use to enhance the counselling and consultancy role of HRD professionals such as in team development and culture change (Richards, 1996) could be problematic (Hague, 1997), that is, unless the NLP practitioner has experienced some training in professional ethics around psycho-dynamic processes.

The ethics of Gestalt in organisations – humanistic and holistic development

Gestalt is usually viewed as a psychotherapeutic tool rather than an HRD intervention. It is also popularly associated with the charismatic, abrasive and narcissistic leadership style of its founder, Fritz Perls (1969), who used confrontation and catharsis in his work with clients as a means of healing painful experiences arising from unfinished business in their inner lives. However, Gestalt as a psychotherapeutic tool has since undergone considerable evolution to become much more concerned with helping the client achieve self-awareness, insight, autonomy and self-support to enable them to achieve their own inner healing (Clark and Fraser, 1982; Clarkson, 1989; Perls *et al.*, 1969), an altogether much more sensitive, grounded and humanistic endeavour than the early approach.

The key concepts are the connection between a 'Gestalt' (a figure that stands out against a background), and the wider 'field' with which it is interconnected through a dynamic interplay of forces and constraints. This 'field' is a unitary concept, indicating the interconnectedness of human experience within a cycle of Gestalt formation and destruction (see Figure 7.1), which incorporates emotions, physical sensations, intuitions and spiritual dimensions as well as thoughts, and is connected with the wider community as well as immediate relationships. Gestalt is concerned with helping individuals with self-discovery from their immediate experience, in the 'here and now'. Mere thinking, without self-awareness of the emotions, and over-rationalising and intellectualising, can become a barrier to development and an impediment to an awareness of feelings and emotions. Thus there needs to be a relationship between the heart/emotions and the head/mind. It can act as an 'interruption' in the cycle of Gestalt formation and destruction (see Figure 7.1) that enables individuals to move beyond patterns of behaviour learned earlier in life, but which have since become inappropriate (for further elaboration of the principles and techniques of Gestalt see Clarkson, 1989 and Yontef, 1988).

FIGURE 7.1   The cycle of Gestalt formation and destruction

While Gestalt was influential in providing the foundations for NLP (there is a strong connection between NLP 'techniques' and the early 'catharsis' school of Gestalt), its authentic use as an HRD technique is still rather limited. The main difference between Gestalt in psychotherapy, and Gestalt in organisations is that whereas individuals look for healing of painful experiences arising from unfinished business, organisations are seen as looking for instruments of change that enable both the development of interpersonal skills and wider organisation development. There is a parallel between unfinished personal business and strategic misalignment of organisational culture.

Gestalt in organisations is based on a paradoxical theory of change, namely that individuals cannot be other than it is in their nature to be, and that attempts to change them otherwise are doomed to failure:

the more you try to be what you are not, the more you stay the same. Growth including assimilation of love and help from others, requires self-support. (Yontef, 1993, p. 26)

So, attempts to get behavioural and attitude change by just working with individuals at the cognitive level are unlikely to be successful. Working on self-support is not about requiring individuals to be self-sufficient and avoid dependency. Rather, it is about helping them to acknowledge the existence and role of others (often holding very different values) and to seek their support. This requires establishing dialogue and supporting self-esteem in oneself and others. Gestalt interventions in organisations are designed to work on interpersonal skills, working with the forces and constraints to remove blocks and avoid controlling both individuals and situations. It is used as an OD tool to understand the dynamics of team working, work with difficult people, transforming resistance into motivation, building confidence and self-esteem, coping with emotional situations, conflict and distress and to help people manage upwards and use coaching skills (Leary, 1998).

Much of the work is done through groups, and particular attention is drawn to the group dynamics and drawing parallels with interpersonal and team issues thrown up in the workplace. However, Gestalt in organisations does not use techniques in the same way as NLP or OMD. It is usually conducted through training groups of 6–12 people under the direction of trained leadership, but with a strong emphasis upon individual interactions and feedback. Most of this is achieved by establishing a 'dialogue' that is inclusive, non-invasive, accepting and is based upon genuine honest communication.

In the UK there are not many Gestalt in organisations practitioners, although the numbers are growing and there is now ENGLO – the European Network for Gestalt in Organisations. Interest in the potential of Gestalt as an HRD tool has been sporadic (Clark and Fraser, 1982; *Training Officer*, 1996). Perhaps Gestalt still suffers from the legacy of its early confrontational style. However, those that do practice have completed extensive training in Gestalt therapy and so are well aware of the codes of ethics for individual practitioners of the Gestalt Association UK and the Gestalt Centre, London. So, unlike the practitioners of OMD, those interviewed for this study did not see any need for additional written codes of practice or value statements. They were very conscious of their values (these include integrity, self-awareness, honesty, compassion, humanity, choice, responsibility and spirituality). For them ethics is the invisible glue that binds like-minded people together.

Contemporary Gestalt in organisations practitioners take psychological safety very seriously, and this is built in from the start, through managing the boundary between organisational and historic family issues, awareness and sensitivity to the needs and fears of others and through flexibility in adjusting material to respond to personal and organisational issues. They aim to avoid pursuing their interventions beyond individual participant capacity to tolerate anxiety, and, if necessary, will take time out from different parts of the programme to support vulnerable people. The aim is not to 'win hearts and minds' but to assist individuals and organisations overcome what is blocking them. Although 'ground rules' are usually established at an early stage:

> The Gestalt approach is not a set of techniques or formulae for discovering self or others: it is an orientation to experience which is dynamic and flexible in which the individual is open to all possibilities. (Clark and Fraser, 1982, p. 24)

Conclusion: how to handle ethics in HRD

This chapter has attempted to bring to the surface the implicit ethical principles and problems inherent in HRD. It is currently fashionable to make a critique of humanistic approaches to training and development for their lack of appreciation of social and political contextual factors. However, the current strategically focused agenda of HRD can make an appeal to the principles of ethical humanism seem quite justifiable.

Manipulation of individuals into acceptance of the 'need' for commitment by displaying certain behavioural competencies, espousing certain values, simultaneously with an acceptance of increased uncertainty and insecurity in the employment relationship, is to invite a very emphatic critique based on the principles of ethical humanism. However, this requires more than a naïve appeal to deontology based upon establishing a list of participant 'rights in development'. There is also the need to establish an ethical moral agency among those involved in development.

Ethical codes of practice such as those used by OMD and Gestalt practitioners can go some of the way. However, codes are usually best when dealing with normal practice and can come unstuck when practitioners face a dilemma (Marsick, 1997). This is where the strength of virtue ethics and the ethics of care come into their own. Their focus upon individual intention and handling of complexity that goes beyond the immediate development context within an organisation and reaches far into interpersonal and even psychological processes, implies that HRD practitioners require a higher level of ethical sophistication than is perhaps required of HRM professionals working in selection and assessment or reward management.

The substance as well as the processes of an intervention can also be issues of ethical concern. The discussion of OMD has shown that an intervention that has a poor ethical image can in fact be conducted in a very ethical manner. Furthermore, techniques such as NLP, which have a large popular following, are potentially dangerous tools in the hands of those with little training in humanistic psychology and with a superficial acquaintance with professional ethics. Finally, little understood methods such as Gestalt might, in the hands of experienced practitioners, offer the most ethically sophisticated and sensitive option for HRD.

References

Alimo-Metcalfe, B. (1995) 'Leadership and assessment' in Vinnicombe, S. and Colwill, N. L. *The Essence of Women in Management*, Hemel Hempstead: Prentice Hall

Alvesson, M. and Willmott, H. (1996) *Making Sense of Management: A Critical Introduction*, London: Sage

Association for Neuro-Linguistic Programming (1998) Information Booklet, Stourbridge: ANLP (UK) Ltd

Bandler, R. and Grinder, J. (1976) *The Structure of Magic I*, Palo Alto, CA: Science of Behaviour Books

Bevan, S. and Thomson, M. (1992) *Merit Pay, Performance Appraisal, and Attitudes to Women's Work*, IMS Report 234, Brighton: Institute of Manpower Studies

Burgoyne, J. and Reynolds, M. (eds) (1997) *Management Learning: Integrating Perspectives in Theory and Practice*, London: Sage

Burleson, L. and Grint, K. (1996) 'The deracination of politics: Outdoor management development' *Management Learning*, 27(2): 187–202

Clark, N. and Fraser, T. (1982) *The Gestalt Approach: An Introduction for Managers and Trainers*, Kent: Roffey Park Management Institute

Clarkson, P. (1989) *Gestalt Counselling in Action*, London: Sage

Development Training Advisory Group (1991) *Statement of Principles* (mimeo), Welwyn Garden City: DTAG

Development Training Advisory Group (1994) *Health Aspects of Development Training* (mimeo), Welwyn Garden City: DTAG

Dilts, R. (1990) *Changing Belief Systems with NLP*, California: Meta Publications

Druckman, D. and Bjork, R.A. (eds) (1991) *In the Mind's Eye: Enhancing Human Performance*, Washington DC: National Academy Press

Ebadan, G. and Winstanley, D. (1997) 'Downsizing, delayering and careers: the survivors' perspective' *Human Resource Management Journal*, 7(1): 79–91

French, R. and Grey, C. (eds) (1996) *Rethinking Management Education*, Sage: London

French, W.L. and Bell, C.H. (1990) *Organization Development: Behavioural Science Interventions for Organization Improvement* (4th edn), Englewood Cliffs, NJ: Prentice Hall

Kolb, D.A. and Fry, R. (1975) 'Towards a theory of experiential learning' in Cooper, C.L. (ed.) *Theories of Group Processes*, London: John Wiley

Gilley, J.W. and Eggland, S.A. (1989) *Principles of Human Resource Development* Reading, MA: Addison-Wesley

Grinder, J. and Bandler, R. (1976) *The Structure of Magic II*, Palo Alto, CA: Science of Behaviour Books

Guest, D. and Davey, K. (1996) 'Don't write off the traditional career' *People Management*, 22: 22–5

Guest, D. and Conway, N. (1997) 'Employee motivation and the psychological contract' *Issues in People Management*, No. 21 London: Institute of Personnel and Development

Hague, H. (1997) 'Strange but true' *Personnel Today*, 3 July, pp. 29–30

Hardiman, R. (1994) 'Neurolinguistic programming: background and issues' *Industrial Relations Review and Report*, No. 560, May

Hardingham, A. (1997) 'Finding a path through training's moral maze' *People Management*, 11 September, pp. 49–50

Herriot, P. and Pemberton, C. (1995) *New Deals: The Revolution in Managerial Careers*, Chichester: John Wiley

Holman, S. (1993) 'Outdoor challenge' *Training Officer*, 29(3): 88–9

Holmes, L. (1995) 'HRM and the irresistible rise of the discourse of competence' *Personnel Review* 24(4): 34–49

Honey, P. and Mumford, A. (1992) *The Manual of Learning Styles*, Maidenhead: Peter Honey

Institute of Personnel and Development (1998) *The IPD Guide on Outdoor Training*, London: Insitute of Personnel and Development

Irvine D. and Wilson, J.P. (1994) 'Outdoor management development – reality or illusion?' *Journal of Management Development*, 13(5): 25–37

Knights, S. (1995) *NLP at Work*, London: Nicholas Brealey

Knowles, M. (1989) *The Adult Learner: A Neglected Species*, Houston: Gulf Publishing

Laborde, G. (1995) *Influencing with Integrity*, Mountain View, CA: Syntony Publishing

Leary, Joyce, J. (1998) Promotional literature from Gestalt Consultancy and Training, St Albans

Lewin, K. (1952) *Field Theory in Social Science*, London: Tavistock

Lyon, U. (1996) 'Influence, communication and neuro-linguistic programming in practice' in Stewart, J. and McGoldrick, J. (eds) *Human Resource Development: Perspectives, Strategies and Practice*, London: Pitman

Mabey, C., Salaman, G. and Storey, J. (1998) *Human Resource Management: A Strategic Introduction*, Oxford: Blackwell

Marsick, V.E. (1997) 'Reflections upon developing a code of integrity for HRD: editorial' *Human Resource Development Quarterly*, 8(2): 91–4

Martin, J. (1992) *Cultures in Organizations: Three Perspectives*, New York: Oxford University Press

Mayon-White, W.M. (1994) 'Focus on business change and ethics: the ethics of change management: manipulation or participation?' *Business Ethics: a European Review*, 3(4): 96–200

McKendall, M. (1993) 'The tyranny of change: organization development revisited' *Journal of Business Ethics*, 12: 93–104

McLagan, R.A. and Suhadolnik, D. (1989) *Models of HRD Practice*, Alexandra, VA: American Society for Training and Development

Myerson, D. and Martin, J. (1994) 'Cultural change: an integration of three different views' in Tsoukas, H. (ed.) *New Thinking in Organizational Behaviour*, London: Butterworth Heinemann

O'Connor, J. and Seymour, J. (1990) *Introducing Neuro-Linguistic Programming*, London: HarperCollins

Perls, F.S. (1969) *Ego, Hunger and Agression*, New York: Basic Books

Perls, F.S., Hefferline, R.F. and Goodman, P. (1969) *Gestalt Therapy: Excitement and Growth in the Human Personality*, New York: Julian Press

Pickard, J. (1998) 'Your own mind business' *People Management*, **4**(17): 46–9

Rapport: The Journal for Neuro-Linguistic Programming (1998), **39**: 58

Reynolds, M. (1997) 'Learning styles: a critique' *Management Learning*, **28**(2): 115–33

Richards, R. (1996) 'Best behaviour' *Personnel Today*, 7 May, pp. 26–7

Rogers, C. (1969) *Freedom to Learn*, Columbus, OH: Charles E. Merrill

Rothwell, W. and Kazanas, H.C. (1989) *Strategic Human Resource Development*, New York: Prentice Hall

Rousseau, D.M. (1995) *Psychological Contracts in Organizations: Understanding Written and Unwritten Agreements*, London: Sage

Schein, E. (1993) 'How can organizations learn faster? The challenge of entering the green room' *Sloan Management Review*, Winter, pp. 85–92

Sparrow, P. (1994) 'Organizational competencies' in Anderson, N. and Herriot, P. *Assessment and Selection in Organizations*, Chichester: John Wiley

Sparrow, P. (1996) 'Transitions in the psychological contract: some evidence from the banking sector' *Human Resource Management Journal*, **6**(4): 75–92

Stewart, J. and McGoldrick, J. (1996) *Human Resource Development: Perspectives, Strategies and Practice*, London: Pitman

Taylor, M. (1992) *Coverdale on Management* (2nd edn), Oxford: Butterworth Heinemann

Townley, B. (1994) *Reframing Human Resource Management*, London: Sage

Training Officer (1996) Series of six articles by Trevor Bentley and Susan Clayton, January/ February to July/August

von Bergen, C. W., Soper, B., Rosenthal, G.T. and Wilkinson, L.V. (1997) 'Selected alternative training techniques in HRD' *Human Resource Development Quarterly*, **9**(4): 81–294

Walter, G.A. (1984) 'Organizational development and individual rights' *Journal of Applied Behavioural Science*, **20**: 423–39

Welch, J. (1997) 'NLP practitioners to face down hypnotist' *People Management*, **3**(25): 13

White, L.P. and Whooten, K.C. (1983) 'Ethical dilemmas in various stages of organization development' *Academy of Management Review*, **8**: 690–7

Winstanley, D. and Stuart-Smith, K. (1996) 'Policing performance: the ethics of performance management' *Personnel Review*, **25**(6): 66–84

Woodall, J. (1996) 'Managing culture change: can it ever be ethical?' *Personnel Review*, **25**(6): 26–40

Woodall, J. and Winstanley, D. (1998) *Management Development: Strategy and Practice*, Oxford: Blackwell

Yemm, G. (1997:) 'What can NLP do for me?' *Training Officer*, **33**(5): 147–9

Yontef G.M. (1988) 'Assimilating diagnostic and psychoanalytic perspectives into Gestalt therapy' *Gestalt Journal*, **11**(1): 5–32

Yontef, G.M. (1993) 'Awareness, dialogue and process' *The Gestalt Journal*, pp. 26–8

CHAPTER 8

Flexible working patterns

Celia Stanworth

Introduction

'Flexibility' in its numerous guises shows no sign of disappearing from the human resource agenda, despite pleas for 'farewell to flexibility' (Pollert, 1991). Flexible working patterns have continued to obsess employers in the 1990s, bolstered by political ideology and moves to deregulate the labour market (Rubery, 1996). The casualisation of labour and the use of non-standard work patterns to create a disadvantaged and marginalised workforce seem set to continue in a context where employers are reacting to powerful supra-national forces of globalisation, competitive pressure in product markets and growing short-termism in capital markets (Purcell and Purcell, 1996). This chapter outlines the context for flexibility in the UK and discusses ethical theory in relation to flexible working patterns. Part-time work, temporary work, self-employment and teleworking are then considered in more detail. The chapter concludes that flexible workers could be included as stakeholders within firms, through the development of a minimum floor of rights, based on equality with 'standard' work.

Flexible working patterns in context

In the 1980s and 90s successive Conservative governments advocated the use of flexible working patterns, which were broadly speaking those which moved away from the standard pattern of:

- working for another in return for a wage
- in a subordinate role
- for one employer
- on a full-time basis
- on the employer's premises
- with an expectation of indefinite employment. (Cordova, 1986)

Insecurity among workers was prompted by attempts to deregulate the labour market and to weaken the institutions which had previously given it stability. This strategy was pursued in the belief that this would create jobs as had appeared to be the case in the US (Rubery, 1996). These flexible practices, some new but others of long standing, were sold as a 'win-win' for both parties to the employment relationship, although the reality was that in the UK most were implemented on employers' terms (Brewster, 1998). The 'New' Labour government has been ambiguous and paradoxical in its pronouncements on flexibility, perhaps because of the need to appease the divergent interests of employers and trade unions for as long as possible. By signing up to European social legislation, the new government signalled acceptance of a floor of employment rights, but this could contradict its view that flexibility should be the means to ensure UK competitiveness, implying that a cost-cutting approach should be the priority, given pronouncements that European legislation likely to increase employers' costs will be strongly resisted.

Despite the criticisms and modifications of Atkinson's flexible firm model, particularly in terms of the thesis of a radical break with the past (Brewster *et al.*, 1993; Pollert, 1988, 1991), the strategic nature of the development of a core/periphery (Hakim, 1990), and the internal 'need' within firms for greater functional and numerical flexibility (Rubery, 1994), there is evidence that it has been used prescriptively by some employers (McGregor and Sproull, 1992), and has acted to give legitimacy to moves which some employers were already making in terms of externalising their labour sources at a time of high unemployment. Employers' interests are reflected in the rhetoric of the duality between a (supposedly) more secure core work-force, where workers are treated as long-term assets, and the periphery of insecure and disposable workers, whose disadvantaged position can be justi-fied as a buffer to protect the core in hard times. The flexible firm also rein-forces the norm of the standard (male) job versus the deviant non-standard (female) worker, which perpetuates the gender stereotype of women's marginal relationship to the labour market, especially married women and those with children (Lindley, 1994).

Deregulation of the labour market alone cannot account for the expansion of flexible work in the UK (Purcell and Purcell, 1996) but it can explain the ways in which UK employers have chosen to use it, compared to their coun-terparts in other EU nation states (Brewster, 1998). Pressures on work organis-ations from global product and labour markets, international competition, as well as sluggish economic growth and recurring recessions, have all been implicated in employers' felt need to adopt more flexible working patterns. Rubery and Horrell (1994) found that firms are experiencing three kinds of competitive pressure: from the more sophisticated consumer, from inter-firm competition and from strict internal budgetary targets. Low growth and recessions have focused employers' minds on cutting labour costs and minimising risk by using temporary contracts, reducing headcount, outsourcing and subcontracting. The buffer of high unemployment and weakened trade unions has allowed employers to offer work very much on their own terms, with little regard to workers' preferences. The attractiveness of the flexible workforce for UK employers is thus mostly associated with disposability and limited attachment (Blyton and Morris, 1992) rather than the developmental aspects centred around multiskilling and long-term investment in people.

The system of labour law, tax and social security in the UK still enshrines the male 'breadwinner' model (despite its *de facto* long-term decline) whereby workers enjoy statutory entitlement to various guarantees and social benefits if they sell their labour on standard terms, and the law imposes contributions and obligations on the employer, employee and the state (Cordova, 1986; European Foundation, 1997). Once workers move away from such standard work relationships, they tend to be excluded from these rights, which generally relate to employment continuity, a trigger level of earnings and the recognition that they are dependent labour. The fewer standard elements present, the fewer guarantees and benefits apply (Stanworth, 1996). This framework of legislation tends to legitimise the inferior treatment of non-standard workers by employers. The avoidance of employment regulation has been a deliberate decision by some employers (NACAB, 1997), encouraged by successive Conservative governments. This means that the risks of maintaining an income flow and the provision of social protection have been pushed onto the individual worker, the family or the state (Stanworth, 1996). The Labour government elected in 1997 has begun to reverse this trend, gradually introducing a floor of basic rights applicable to both standard and non-standard workers.

Ethics and flexible work

The Friedmanite free market economic position applied to flexible working in organisations is that managers act morally only if they maximise the firm's profits, so that whichever route achieves this end, within existing legal limitations, is moral. Using peripheral workers in this way, as factors of production in the hard version of the HRM model, generally leads to flexibility driven by short-termism and cost cutting that may undermine the HRM goals of commitment and quality (Blyton and Morris, 1992). This approach also contradicts the need of employees for stability and security (Heery, 1996). The development of flexible working practices in terms of insecurity and deregulation leading to 'junk jobs' (Crompton *et al.*, 1996) is not inevitable, but is the likely consequence in a situation where labour market institutions have been undermined (Rubery, 1996), and employers can adopt this approach to labour deployment with little apparent resistance from trade unions and the workforce (Heery and Salmon, 1998).

A contrasting view of the firm is based around the duty of care, one version of which is paternalism, the traditional 'master–servant' contract of security and stability in return for loyal devotion, that Anthony considers is morally superior (1986, cited in Warren, 1998), but which is clearly in decline. Only the core workforce has the possibility of this kind of relationship, with most or all peripheral workers excluded, and in the current business environment, this divide is believed by some to be the only alternative to a free-for-all in employment contracts (Warren, 1998). The trend to shrink the standard workforce and enlarge the flexible periphery means that there is a smaller and smaller number to whom employers may extend a paternalistic, developmental or stakeholder relationship. Warren (1998) feels that the young and well qualified may relish a state of insecurity, but these are hardly majority cases. For the rest, the more powerful are shifting the risk onto the less powerful. It is the individual worker who may live with intermittent or fluctuating earnings, or increasingly shoulder the responsibility for training for the reproduction of skills.

Academics may adopt a negative normative stance of merely berating employers for going down the exclusion/insecurity route, but a more positive alternative is to look at the possibility of better actions through morality in the firm. The concept of the virtuous organisation (Collier, 1995) moves towards the idea of encouraging employers to develop purposeful organisations with committed members. Companies with employment policies which attempt to add value to employee skills, which encourage employees to take initiatives, and which take consultation seriously are exercising virtue (Collier, 1995). Management becomes concerned with the manufacturing of meanings, the shaping of a culture 'in which people find it possible to find meaning and fulfilment in excellence as defined in performance terms' (Collier, 1995, p. 146).

But what of employers operating a bifurcation of employment systems with motivational systems for some, instrumental systems for others? Can they still be seen as good, caring employers? Goodness is difficult to define in a business context of increasing competition and postmodernist rationality in which there is no one correct view on anything (French and Allbright, 1998). Can moral conflict situations be resolved satisfactorily in this context, or is it likely that justice is absent and that the most powerful voice in the organisation will win? In terms of flexible work, where the workforce is often in a weak situation, the outcome is likely to be second-class jobs, justified by the firm's economic position where 'people can exit if they don't like what is on offer'. Alternatively, employers may only include flexible workers in high-commitment arrangements if they can see demonstrable economic benefits in so doing, treating them instrumentally as means to ends. So far, research linking high commitment developmental 'soft' HRM employment policies to better corporate performance has found that productivity improvements are commonly achieved by increased control and surveillance rather than by developing a welfare–humanist relationship with employees (for a discussion see Mabey *et al.*, 1998).

Another approach to the moral development of organisations, using Kohlberg's (1976, 1981) work (Logsdon and Yuthas, 1997) suggests that the concept of moral development in individuals can be modified and applied to work organisations. This has the attraction of linking the theory of business ethics to empirical business research. An organisation's stage of moral development can be indicated with reference to its responses to stakeholders. According to Logsdon and Yuthas, there is not one stakeholder theory, but several, ranging from narrow orientations focusing on benefits to one group, through to broader orientations that encompass a wider range of stakeholders. They set out three levels of moral development, pre-conventional, conventional and post-conventional. In the pre-conventional stage corporate decisions are made in top managers' interests, to the detriment of other supposed stakeholders. At the conventional stage, decisions tend to be made in terms of negative duties, including compliance with society's legal standards, such as employment laws. Positive duties to promote the welfare of a wide range of stakeholders, based upon respect for others, typifies post-conventional moral reasoning in organisations.

The development of organisations is not uni-directional, firms can reverse their moral development, although Logsdon and Yuthus (1997, p. 8) argue that:

> Most of the social legislation and regulation during the 1960s and 1970s were efforts to shift new social norms and knowledge that had originated in post-conventional ethical analysis into the peer expectations and legal requirements of conventional thinking.

Thus one influence (among others) on an organisation's moral development is legal regulation, that can make unethical behaviour illegal behaviour. Public pressure for more responsible corporate action should lead to corporate compliance in the short term, but holds out the possibility of moral commitment in the long run.

Using this framework, certain actions, such as treating the non-standard workforce as being of lesser worth than standard workers, and not including them as full stakeholders of the organisation, may come to be considered unethical by society as a whole. This may develop into public pressure on employers to alter their behaviour, and the beginnings of this are discernible in the improvement in the lot of part-time workers through domestic and

European legislation, which is discussed more fully in the next section. Compliance with laws could lead to attitude change and eventually to a re-orientation of the labour market which accommodates diversity, rather than treating the non-standard as deviant (Lindley, 1994).

Part-time work

This is by far the most common non-standard work form in the UK, affecting more than a quarter of the workforce. It has steadily grown relatively inde-pendently of the trade cycle since the 1950s, and is forecast to affect 31 per cent of the workforce by the year 2006 (DfEE, 1996). Four out of five part-time workers are women, although male (mostly involuntary) part-time work has increased recently, but from a low base. Recent entrants to this workforce are impecunious students in full-time education and just under a million of them are working part-time, mostly in low-paid service sector jobs (IDS, 1997). Part-time work is a tradition, and concentrated in the public and private services sector, especially health, education, hotels, catering and retailing, and most of the recent increase in this form of work can be explained by the growth in serv-ices (Pollert, 1991). The financial services sector has seen a dramatic rise in part-time work since 1994 (Emmott and Hutchinson, 1998). Part-time working is concentrated in low-skill, low-wage occupations, with part-timers accounting for three-quarters of the low paid. Short-hours workers earning below the National Insurance threshold are debarred from Statutory Sick Pay and Statutory Maternity Pay (Labour Research Department, 1996a), but the rights of this group have improved in recent years, despite opposition from Conservative governments. A House of Lords ruling implemented in 1995 (*R. v. Secretary of State for Employment, ex-parte EOC* [1994] IRLR 176) removed the differential access to employment protection and a European judgement (ECJ, Vroege case, September 1994, DCLD22, under Article 119 of the EC Treaty covering equal treatment) entitles part-timers to pension rights on a pro-rata basis with full-time workers. The Fairness at Work legislative programme will bring UK practice into line with the Part-time Workers' Directive, which outlaws less favourable treatment of part-timers by employers.

The vast majority of part-time jobs are permanent, and many women part-time workers have long service, constituting a relatively stable workforce. But it is clear that many part-time workers neither feel nor are treated as fully inte-grated stakeholders of the employing organisation. They are rarely offered advancement of any kind (Gallie and White, 1994) and have in the past been excluded from company fringe benefits (Dex and McCulloch, 1995). Other drawbacks include downward occupational mobility and deleterious effects on lifetime earnings and consequently pensions. Part-time work is used by employers to avoid paying overtime premia to full-time staff, part-time workers are often expected to work 'unsocial' hours and hours of work are sometimes changed at short notice, resulting in unpredictable earnings (Lynch and Stanworth, 1997). Although there is some evidence of more high-status work now being undertaken on a part-time basis, most UK employers create part-time work only in low-skilled work and careerless occupations.

For many women, part-time work can be seen as both a threat and an opportunity – more specifically the only way that most women can combine paid work with family commitments. Women's recorded high levels of satisfaction with low-grade part-time work (Hakim's (1990) 'grateful slaves') can be explained by their constrained choice in a situation in the UK where affordable childcare is in short supply. Genuinely 'family friendly' reduced hours working patterns are offered to women – and occasionally to men too – by exemplar firms (Lewis and Lewis, 1996), enabling workers to avoid occupational downgrading and to return to full-time work when children are older. Job sharing in managerial work was pioneered by the public sector, although only two per cent of managers in the UK work part time (New Ways to Work, 1997).

The quality of part-time jobs has declined in the 1990s, with the increasing use of short-hours part-time work (TUC, 1994), that further loosens the tenuous grip of these workers on the labour market. Employers' costs are reduced by keeping earnings below the National Insurance threshold and paying part-timers less than full-timers for equivalent work (Labour Research Department, 1996a). Zero-hours contracts, used in retailing, represent the ultimately flexible work pattern, guaranteeing no minimum hours, no stable level of earnings and precluding workers' planning their lives (NACAB, 1997). Compulsory competitive tendering (CCT) in local government has undermined the pay and working conditions of already disadvantaged part-time women workers (Escott and Whitfield, 1994). Lengthening trading hours, Sunday opening in retailing, and 24-hour working in some call centres have all led to more evening, night and weekend part-time jobs. In a recent call-centre survey employers predicted that, because of high levels of job stress, half of all workers would in future be part time compared to one-third currently (Taylor and Bain, 1998).

Despite the low quality of most part-time work, employers often expect high standards from these workers. In food retailing, basic grade part-time staff are expected to deliver greater customer care despite intensification of work (Lynch and Stanworth, 1997; Ogbonna, 1992). In a situation where plentiful external sources of labour are available to employers, because of supply-side segmentation, and limited alternatives for workers, employers can 'have it all' in terms of offering low pay and prospects, but getting relatively high levels of employee commitment and productivity from part-time staff (Crouch, 1997; Rubery, 1994).

Despite recent legislative changes improving the situation of part-time workers, they still suffer second-class treatment. Specifically, more protection needs to be given from arbitrary changes to terms and conditions, equal pay and treatment must be assured, and changes made to National Insurance rules so that short-hours part-time workers are not excluded from some state benefits. The National Association of Citizen's Advice Bureaux (NACAB, 1997) would like zero-hours contracts to be made illegal, or employers to be required to specify minimum contractual working hours, such as in the recent agreement between Tesco supermarkets and the shopworkers' union USDAW. Employers might also be encouraged to provide inclusivity rather than marginalising part-time work by demonstrating that genuinely family friendly policies such as those of Midland Bank (now HSBC) (Lewis and Lewis, 1996) can have advantages for both parties.

Self-employment

One of the most profound changes in the UK workforce structure in the 1980s was the expansion of self-employment, which grew from seven to over 13 per cent of the workforce. Seventy-five per cent of the self-employed are male, with women increasing their proportion of this workforce recently (Emmott and Hutchinson, 1998). The self-employed tend to be concentrated in construction, hotels and restaurants, agriculture and fishing. The growth of this workforce is mainly due to exclusion of workers from the mainstream labour market, because of unemployment, outsourcing by firms, as well as the tax advantages of self-employment (Rubery, 1989). Numbers are predicted to increase by a further 800,000 by the year 2006 (DfEE, 1996) mainly due to further outsourcing by large companies. The Thatcher governments promoted the moral superiority of working for oneself (Rainnie, 1989) and placed great faith in the ability of new small firms to be the engine of economic regeneration in the UK.

The number of self-employed with employees in the UK actually fell from over one million in 1985 to 860,000 in 1997, whereas the number of self-employed without employees grew from 1.7 to 2.5 millions (Stanworth, 1998a). The situation of a significant proportion of self-employed without employees is that of 'disguised wage workers'. These include some self-employed in construction (Druker and Macallan, 1996), freelancers in book publishing (Stanworth and Stanworth, 1997), chair-renters in hairdressing (Druker *et al.* 1997) and milk distribution (Boyle, 1994) where 8000 dairy rounds people were pushed into franchised self-employment in the late 1980s. Many traditional homeworkers are also treated as self-employed, but are clearly dependent labour. Labour Force Survey figures identify about one-third of a million homeworkers (Felstead, 1995) but just over one million is probably a more realistic figure (Huws, 1994). There is evidence that homeworking is expanding, not declining (Felstead, 1995; Stanworth, 1996). Homeworkers are the most exploited in the UK, with low pay, fluctuating earnings and exclusion from the benefits and employment protection associated with incorporation. For the genuinely independent self-employed, who may have scarce technical or professional skills to sell, or the small business in an affluent region of the UK with buoyant demand for the product or service, there are advantages, including tax breaks, but for many new entrants to this workforce in the recent past, self-employment has hardly been a positive choice.

Self-employment is being used by some organisations to turn fixed into variable costs, as a strategy of avoidance of responsibility for the workforce (Anthony, 1986, cited in Warren, 1998), using the argument that this is the only possible choice in a globally competitive situation (Warren, 1998). For the dependent self-employed, perpetual insecurity is the outcome, with none of the advantages of independent entrepreneurship, but none of the benefits of employment either. Where employers are keen to reduce their legal obligations, there may be little choice between bogus self-employed status or no work. NACAB feel that the legal loophole allowing this to happen should be closed, with employers encouraged to incorporate the self-employed, with the burden of proof on the employer to demonstrate that a worker is self-employed (NACAB, 1997). Moves in this direction in UK law are already in train, although there are likely to be considerable problems of enforcement. If economically dependent self-employed workers are able to enjoy the legal rights accorded to standard employees, the mutual moral obligations of both parties can be recognised (Warren, 1998).

Temporary work

The temporary workforce currently makes up more than seven per cent of the UK workforce, and takes several forms: casual, seasonal, fixed-term contract, engagement until project completion, and agency temping. There has been a significant increase in temporary working since 1992, due to the growth in use of fixed-term contracts, but agency work has also shown a dramatic increase (Emmott and Hutchinson, 1998). Most temporary workers are found in the service sector, and the occupations of temporary workers tend to be polarised between teaching and health professionals on the one hand, and routine clerical and other low-skilled occupational groupings on the other. Many of the new jobs in the labour market are offered on a temporary basis and, although the most popular reasons for using temporary workers are still the traditional ones of matching demand to supply of labour and providing short-term cover for absence, there are two new trends in temporary work.

One is an increasing use of short-term contracts, for example in further and higher education, resulting in deleterious outcomes for individuals and institutions (Bryson and Barnes, 1997). The second is a new demand from large, often blue chip companies, for high volumes of agency staff supplied by intermediaries, known as insourcing (IES, 1995; Purcell and Purcell, 1996). The supply of such staff is governed by cost-competitive contracts between the client firm and agency, often of only one year's duration. In some cases large numbers of agency workers (sometimes more than half the workforce) are found alongside permanent staff, on much less favourable pay and conditions (Purcell and Purcell, 1996). Call-centre work is another area where there are large numbers of agency temporary staff (IES, 1995; Purcell and Purcell, 1996), which has led to collective agreements between trade unions and agencies (for example BIFU, CWU and Manpower). This new departure towards the permanent use of temporary working on a large scale within well-known companies and institutions indicates a strategic restructuring towards a situation where a dwindling number of permanent employees are supplemented by an insecure mass of temporary and agency staff performing not only routinised work tasks (Purcell and Purcell, 1996), but also 'core' functions. Besides the likelihood of poorer pay and conditions and job insecurity, there are concerns with temporary work in terms of a training deficit (CBI, 1994).

As with dependent self-employment, the growth areas of temporary work represent a withdrawal by employers from employment obligations, a way to lower labour costs and a buffer in times of uncertainty. To improve the rights and situation of temporary workers, a number of legal changes could raise basic standards. Stronger equal treatment legislation could prevent discrimination in terms of pay and conditions for temporary and casual workers. Waiver clauses forfeiting entitlement to employment rights are likely to be deemed invalid in future, and better regulation of temporary employment agencies (NACAB, 1997) is advocated by the current government, as well as moves to ensure that temporary agency workers enjoy full employment rights. These developments would emphasise the moral obligations of employment (Warren, 1998) and, while not outlawing the use of temporary work, would encourage its better-regulated use in situations where jobs are genuinely short term in nature (such as project work or cover for maternity absence).

Teleworking

Remote work facilitated by information and communications technologies (ICTs) has been feasible since the 1970s, but has only started to grow in the UK in the 1990s. Labour Force Survey figures show that there are now just under a million teleworkers in the UK (*The Teleworker*, 1998, Jan–Feb, p. 18). If workers in remote offices and call centres are included, who will represent two per cent of the UK workforce by 2000, this adds up to a not inconsiderable total.

Teleworking was promoted by the Conservative government (DTI, 1994; Employment Department, 1993, 1994) and by the telecommunications and IT industry (for example Gray *et al.*, 1993). It has been presented as a liberating, flexible work pattern giving individuals autonomy to organise their own time and freedom to manipulate the hard and software (McGrath and Houlihan, 1996). Teleworkers are frequently presented working in comfortable, leafy surroundings, and although physically remote from colleagues and clients, able to make meaningful global contacts through ICTs. If they are employed, they are assumed to be managed in a high-trust context where bosses motivate and lead rather than closely control. They retain the benefits of the internal labour market – training, advancement, equality of pay and conditions with their office-based counterparts – and are treated as long-term human assets.

Self-employed teleworkers are portrayed as part of the 'enterprise culture' (Huws, 1991) where telework facilitates voluntary moves into self-employment, with the expectation of growth into a small business. The prevailing archetype (for example Handy, 1989; Toffler, 1981) is the highly paid professional or technical consultant, possessing scarce skills, and operating from an Arcadian country cottage (Stanworth and Stanworth, 1992). Telework is also associated with the 'virtual' organisation in the 'knowledge' society (Crouch, 1997; Stanworth, 1998b) where workers are self-directing and self-disciplined, coming together in 'virtual teams', sometimes global, to work on short-term projects (Barnatt, 1996; Birchall and Lyons, 1995; Negroponte, 1995).

In all these ways telework fits with HRM theory. It is adaptable, not only in terms of time and location, but also contract. Telework can be conventional employment, short-term contract work or self-employment. It emphasises the individualisation of the employment relationship, as teleworkers are often spatially isolated, with their performance measured by individual output. The technology facilitates the decentralised or 'federal' organisation (Handy, 1989), rapidly responsive to change, allowing unlimited geographical dispersion alongside central control. This restructures 'outdated' bureaucratic command and control organisations towards adhocratic, innovative forms said to reflect current human resource contingencies (Kanter, 1984; Mintzberg, 1979). But what is the reality of teleworking?

The first teleworkers in the UK were technical specialists and professionals, and the IT sector was the first to use this work pattern to any extent (Judkins *et al.*, 1985; Kinsman, 1988). More recent research shows that telework has become more widespread in other sectors, and in a very broad range of occupations (Huws, 1993). There is also anecdotal evidence that telework has grown more rapidly in the self-employed workforce than among corporate employees. Far less attention has been paid in the UK literature (except for Brocklehurst, 1989; Huws, 1984) to home-based teleworkers performing clerical functions of a routine nature. Word processor operators and data entry clerks have easily replaceable skills and a weaker bargaining position. For these workers telework at home is likely to be low paid, careerless and marginalised. They are often women constrained to work in this way to combine employment with childcare and there is evidence of a growth in this type of telework. Felstead (1995) found that well over half UK homeworkers were in clerical occupations, and he feels that they are often subject to the same exploitative employment relationships as those in the old 'sweated' trades. Although often treated as self-employed, they are in reality disguised wage workers, insecure and unprotected (Stanworth, 1996).

Telework in back offices and call centres is a rapidly growing area of work in the UK, facilitated by automatic call distribution (ACD) technology. It includes customer interface work, or processing correspondence, mortgage applications or credit card payments. Many of these offices are located in lower cost regions, tapping into a pool of married women seeking local shift or part-time employment. Most retail banks have opened long-hours, direct telephone banking centres in such locations, as have insurance companies. Some retail banks have opted to centralise their paperwork on such sites, often using twilight shifts (Cressey and Scott, 1992), in parallel with job reductions in branches. A new, deskilled workforce is often being created in these centres, where there is no longer a need for qualifications, staff are recruited over the telephone and trained in three weeks (BBC2, 1995). There is a high intensity of work, call rates are monitored and the software prompts standardised responses to customers. Typically, there is shift and night work, and in some centres there is a high proportion of agency temporary workers. The banking union, BIFU (now Unifi), reports that call-centre workers are often excluded from better employment policies which applied to branch workers, the work careerless and the workforce disposable.

Even where teleworkers appear to have scarce, valuable skills and high education levels, they are being employed as a contingent workforce. In UK book publishing the use of home-based, freelance editors and proof-readers has expanded in parallel with the contraction of in-house editorial teams. Mergers and downsizing have created an externalised workforce and many now work for their former employers on a self-employed basis (Stanworth and Stanworth, 1997). Fluctuating earnings and work flow, low and slow pay, social isolation and a training deficit were also experiences shared by free-lance, home-based translators (Huws *et al.*, 1996). At IBM a two-tier staffing model has been created. Project managers are permanently employed, but project team workers can be easily discarded, being on short-term contracts with no rights to pension or redundancy payments. For this 'supplementary' workforce training tends to be task specific and workers are expected to have the skills required at the time they are needed – a just-in-time workforce.

In another major computer company, half the workforce have been shed in a massive cost-cutting programme and offices disposed of, replaced by shared offices, 'hot-desking' arrangements and working at home. Hours of work were longer and they felt constantly on call (BBC2, 1995). Hot desking (desk sharing) and homework are used where staff are mobile and visit clients and other sites as part of their work. It has been adopted by management consultancies, sales representatives in insurance and British Gas Services where offices have been reduced from 120 to 37 by compulsorily moving the managers to homework and their teams to mobile work, receiving their daily schedule of work directly into their vans (Labour Research Deparment, 1996b).

Looking at UK telework as a whole, some better qualified, professional and technical teleworkers may be given discretion in their work, and in some cases where skills and experience are in short supply telework can be liberating and well rewarded. For this group, the approach of Schwoerer *et al.* (1995) whereby 'knowledge' workers can demand rights to fair treatment in the work situation applies. Many teleworkers, however, are not privileged – they have easily replaceable routine skills. Some are vulnerable outworkers, whose situation has limited possibility of improvement even with legislation. This could encompass adoption of the 1996 ILO Convention on Homeworking (Stanworth, 1996), which has similarities with government policy that economically dependent workers should be accorded the legal rights of employees, unless the employer can prove that the worker is genuinely self-employed.

Teleworkers, in all socio-economic groups, often have inferior employment conditions if they are remote from the workplace. They often have no choice about using their home as an office. Comprehensive collective agreements, such as BT's agreements with the CWU and the STE, are successful at protecting teleworkers (Stanworth, 1996) and should be promoted as examples of good practice, but where employers are determined to outflank trade unions, they are succeeding. Unions find representing teleworkers more difficult than conventional staff, because they are physically remote from the workplace, or turnover rapidly as in many call centres (BIFU, 1993, 1996) and an increasing number of teleworkers are in non-union environments.

The treatment of teleworkers to reflect a morally highly developed stakeholder approach could be based on the following tenets (Moon and Stanworth, 1997). Moves to homework should be voluntary, teleworkers should not be given inferior terms and conditions, and homeworking should not be a substitute for childcare. Telework should not mean casualisation, by changing to self-employment or short-term contracts, and teleworkers should maintain rights to union representation. Telework represents a (relatively) new division of labour (Guest, 1998) between those who need to be physically present in the workplace and those who do not, with challenges for personnel practitioners to develop appropriate new policies (Stanworth and Stanworth, 1991), recognising and safeguarding teleworkers' rights, but this may need to be supplemented by legislation for vulnerable groups of teleworkers, which is under consideration by the European Commission.

Conclusions

For many workers on the periphery – in non-standard jobs in the UK today – life is insecure, training minimal, opportunities for development and promotion severely limited. Casualisation is affecting professional and white collar workers as well as blue collar. Even where highly qualified workers are using up-to-date technology in expanding sectors, they are sometimes treated by their organisations as contingent workers, subject to disposal at short notice, absorbing the fluctuations in the organisation's competitive position. Work organisations are often operating between a managerial prerogative position emphasising only top managers' interests, and narrowly based stakeholder relationships, with shareholders interests dominant (Logsdon and Yuthas, 1997). Organisations (with some exceptions) tend to consider non-standard workers as a lesser breed and to build penalties for workers into the employment relationship, besides using them as a means of cost minimisation and/or withdrawing from the employment relationship entirely, in order to shift risks from the firm onto the individual (Stanworth, 1996; Warren, 1998). Taking a normative position, this means missed opportunities – to offer men and women greater family and lifestyle choices (Lewis and Lewis, 1996), or to create a feeling of inclusion and loyalty among workers, however fleeting their stay, to the employing entity.

Recent legal changes to the position of the flexible workforce could affect employer behaviour, initially in terms of compliance by organisations with external constraints (Logsdon and Yuthas, 1997). The 'equal rights' approach advocated by the EOC and NACAB, and largely adopted by the current Labour administration, does not seek to abolish flexible work patterns, but to give all non-standard workers equality with standard workers in terms of employment protection, rights to fringe benefits and opportunities for training and development. Some further development of these regulations would be necessary to continue to improve the situation of various groupings of non-standard workers. Such a floor of rights may also have societal pay-offs, in terms of facilitating movement between jobs in a volatile labour market without disadvantaging workers. It would also prevent the shifting of risk onto the weakest in the labour market, and instead would encourage firms to build a high-skill, high-added-value workforce.

The costs of employing flexible workers is increasing, which could inhibit job creation, encourage a growth in the unregulated, hidden economy, or drive companies to relocate to cheaper labour markets abroad, particularly where work can be facilitated by ICTs (Stanworth, 1998b). Legislation might provoke avoidance by some employers operating on the pre-conventional moral level. However, higher cost 'equal rights' flexible work would still be cost-effective, for example in high-stress work such as in call centres, or when it retains staff at the family-building stage in whom a training investment has been made

(Lewis and Lewis, 1996), or where it is used to access scarce skills only needed intermittently by using temporary or self-employed workers. The recent extension of rights to part-time workers has not been accompanied by a numerical decline in part-time work, despite dire predictions by politicians at the time.

The adoption of 'equal rights' flexibility could alter the level of moral development of firms from the pre-conventional to the conventional. By complying with legislation, organisations would be conforming to their negative duties to others, in line with peer expectations and social controls (Logsdon and Yuthas, 1997). In the longer term, however, as with sex and race equality legislation of the 1970s, some firms would begin to internalise this surface compliance into a deeper change of attitudes, encompassing respect for others and a duty to promote the welfare of all those who undertake work for the firm. Flexible workers would be recognised as full stakeholders of the firm, reflecting Rawlsian theory, moving towards universal ethical principles. This recognition of non-standard workers as having rights and legitimate interests could be a powerful incentive for employers to initiate and maintain investment in human capital (Warhurst and Thompson, 1998).

The development of a floor of rights for non-standard workers is a welcome step towards ensuring that they are accepted as valuable members of the organisation, although the mere passing of statutes is no guarantee that the law will be enforced. The onus is often on the individual worker to ensure that fair standards are operated, but this is problematic given the often powerless position of these workers. Pressure on employers to enforce the rights of flexible workers will continue to come from trade unions, although coverage by collective agreements has shrunk and they have had limited success in representing some groups of non-standard workers. Or it may come from new representative bodies such as Citizen's Advice Bureaux (Heery and Salmon, 1998). Without the *de facto* implementation of minimum legal rights the weak bargaining position of most flexible workers *vis-à-vis* their employers means that they will not be treated with the respect they deserve and will continue to be subordinate to more powerful voices in the organisation.

References

Anthony, P. (1986) *The Foundation of Management*, London: Tavistock

Barnatt, C. (1996) *Cyber Business: Mindsets for a Wired Age*, Chichester: John Wiley

BBC2 (1995) *Working All Hours – Brave New Work*, broadcast on 30 September

BIFU (1993) *Homeworking: Potential Applications and Possible Consequences for BIFU*, revised edn, London: Banking, Insurance and Finance Union

BIFU (1996) 'Dialling the Future? Phone Banking and Insurance', London: Banking, Insurance and Finance Union, July

Birchall, D. and Lyons, L. (1995) *Creating Tomorrow's Organization*, London: Pitman

Blyton, P. and Morris, J. (1992) 'HRM and the Limits of Flexibility', in Blyton, P. and Turnbull, P. (eds) *Reassessing Human Resource Management*, London: Sage, pp. 116–30

Boyle, E. (1994) 'The Rise of the Reluctant Entrepreneurs' *International Small Business Journal*, **2**(2): 63–9

Brewster, C. (1998) 'Flexible Working in Europe: Extent, Growth and the Challenge for HRM' in Sparrow, P. and Marchington, M. (eds) *Human Resource Management: The New Agenda*, London: Pitman, pp. 245–58

Brewster, C., Hegewisch, C. and Mayne, L. (1993) *Flexible Work Patterns in Europe*, Institute of Personnel Management, Issues in People Management Series No. 6, London: IPD

Brocklehurst, M. (1989) 'Homeworking and the New Technology', *Personnel Review*, **18**(2): 2–70

Bryson, C. and Barnes, N. (1997) 'Professional Workers and Fixed-Term Contracts: a Contradiction in Terms?' Paper given to The Insecure Workforce Conference, Cardiff Business School, 11–12 September

CBI (1994) *The Flexible Workforce: Who Pays for Training?*, London: Confederation of British Industry

Collier, J. (1995) 'The Virtuous Organization', *Business Ethics: A European Review*, **4**(3): 143–8

Cordova, E. (1986) 'From Full-Time Wage Employment to Atypical Employment: a Major Shift in the Evolution of Labour Relations?', *International Labour Review*, **125**(6): 641–57

Cressey, P. and Scott, P. (1992) 'Employment, Technology and Industrial Relations in the Clearing Banks: is the Honeymoon over?' *New Technology, Work and Employment*, Autumn, pp. 83–96

Crompton, R., Gallie, D. and Purcell, K. (1996) 'Work, Economic Restructuring and Social Regulation' in Crompton, R., Gallie, D. and Purcell, K. (eds) *Changing Forms of Employment: Organisations, Skills and Gender*, London: Routledge, pp. 1–20

Crouch, C. (1997) 'Skills-based Full Employment: the Latest Philosopher's Stone', *British Journal of Industrial Relations*, **35**(3): 367–91

Dex, S. and McCulloch, A. (1995) *Flexible Employment in Britain: A Statistical Analysis*, Research Discussion Series No. 15, Manchester: EOC

DfEE, (1996) *Labour Market and Skill Trends 1997/1998*, Nottingham: Skills and Enterprise Network, Department for Education and Employment

Druker, J. and Macallan, H. (1996) *Work, Status and Self-Employment in British Construction Industry*, Milton Keynes: Small Business Research Trust

Druker, J., Stanworth, C. and Conway, J. (1997) 'The Self-Employed without Employees – an Unexplored Growth Area – Cases from the UK'. Paper presented to the Canadian Industrial Relations Association Conference, St John's, Newfoundland, June

DTI (1994) *DTI Teleworking Study (1992/3) Summary of Conclusions and Recommendations*, DTI/MTA/Brameur Ltd

Emmott, M. and Hutchinson, S. (1998) 'Employment Flexibility: Threat or Promise?' in Sparrow, P. and Marchington, M. (eds) *Human Resource Management: The New Agenda*, London: Pitman, pp. 229–44

Employment Department (1993) *Be Flexible*, Rotherham: Employment Department Group

Employment Department (1994) *A Manager's Guide to Teleworking*, Rotherham: Employment Department Group

Escott, K. and Whitfield, D. (1994) *The Gender Impact of CCT in Local Government*, Research Discussion Series No. 12, Manchester: EOC

European Foundation (1997) *The Social Implications of Teleworking*, EF/97/23/EN, Dublin: European Foundation for the Improvement of Living and Working Conditions

Felstead, A. (1995) 'Concepts, Definitions and Estimates of the Extent and Characteristics of Homeworking in Britain'. Paper given to the 17th Working Party on Labour Market Segmentation Conference, University of Siena, July

French, W. and Allbright, D. (1998) 'Resolving a Moral Conflict through Discourse', *Journal of Business Ethics*, **17**: 177–94

Gallie, D. and White, M. (1994) 'Employer Policies, Employee Contracts, and Labour Market Structure', in Rubery, J. and Wilkinson, F. (eds) *Employer Strategy and the Labour Market*, Oxford: Oxford University Press

Gray, M., Hodson, N. and Gordon, G. (1993) *Teleworking Explained*, Chichester: John Wiley

Guest, D. (1998) 'Beyond HRM: Commitment and the Contract Culture', in Sparrow, P. and Marchington, M. (eds) *Human Resource Management: The New Agenda*, London: Pitman, pp. 37–51

Hakim, C. (1990) 'Core and Periphery in Employers' Workforce Strategies: Evidence from the 1987 ELUS Survey', *Work, Employment and Society*, **4**(2): 157–88

Handy, C. (1989) *The Age of Unreason*, London: Hutchinson

Heery, E. (1996) 'Risk, Responsibility and the New Pay', *Personnel Review*, **25**(6): 54–65

Heery, E. and Salmon, J.(1998) 'Introduction: The Insecure Workforce', in Heery, E. and Salmon, J. (eds) *The Insecure Workforce, Management Research News*, **21**(2/3): 7–8

Huws, U. (1984) *The New Homeworkers*, London: Low Pay Unit

Huws, U. (1991) 'Telework: Projections', *Futures*, Jan–Feb: 19–31

Huws, U. (1993) *Teleworking in Britain: A Report to the Employment Department*, Research Series No. 18, Sheffield: Employment Department

Huws, U. (1994) *Key Results from a National Survey of Homeworkers*, Leeds: National Group on Homeworking, Report No. 2

Huws, U., Podro, S., Gunnarsson, E., Weijers, T., Arvanitaki, K. and Trova, V. (1996) *Teleworking and Gender*, Report No. 317, Brighton: Institute for Employment Studies

IDS (1997) 'Viewpoint: More and More Full-time Students join the Workforce', *IDS Report 749*, November: 1

IES (1995) *Temporary Work and the Labour Market*, Report No. 311, Brighton: Institute for Employment Studies

Judkins, P., West, D. and Drew, J. (1985) *Networking in Organisations*, Aldershot: Gower

Kanter, R.M. (1984) *The Change Masters*, London: Allen & Unwin

Kinsman, F. (1988) *The Telecommuters*, London: John Wiley

Kohlberg, L. (1976) 'Moral Stages and Moralization', in Likona, T. (ed.) *Moral Development and Behaviour*, New York: Holt, Rinehart & Wilson

Kohlberg, L. (1981) *Essays on Moral Development*, Vol. 1. *The Philosophy of Moral Development*, San Fransisco: Harper & Row

Labour Research Department (1996a) *Part-Time Workers*, London: LRD, March

Labour Research Department (1996b) 'Home is Where the Computer is', *Labour Research*, October: 13–14

Lewis, S. and Lewis, J. (eds) (1996) *The Work–Family Challenge: Rethinking Employment*, London: Sage

Lindley, R. (ed.) (1994) *Labour Market Structures and Prospects for Women*, Manchester: EOC

Logsdon, J. and Yuthas, K. (1997) 'Corporate Social Performance, Stakeholder Orientation, and Organizational Moral Development', *Journal of Business Ethics*, **16**: 1213–26

Lynch, S. and Stanworth, C. (1997) 'Measuring Insecurity: the Case of Part-time Workers in Retailing'. Paper given to The Insecure Workforce Conference, Cardiff Business School, 11–12 September

Mabey, C., Salaman, G. and Storey, J. (1998) *Human Resource Management – A Strategic Introduction* (2nd edn), Oxford: Blackwell

McGrath, P. and Houlihan, M. (1996) 'Conceptualizing Telework: Modern or Post-Modern?' Paper given to the New International Perspectives on Telework Conference, Brunel University, July–August

McGregor, A. and Sproull, A. (1992) 'Employers and the Flexible Workforce' *Employment Gazette*, May: 225–34

Mintzberg, H. (1979) *Structure in Fives*, Chichester: John Wiley

Moon, C. and Stanworth, C. (1997) 'Ethical Issues of Teleworking', *Business Ethics: A European Review*, **6**(1): 35–45

NACAB (1997) *Flexibility Abused, A CAB Evidence Report on Employment Conditions on the Labour Market*, London: National Association of Citizen's Advice Bureaux, September

Negroponte, N. (1995) *Being Digital*, London: Coronet/Hodder & Stoughton

New Ways to Work (1997) *Part-Time Work*, Flexibility, Choice and Quality of Life Factsheet, London: New Ways to Work

Ogbonna, E. (1992) 'Organization Culture and Human Resource Management: Dilemmas and Contradictions' in Blyton, P. and Turnbull, P. (eds) *Reassessing Human Resource Management*, London: Sage, pp. 74–96

Pollert, A. (1988) 'The Flexible Firm: Fixation or Fact?' *Work, Employment and Society*, **2**(3): 281–316

Pollert, A. (ed.) (1991) *Farewell to Flexibility?* Oxford: Blackwell

Purcell, K. and Purcell, J. (1996) 'In-Sourcing, Outsourcing and the Growth of Contingent Labour as Evidence of Flexible Employment Strategies'. Paper given to the 14th Annual International Labour Process Conference, Edinburgh, April

Rainnie, A. (1989) *Industrial Relations in Small Firms: Small isn't Beautiful*, London: Routledge

Rubery, J. (1989) 'Precarious Forms of Work in the United Kingdom' in Rodgers, G. and Rodgers, J. (eds) *Precarious Jobs in Labour Market Regulation*, Geneva: ILO

Rubery, J. (1994) 'Internal and External Labour Markets: Towards an Integrated Analysis' in Rubery, J. and Wilkinson, F. (eds) *Employer Strategy and the Labour Market*, Oxford: Oxford University Press, pp. 37–68

Rubery, J. (1996) 'The Labour Market Outlook and the Outlook for Labour Market Analysis' in Crompton, R., Gallie D. and Purcell, K. (eds) *Changing Forms of Employment, Organisations, Skills and Gender*, London: Routledge

Rubery, J. and Horrell, S. (1994) 'The New Competition and Working Time', *Human Resource Management Journal*, **3**(2): 1–11

Schwoerer, C., May, D. and Rosen, B. (1995) 'Organizational Characteristics and HRM Policies on Rights: Exploring the Patterns of Connections', *Journal of Business Ethics*, **14**: 531–49

Stanworth, C. (1996) *Working at Home – A Study of Homeworking and Teleworking*, London: Institute of Employment Rights

Stanworth, J. (1998a) *The Role of Small Business in the UK*, Inaugural Lecture Series, London: University of Greenwich Press

Stanworth, C. (1998b) 'Telework and the Information Age', *New Technology, Work and Employment*, **13**(1): 51–62

Stanworth, J. and Stanworth, C. (1991) *Telework: The Human Resource Implications*, London: Institute of Personnel Management (now the IPD – Institute for Personnel and Development)

Stanworth, J. and Stanworth, C. (1992) 'Problems of Definition and Marketing of High Technology Homework' in Robertson M., Chell, E. and Mason, C. (eds) *Towards the 21st Century: the Challenge for Small Business*, Macclesfield: Nadamal Books

Stanworth, C. and Stanworth, J. (1997) 'Reluctant Entrepreneurs and their Clients: the Case of Self-employed Freelancers in the British Book Publishing Industry', *International Small Business Journal*, **16**(1): 58–73

Taylor, P. and Bain, P. (1998) 'An Assembly Line in the Head: The Call Centre Labour Process'. Paper given to The Sixteenth Annual International Labour Process Conference, Manchester, April

Toffler, A. (1981) *The Third Wave*, London: Pan

TUC (1994) *Part-Time Work*, London: TUC

Warhurst, C. and Thompson, P. (1998) 'Shadowland: the Real Story of Knowledge Work and Workers'. Paper given to The Sixteenth Annual International Labour Process Conference, Manchester, April

Warren, R. (1998) 'Between Contract and Paternalism'. Paper given to the Second Conference on Ethical Issues in Contemporary HRM, Kingston University, January

CHAPTER 9

Presenteeism and the impact of long hours on managers

Ruth Simpson

Introduction

In the UK the culture of downsizing, fuelled by new technology, takeovers and global market pressures, has been facilitated by a government which has been attempting throughout most of the 1980s and 90s to encourage more flexibility in the labour market, as discussed in Chapter 8. This has involved a variety of reforms designed to free the labour market from legal and other constraints which are intended to increase the willingness of employers to hire labour and create the flexible employment practices crucial for a competitive economy. According to Beatson (1995), such 'flexibility' has contributed to the development of a dual labour market, characterised by a small 'core' of permanent and increasingly overworked employees who put in long hours and an outer ring of 'peripheral' workers who may be on a variety of short-term, project-based casual contracts with little security of tenure. Concern over this has led the government of the late 1990s to incorporate some employment protection for flexible workers in employment legislation. These trends in flexibility were discussed in more detail in Chapter 8.

Such developments have raised ethical issues concerning the moral obligations of organisations, the rights of workers and the treatment of employees. However, an extra ethical dimension has been introduced by the possible inclusion of managers, as core workers, into the realms of the periphery as they experience increasing insecurity and uncertainty at work. As employees, managers are subject to the same 'moral climate' of the organisation as other workers and increasingly prey to similar pressures, while as senior personnel and decision makers they may have a moral obligation towards the members of their teams. This chapter discusses the findings of a research project on the effects of this 'dual status' (Wood, 1989) on managers' working lives, together with the ethical implications of these developments.

Recent research suggests that being part of a reduced and increasingly insecure 'core' places a double burden on managers both of which impact on hours worked. First, in the face of restructuring, new technology and loss of key personnel, their workload is considerably increased which in turn leads to longer hours (IM, 1996; Wheatley, 1992). A recent Institute of Management survey (IM, 1996) found that 84 per cent of managers claimed to work in excess of their official hours regularly, with the average working week varying between 50 and 60 hours. In two studies of restructuring, 80 per cent of senior managers and 75 per cent of middle managers had been personally affected in terms of increased workloads and responsibilities (Benbow, 1996; Lockwood *et al.*, 1992). Similarly, after restructuring at BT the proportion of employees working more than 46 hours a week increased from 39 per cent in 1991 to 51 per cent in 1995 (Newell and Dopson, 1996).

Second, given that firms are less willing to promise job security in the face of tighter cost controls, and given the likelihood of reduced promotion opportunities in flatter organisations, many managers react to the insecurity and fear of redundancy by staying at their desk for long periods of time in order to demonstrate visible commitment to the job and to gain an advantage over others (Goffee and Scase, 1992). Brockner *et al.* (1993) see such behaviour as part of a 'survivor syndrome' that affects many managers who have experienced restructuring and downsizing in their organisations. Characteristics include stress, heightened anxiety and, according to Clarke (1994), fear of being next in line for redundancy which drives its victims to work harder than necessary. Cooper (1996) refers to this as 'presenteeism' which he defines as 'being at work when you should be at home either because you are ill or because you are working such long hours that you are no longer effective' (Cooper, 1996, p. 15). A survey by Austin Knight (1995), recruitment consultants, found a fifth of managers surveyed worked long hours, either out of fear of job losses or because they felt under direct line manager pressure, while over a half felt pressurised by a prevailing culture of presenteeism. A similar outcome emerged from a survey by Hays Accountancy Personnel (1996, p. 4) whose Managing Director commented:

> The combination of competitive aggression which was the hallmark of much of the 1980s' culture and the desperate need not to be at the top of the redundancy list in the early 1990s have combined to form a work ethic of making sure you are never first to leave the office.

Similarly, at BT career movement changed after restructuring from clearly defined paths to ones based on proof of performance, efficiency and above all visible commitment. The latter was often cited as a key factor in terms of improved career chances so that an important measure of success was the number of hours worked despite the fact that there was a strong feeling that these extra hours were not really necessary (Newell and Dopson, 1996). In fact, nine out of ten managers in the Austin Knight survey felt their performance suffered with increased hours and half the accountants surveyed by Hays Accountancy Personnel agreed that their productivity dropped after 7pm. Nevertheless, it was important to be seen to be at your desk for long periods of time both to advance your career by demonstrating a heightened commitment and to avoid future rounds of redundancies. In addition, both the IM and the Austin Knight survey gave evidence of the negative impact of these long hours on personal lives. Two-thirds of managers in the IM (1996) survey felt they had not achieved a good balance between work and home and 45 per cent of male respondents claimed that not seeing enough of their children was a major source of stress. Over a half of both the IM and the Austin Knight survey felt that their relationships were badly affected by long hours.

While it may seem reasonable to suppose that long hours impact more on women than on men as they cope with the conflicting demands of home and work, Goffee and Nicholson (1994) suggest that restructuring may have greater effect on the careers of men. They argue that restructuring has led to the dismantling of orderly and predictable career structures on which men have traditionally relied so that their climb up the corporate hierarchy has become more uncertain. In other words, career experiences of men and women could well be converging as men encounter the same levels of insecurity and unpredictability that women have typically faced as they cope with the effects of career breaks and the glass ceiling (Burke and McKeen, 1994; Goffee and Nicholson, 1994). Consequently, the so-called proletarianisation or dual status of managers together with associated pressures of insecurity and overload may well have a different gendered impact with men, given their earlier advantages, feeling the changes more keenly. Dysfunctional outcomes such as long hours and, in particular, presenteeism may, according to Burke and McKeen (1994) arise from the intensification of managerial work and it is possible that these dysfunctions, while affecting men and women alike, originate in men's feelings of insecurity and uncertainty.

Whatever the cause, increased hours and increased workloads experienced by managers raises several ethical issues. These concern, from a deontological perspective, the treatment of individuals at work and individual rights. Teleology, however, focuses on the morality of action in relation to the outcome and carries with it the implication that people can be used as a means to the end of achieving the greatest good. By contrast, care ethics suggests that organisations have a moral responsibility towards all stakeholders including employees. If organisations care for employees as well as other stakeholders they may be described as exercising 'virtue' which indicates the existence of a corporate identity and the possibility of organisations, as opposed to individuals within it, acting as a moral agents. These and related issues are discussed in the summary.

The research project

The project on which this chapter is based aimed to assess the impact of restructuring on workloads and working hours of male and female managers. Data were collected through questionnaires and interviews. The questionnaire sample consisted of 90 female and 130 male managers who were asked to provide information on their personal status, labour market position and work pressures. Three-quarters of men and a half of women were working in the private sector with the remainder in the public sector. Women managers were concentrated in services such as education and training while men tended to work in manufacturing production and finance. In terms of management level, approximately 40 per cent of both men and women were in senior management with the remainder spread between middle and junior management and professional/technical roles. From this sample, follow-up interviews with 15 female and 10 male managers were conducted to allow a more in-depth analysis to take place of the impact of restructuring on workloads, working hours and the implications for personal as well as working lives.

Long hours as a key work pressure

From the survey, two-thirds of men and women experienced long hours as a pressure with just over a quarter of both men and women choosing it as the single largest pressure. Little difference emerged between the private and public sector, although financial services and retail emerged as the activities most associated with long hours. Senior managers were more vulnerable to long hours than middle or junior manager as, perhaps surprisingly, were childless women over women with children. In the latter case, 34 per cent of childless women chose long hours as the single largest pressure compared to only 12 per cent of women with children. While one might expect women with children to feel worktime pressures more keenly, from the interview data it was these women who were more ruthless than childless women in their determination to put in the hours contracted and no more. Therefore, in the conflicting demands made on them between home and work, women with children gave non-work activities more priority than childless women in terms of allocation of time.

Gender mix of organisations

For women, gender mix of the employing organisation was strongly associated with long hours. This was explored at two levels. First, the female sample was divided into 'token' and 'non-token' women according to the ratio of men to women working at the same or similar level to the women themselves. Where the male/female ratio was 5:1 and over the woman was defined as a 'token' while a ratio of less than 5:1 defined her as 'non-token'. Male-dominated organisations, defined as those organisations in which women managers were of a 'token' status, emerged as being associated with long hours, more so than those organisations where the gender mix was more balanced. For example, a higher proportion of 'token' women claimed long hours to be a pressure (64.8 per cent) compared to just over a half of 'non-token' women.

However, larger differences emerged at the second level of the inquiry where organisations were divided into 'top heavy' and 'very top heavy' to describe the gender mix at management levels higher than the women themselves where, again, the ratio of 5:1 was used. In this case, where divisions were made according to the gender mix at the top of the organisation, nearly three-quarters of women claimed long hours as a pressure in 'very top heavy' organisations as opposed to only 62 per cent of women in the less unequal 'top heavy'. So whereas gender mix appeared to be a factor behind the incidence of long hours, it was male dominance at the top of the organisation which appeared to be more important over gender imbalances further down the hierarchy.

Reasons for long hours

Workloads and presenteeism

Reasons given for working long hours were taken to indicate the extent of presenteeism in the organisation that is the extent to which managers remained at work when the demands of the job did not require it. From the interview data three main reasons emerged for working long hours which conformed largely with previous studies in this area (Austin Knight, 1995; Hays Accountancy Personnel, 1996; IM, 1996).

First, some managers worked long hours simply because the job demanded it especially if there were sudden deadlines to meet or if the job were a relatively new one. Long hours were under these circumstances seen as a one-off necessity or as a temporary phenomenon while new skills or procedures were being learned. Second, managers worked long hours because restructuring led to higher workloads either because of loss of staff or because of the demands of continual job changes, as reported by the following female manager:

> I can't do the job until I understand what there's to do because I've got to understand what's needed because things keep changing. So there's a lot more work to do if it's a changing organisation than if it's a stable organisation.

Third, many managers who had been through restructuring were made to feel that they could only retain their position by working long hours as a way of demonstrating visible commitment to the job. In other words they were under pressure 'to be seen to be working long hours'. Such presenteeism, however, was much more likely to be recognised by women than by men and was more likely to be a feature of male behaviour although women were clearly affected by it. Men tended to accept long hours as part of the job ('I don't think about it – I just get on with it') or to deny working longer hours than necessary. One common theme that emerged from the interviews with women was the relationship between long hours and a masculine culture:

> And there's this well 'who's looking over my shoulder' and 'am I being seen to be doing enough' and it gets quite macho, they all compete with each other sort of thing.

Such competition was found to occur in large, male-dominated organisations where career structures had been significantly reduced. A similar situation was observed by Cockburn (1991) in her study of a male-dominated computer division within a retail organisation. Here the change to a flatter hierarchy led to competitive relations between men particularly over technical expertise and, significantly, over career pace. This heightened competition between men could well reflect the greater impact of restructuring on male careers in terms of uncertainty and reduced promotion opportunities referred to earlier (Goffee and Nicholson, 1994) and could also lead to dysfunctional outcomes such as presenteeism. Where the gender mix was more balanced and where restructuring had also occurred, presenteeism was not recognised to the same extent.

Competitive presenteeism

> I stay as long as I have to stay to do something, but I find I try very hard not to be pressurised into staying late if I'm not busy sometimes. But it's very difficult if all the others are still around... I feel quite guilty, and I'm sure they all notice and think... There, she's off home again! (Female manager)

Those women who encountered heightened competition in their organisations therefore saw it as a male phenomenon with long hours associated with 'macho' behaviour and attitudes. This is supported by Collinson and Collinson (1995) who found that long hours could become a test of manhood with some male managers enjoying the buzz of staying at the office late into the evening. This also helped to 'recolonise' management as a male preserve as few women were willing to compete on these terms. Such 'competitive presenteeism' can also pressurise those lower down the hierarchy to adopt the same practices, helping it to become an endemic part of the organisational culture. Young men emerged from this study as being particularly vulnerable to the pressure to work long hours (80 per cent of men aged between 25 and 34 claimed this to be a major pressure compared to only 55.5 per cent in the 45–54 age bracket). This may reflect the fact that young men identify more with the organisation as a means of achieving career success and are therefore subject to pressures to stay for long periods of time in the office.

> I feel sorry for the [male] graduates. They're here until 7 or 8. And they do seem to find it difficult if two or three are working and their boss is still here... You tend to find there's pressure on the others. (Senior male manager)

Competitive presenteeism was found to involve the sacrifice not just of leisure time after work but also of recuperation time such as after working trips abroad (one male manager returned from an Australian business trip in the morning and arrived at the office in the afternoon) or of holiday entitlements which the men frequently did not take up. Many women tried hard to resist the culture without appearing to be 'shirking'.

Project rivalry

> People are more competitive all round, and you've got to demonstrate that you can do your job because another five people are queuing up for it. It's very much we've got to do that – we've got to demonstrate that we can do that. (Female manager)

> Everyone is trying to demonstrate that they're doing a good job and it's not a sharing culture at all. You have to be able to demonstrate that you can do this all yourself. So there's an awful lot of jockeying for position. (Senior woman manager)

Competition over hours worked was not the only area of rivalry between men in male-dominated organisations. A second area of competition concerned the ownership of projects or tasks with managers anxious to display their commitment and their ability to perform effectively. This was often linked to growing uncertainty over job security and to fear of redundancies. Under these conditions it was important to be seen to be doing the job and doing it well with as little outside help as possible so as to prevent the credit for effective performance being claimed elsewhere. This helped to create an individualistic, non-cooperative culture, which often meant work was repeated. Territorial battles occurred over areas of work, which Goffee and Nicholson (1994) see as part of the increased emphasis on managerial performance with managers anxious to meet performance targets and claim credit for successful projects or outcomes for themselves.

Presenteeism as a form of male resistance

> Most companies have moved away from such things as drinking at lunchtimes – but people would go out after work and they tend to and it tends to be later on. So it's not shall we go out for a drink at half five. It's like when we've finished work at maybe 7 o'clock, and it's not the sort of thing I could get into if I have the children to pick up. (Female manager)

In several studies of women in management, men have been found to be culturally active in creating an environment where women do not flourish (Kanter, 1977; Maddock and Parkin, 1993; Marshall, 1984). As Cockburn (1991) suggests, the encroachment of women into the male hierarchy can lead to heightened resistance by men as they feel their positions of power and 'sex right' threatened. On this basis, increased insecurity and reduced promotion opportunities through restructuring may not only have created greater rivalry among men in terms of heightened competitive behaviour but also have actively lead to a hardening resistance to women in the organisation and, as Woodall *et al.* (1997) suggest, a looser commitment to equal opportunities.

According to Collinson and Collinson (1995) long working hours can serve to recolonise management as an inherently masculine function, confirming in men's eyes their sense of 'owning the organisation' (Cockburn, 1991 p. 46). This was recognised by Watson (1994) in a study of managerial practices where working long hours into the evening was found to marginalise many women. In fact, male managers deliberately stayed late at work into the evening, artificially extending meetings and then criticising those managers, especially women, who left earlier even although this may in fact be well after the official end of the day. One impact of extending office hours in this way is the timing of informal socialising which, as one woman senior manager complained, meant a trip to the pub at 7pm rather than 5.30 – an impossible situation for women with children.

Informal networks have been shown to be important in terms of gaining insight into the politics of the organisation – not simply in terms of gathering valuable and up-to-date information, although this is important enough in its own right, but also in terms of establishing relations, evaluating colleagues and obtaining feedback on work-related issues. Lack of opportunity to build important networks and relationships emerged from this study as one major area of disadvantage as the following woman manager confirmed:

> It [socialising after work] means you've got a much closer relationship with some people – and if there's a problem or if there's an opportunity then they'll go to the person they know better which is likely to be another man because that's who they go drinking with.

With promotion opportunities in short supply and given the increased emphasis on managerial performance referred to earlier, a competitive edge can be gained over other colleagues by finding out about new jobs or new responsibilities as early as possible and by speaking to the right people in an informal setting. As one woman middle manager pointed out, the allocation of promotions and of key tasks would ultimately depend on who you had made contact with on an informal basis.

A masculine culture, or what has been referred to as the Men's Club (Coe, 1992), therefore marginalised and excluded many women from key sources of information and networking. Not only were there practical problems in terms of timing to joining such groups but cultural problems too. As Cockburn pointed out in her study (1991), women are often reluctant to take part in these all-male sessions even if their circumstances permit it. This reluctance may mean that such sessions become a permanent part of the organisational culture and the ability of women to resist that culture remains extremely limited.

Resisting worktime pressures: strategies and priorities

While men complained of long hours as a pressure experienced in their working lives, they largely conformed to the demands made upon them. Women, on the other hand, tried hard to resist the pressure to stay late at the office. They were constrained in their resistance, however, by the danger of being stereotyped as the 'whinging woman' which meant they could not openly voice their concerns about workloads or working hours. While women, especially those with children, had to adapt to prevailing masculine norms, men were generally seen as having an easier time in terms of workloads and domestic responsibilities.

Childless women accommodated the demands of long hours more easily than women with children and this is somewhat at odds with the survey data which show that it is childless women who are more likely to experience long hours as a pressure in their working lives. However, a clear picture emerged from the interviews of the boundaries that women with children drew between work and home and of their priorities. Limits were set in terms of how much time women were prepared to give up at the expense of their children and they were firm in their commitment to keep to those limits. Single women were less rigorous in this respect and may therefore be more vulnerable to the pressures to stay at the office for long periods. As one single women put it:

> It can become a habit… rather than saying right I'm going home now you sort of fall into someone's office and have a chat about some problem or other.

For another woman with no children:

> I know that on occasions when I've got to get home to something I will get on with it [the work] and go.

Not only does this raise issues concerning the productiveness of working late (does having a 'chat' count as work? Why stay late when the work could have been finished anyway?), it also suggests that women with children have managed with a certain determination to carve out time for themselves and their families. The following comments support this view:

> I won't compromise my time with the kids so what I do is I'll spend time with the kids and they go to bed at 8.30 and at 9 I sit down and start working.

> I mean I'm not prepared to work 50, 60, 70 hours a week. I'm supposed to do a 42-hour week.

> I'm not militant in that sense but I want to have a flexible job – particularly with children and that and I have other interests outside work as well which I want to have time for. I don't want to spend my holidays doing work – I'm not prepared to do that.

At the same time women developed their own strategies to circumvent the problems of keeping enough time for their families and this often involved some element of subterfuge. One strategy was to create a sense of uncertainty concerning worktime location so that time taken to attend non-work activities went unnoticed. Other women were deliberately vague about reasons for absence if this involved some childcare activity such as a visit to the doctor. One woman manager commented that although the organisation she worked for had an equal opportunities policy and was very keen to be flexible, in practice she felt it was not the 'done thing' to take time off for children. If children were ill, some women preferred to take sick leave themselves on the grounds that this reason for absence was more acceptable.

Maintaining a balance between work and home while avoiding the traditional criticism that women with families are not suited to senior managerial positions was therefore not easy, particularly as women felt silenced on the issue of work/home commitments and on the problems created by long hours. Fear of being considered a shirker or unsuitable material for senior management helped to create a conspiracy of silence and reinforce the feeling that women do not belong. One woman summed up the issue:

> I don't feel I can bring home to work and talk about it because I do feel then in people's minds that will create an impression of me – all those bloody women in here, all they want to do is whinge about what they've got to do at home.

The price of silence, however, could be a high one. Several women had already decided to leave their jobs because of the pressures of long hours – either to set up their own businesses, where they would have greater control over working conditions, or to work part time. Two women with younger children were considering giving up work altogether despite the acknowledged career sanctions that would result. None felt able to confront the issue or to discuss the problems she was having with line managers.

Summary

In summary, one impact of restructuring has been the emergence of a 'dual status' for many managers as they experience similar levels of uncertainty and insecurity normally associated with 'periphery' workers. At the same time increased workloads and fear of redundancy can create an imperative to appear visibly committed to the job. Presenteeism itself can become a source of competition as promotion opportunities are reduced. Presenteeism has emerged as being highly gendered: it emanates mainly from men, it imposes heavier costs on women and it can be a source of disadvantage for women managers in the development of their careers.

The pressures created by organisational change on managers, particularly relating to the intensification of managerial work, raises several ethical issues.

While utilitarianism and to some extent stakeholder theory might argue that the detrimental effects these pressures impose on managers are more than compensated for by the outcome, deontology suggests people have rights and should be treated with respect, irrespective of the consequences. This Kantian approach emphasises the immorality of self-interested behaviour and the importance of moral rules which should be capable of being universalised. Deontologists would see long working hours and associated pressures as immoral and, regardless of the consequences in terms of increased costs or reduced competitiveness, would advocate a universal rule similar to the European worktime directive which, with certain exceptions, limits working hours to 48 hours a week.

By contrast, utilitarianism, or the teleological approach, argues that the morality of action should be judged by the outcome which is the greatest good to the largest number. This implies that individuals can be treated as a means to an end if the end involves higher overall welfare. Therefore, regardless of what downsizing, overwork and long hours implies for individuals and their own personal well-being, it is perfectly ethical to use people in this way if it provides the greatest good for the majority in the form, for example, of greater competitiveness which ensures the organisation's survival. However, as Celia Stanworth pointed out in Chapter 8, this creates a problem of where boundaries should be drawn. The logical inference is that as long as the greater good is guaranteed, there are no limits to the treatment of workers nor to the sacrifice required of agents in terms of their personal well-being in the achievement of the best possible outcome. This conforms to what has become known as 'hard HRM' which uses human resources for an end with little regard for personal well-being.

There are some resonances here with stakeholder theory which suggests that it is morally acceptable for some stakeholders such as employees or groups of employees to lose out so that others such as customers or shareholders can benefit. If survival of the enterprise is paramount, given that all parties are consulted, actions that damage some stakeholders can be justified. Consultation, however, is important to the morality of the action: all groups involved must participate in decisions relating to overall welfare.

Aspects of 'hard HRM' may be seen in the treatment of senior personnel by organisations where pressures caused by the intensification of managerial work and associated worktime pressures are accepted as the inevitable price to pay for greater productivity and efficiency. However, taking on board stakeholder theory's emphasis on participation, there appears to be little evidence of opportunity for consultation or participative decision making. This would be particularly the case for new staff who, coming into the organisation, would be expected to conform to the cultural norms concerning working hours and, as this study has shown, women managers in particular, far from being able to voice concerns over pressures experienced, may be silenced by the need to maintain their credibility as senior personnel.

While the frameworks discussed have some application for the general issue of employee rights and worker well-being which emerged from this study, they cannot incorporate some of the more complex elements. These concern the impact of organisational demands on relationships and networks, on levels of conflict and competition, on culture and power structures and on the actions of agents to reconcile differences and cope with dissonance. Two approaches which carry an emphasis on agency rather than outcome incorporate the factors referred to to different degrees. These are the first the ethics of care and second virtue ethics which makes use of the concept of the 'virtuous organisation'.

In terms of the former perspective, Gilligan (1982) argues that organisations have a moral responsibility towards all stakeholders. The ethics of care takes as its basis the relatedness of people and focuses on their needs set within different contexts or circumstances. Networks and relationships are seen as important and employee communication and participation are central elements to this perspective. Organisations have a responsibility to strive for employee communication and participation and to do justice to the genuine needs of individuals. This approach would therefore have difficulty with organisations' apparent lack of concern for well-being, shown in this study, as managers strive to fulfil their commitments both at work and at home. The extra burden that long hours imposes on women, particularly women with children, would be seen as evidence of the neglect of individual circumstances or contexts. Such an approach would suggest not only that workloads and hours worked be reduced to alleviate the burden on managers but also that women, whose circumstances may make such demands more onerous and difficult to fulfil, be facilitated by, for example, the provision of flexible working practices or job-share agreements.

Of central importance to both stakeholder theory and to the ethics of care is the desirability of discourse both as a means of participation and as a means of voicing concerns. The silence of women over the conflicts experienced, engendered by a culture of endurance and competitiveness, indicates not only a lack of transparency in that line managers may not be aware of these conflicts but also suggests that such silence can be an effective means of reinforcing the status quo. At the same time the isolation of women and the individualisation of their experiences may serve to undermine the development of a collective voice which is necessary for challenges to the prevailing norms and attitudes to be made.

Like the ethics of care, virtue ethics arose out of a dissatisfaction with the emphasis of deontology and teleology on act evaluation and instead has a focus on agency. It is concerned with what a 'good' moral character would see as appropriate. Incorporated into virtue ethics is the idea that corporations have an identity distinct from individuals (French, 1994). Corporate moral agents manifest intentionality through the corporate internal decision (CID) structure. The existence of a CID structure demonstrates the presence of a corporate moral actor as opposed to a collection of individual moral agents and, according to Anscombe (1958), it is possible for moral agents to be held accountable. Therefore it is possible to have a 'virtuous organisation', one element of which may be a commitment to the welfare of stakeholders including employees. Companies which care for employees as well as shareholders and customers are exercising virtue and can be seen as 'good' employers while companies that fail to care for stakeholders and impose disproportionate demands on workers and managers, for example, can be deemed to be 'bad' employers. By the same token, criteria will develop concerning what it means to be a good or 'virtuous' employee and this may include the fulfilment of the expectations of the organisation. However, if, as Burke and McKeen (1994) suggest, restructuring impacts more on men than on women in terms of the disruption it engenders in men's careers, and if one dysfunctional outcome is for men to compete over hours worked and over project ownership to maximise their chances of promotion success, then it is possible that these attitudes and practices become internalised by other groups within the organisation who do not necessarily share the same imperatives. Accordingly women, who through past experience of the glass ceiling may be able to accommodate uncertainty and insecurity more easily into their working lives, internalise the norms of competitiveness and presenteeism despite their different orientations to work and the different demands that these norms make on their personal lives.

Not only do virtue ethics incorporate the concepts of what it means to be a 'good' employer and a 'good' employee, but, according to Hampden-Turner (1994), also involve qualities necessary to achieve 'good' management such as the shaping of culture in which people find fulfilment and meaning, effective management of diversity and the management of dilemmas between conflicting values. Corporate culture provides members with values and with rules for behaving within the organisation. These values are often expressed informally through, for example, working late and participation in extra-curricular activities. Insofar as corporate cultures may tend to express male values and reflect male interests (Cockburn, 1991), an organisation which is unaware of, or chooses to ignore, the impact of that culture on a group of workers such as women cannot be said to be facilitating fulfilment, to be effectively managing diversity of interests or to be providing the means by which members can accommodate conflicting demands of, for example, home and worktime without the need to resort to subterfuge (as some women did in this study). In other words, this cannot be seen as a virtuous organisation.

Finally, while culture is something that can be seen as separate from the individuals that make up an organisation, upper management has a strong influence on that culture by indicating behavioural expectations to employees. This means that many managers at senior and at middle management level will occupy a dual position: as employees they are subject to the expectations and 'moral rules' of their organisations while as managers they are not only able to influence that culture but also convey expectations of behaviour to more junior staff. The way managers react to external change can therefore have profound effects not only for their own well-being but also for the organisational 'climate', for pressures experienced by and overall welfare of fellow colleagues and others further down the hierarchy.

Note

An earlier version of this chapter was published as an article 'Presenteeism, Power and Organizational Change: Long Hours as a Career Barrier and the Impact on the Working Lives of Women Managers' *British Journal of Management* **9**: 37–50.

References

Anscombe, G. (1958) 'Modern Moral Philosophy' *Philosophy*, **33**: 1–19

Austin Knight UK (1995) *The Family Friendly Workplace*, London: Austin Knight

Bassett, P. (1995) 'Job Deregulation Rules UK' *The Times*, 2 January 1995: 30

Beatson, M. (1995) *Labour Market Flexibility*, London: Employment Department Research Series No. 48

Benbow, N. (1996) *Survival of the Fittest: A Survey of Managers, Experiences of and Attitudes to Work in the Post Recession Economy*, Corby: Institute of Management

Brockner, J., O'Malley, M., Reed, T. and Glynn, M. (1993) 'Threat of Future Layoffs, Self Esteem and Survivors' Reactions: Evidence from the Laboratory and the Field' *Strategic Management Journal* **14**: 153–66 (special issue)

Burke, R. and McKeen, C. (1994) 'Career Development among Managerial and Professional Women' in Davidson, M. and Burke, R. (eds) *Women in Management Current Research Issues*, London: Paul Chapman

Clarke, S. (1994) 'Presentees: New Slaves of the Office who run in Fear' *Sunday Times*, 16 October: p. 9

Cockburn, C. (1991) *In the Way of Women: Men's Resistance to Sex Equality in Organisations*, London: Macmillan

Coe, T. (1992) *The Key to the Men's Club*, Corby: Institute of Management

Collinson, D. and Collinson, M. (1995) *Corporate Liposuction and the Remasculinisation of Management*. Keynote address at Gender and Life in Organisations Conference, University of Portsmouth, September

Cooper, C. (1996) 'Hot Under the Collar' *The Times Higher Education Supplement*, 21 June: p. 12

Freeman, S. (1992) *Managing Lives: Corporate Women and Social Change*, Amhurst, MA: University of Massachusetts Press

French, P. (1994) *Corporate Ethics*, New York: Harcourt Brace

Gilligan, C. (1982) *In a Different Voice*, Cambridge, MA: Harvard University Press

Goffee, R. and Nicholson, N. (1994) 'Career Development in Male and Female Managers – Convergence or Collapse?' In Davidson, M. and Burke, R. (eds) *Women in Management Current Research Issues*, London: Paul Chapman

Goffee, R. and Scase, R. (1992) 'Organisational Change and the Corporate Career: the Restructuring of Managers Job Aspirations' *Human Relations*, April, **45**: 363–85

Hampden-Turner, C. (1994) *Charting the Corporate Mind: From Dilemma to Strategy*, Oxford: Blackwell

Hays Accountancy Personnel (1996) *The British Fear of Leaving on Time*, London: Hays Accountancy Personnel, The Communication Group

IHSM Consultants (1994) *Creative Career Paths in the NHS*. Report No. 1 – Top Managers. Study conducted for the NHS Women's Unit, London: NHS Executive

Institute of Management (IM) (1996) *Are Managers Under Stress: A Survey of Management Morale*, Corby: Institute of Management

Kanter, R.M. (1977) *Men and Women of the Corporation*, New York: Basic Books

Lockwood, J., Teevan, P. and Walters, M. (1992) *Who's Managing the Managers? The Reward and Career Development of Middle Managers in a Flat Organisation*, Corby: Institute of Management

Maddock, S. and Parkin, D. (1993) 'Gender cultures: Women's Choices and Strategies at Work' *Women in Management Review*, **8**(2): 3–9

Marshall, J. (1984) *Women Travellers in a Male World*, Chichester: Wiley

Meyer, J. and Allen, N. (1984) 'Testing the Side-bet Theory of Organisational Commitment: Some Methodological Considerations' *Journal of Applied Psychology* **69**: 372–8

Morrison, A., White, R. and Van Velsor, E. (1987) *Breaking the Glass Ceiling*, Reading, MA: Addison-Wesley

Newell, H. and Dopson, S. (1996): 'Muddle in the Middle: Organisational Restructuring and Middle Management Careers' *Personnel Review* **25**(4): 4–20

Nicholson, N. and West, M. (1988) *Managerial Job Change: Men and Women in Transition*, Cambridge: Cambridge University Press

Scase, R. and Goffee, R. (1989) *Reluctant Managers Their Work and Lifestyles*, London: Unwin

Wajcman, J. (1996) 'Women and Men Managers: Careers and Equal Opportunities' in Crompton, R., Gallie D. and Purcell, K. (eds) *Changing Forms of Employment*, London: Routledge, pp. 259–77

Watson, T. (1994) *In Search of Management: Culture, Chaos and Control in Managerial Work*, London: Routledge

Wheatley, M. (1992) *The Future of Middle Management*, Corby: Institute of Management

Wood, S. (1989) *The Transformation of Work*, London: Unwin Hyman

Woodall, C., Edwards, C. and Welchman, R. (1997) 'Organisational Restructuring and the Achievement of an Equal Opportunity Culture' *Gender, Work and Organization* **4**: (1): 2–12

CHAPTER 10

The new pay: risk and representation at work

Edmund Heery

Introduction

The last decade has witnessed extensive and continuing experimentation in the field of pay. A new vocabulary of 'reward management' has gained currency (Smith, 1992b), new models of good practice have been propounded by management consultants (Armstrong and Murlis, 1994; Palmer, 1996) and, while management practice has inevitably changed at a slower pace, there is evidence of considerable experiment across much of the economy. Performance pay and other contingent systems of reward have become more widespread, there has been some flattening of pay structures with organisations introducing fewer but broader pay grades and there are indications that benefit systems are becoming more flexible (CBI, 1995; IPD, 1998). These developments have not gone unchallenged and have elicited a critical response from academic researchers in the fields of management and employment relations. Two criticisms have been predominant. First, it is widely claimed that recent developments in pay have perverse effects and are counterproductive from the perspective of the employer because they demotivate workers, multiply transactions and erode team working (Geary, 1992; Randle and Rainnie, 1997). Second, and relatedly, it is claimed that new and more fragmented systems of reward promote 'disorder' in the work-place and generate inflationary pressure in the wider economy (Brown, 1997; Walsh, 1993).

The perspective of this chapter is critical but the burden of criticism rests not on the disutility of the 'new pay' but on its ethical deficiencies. In partic-ular, it is argued that two aspects of the new pay should excite the concern of ethicists interested in contemporary human resource management. These are the movement towards greater risk in remuneration, such that salaries and benefits become less secure and predictable from the perspective of employees, and the movement away from employee representation in the process of selecting and applying reward systems. The chapter contends that neither development is compatible with a system of reward which is socially just and responsive to the interests of employees, as well as employers, and concludes with a new set of recommendations for ethical pay management.

The new pay

The 'new pay' is a term coined by Edward E. Lawler III and popularised by Schuster and Zingheim (1992) in their book of the same name. Although of American provenance, it is a term which has begun to be used here (Corbridge and Pilbeam, 1998, p. 152) and many of the themes enunciated by new pay writers in the USA have been echoed by pay specialists in Britain (Armstrong, 1996; Hewitt Associates, 1991; Murlis, 1996).

Like many fashionable management concepts, the new pay is based on a perceived dichotomy. The old pay of job-evaluated grade structures, payment by time, salary progression on the basis of seniority, and service-related benefits was developed, it is argued, to suit hierarchical organisations, designed on Taylorist principles, which operated in predictable environments. Its natural home was the large manufacturing company or government bureaucracy. The new pay, in contrast, matches a new, less certain organisational environment which demands a more fluid organisational form. The shift from the old to the new pay is thus presented as a functional adaptation to a prior shift in business environment and structure: 'innovative reward systems', according to one recent American textbook, are required 'for the changing workplace' (Wilson, 1995; see also Lawler, 1990; Mahoney, 1992; Schuster and Zingheim, 1992).

The new pay embraces a number of themes. Emphasis varies from author to author but these themes are identifiable across much of the prescriptive pay management literature and together form the now dominant model of best practice offered to managers. The first theme is that of 'strategic pay', the notion that the design of reward policy should flow from and seek to implement the organisation's business strategy. According to Lawler (1995), 'the new pay propounds a pay-design process that starts with business strategy and organisational design. It argues against an assumption that certain best practices must be incorporated into a company's approach to pay'. Similar advice is now given routinely by British pay specialists (Armstrong and Murlis, 1994; Stevens, 1996) and represents a version of the familiar argument for the strategic integration of human resource practices. For Lawler, and other new pay writers, discrete business strategies require particular behaviours and attitudes from employees and strategic pay management involves selecting pay policies which will secure these. It is also regarded as essential that the various pay policies are themselves integrated so that they do not stimulate contradictory responses from employees.

The opposite of strategic pay is a pay policy which is simply inherited from the past and continues to be applied regardless of changes in business strategy (Lawler, 1990, p. 3). Inertia of this kind may result from trade union or legislative pressure or because of conformance to an outdated notion of 'best practice'. Because of the danger of inertia, managers are advised to review pay practices continually and apply tests for strategic integration. There is a bias for action in this literature and for the continual updating and renewal of pay policy as business strategy evolves (Ledford, 1995, p. 47).

While new pay theorists argue that pay policies should be contingent on business strategy, they also propose models of good practice. The seeming contradiction is resolved by arguing that the business environment is changing, requiring new strategies from firms and new approaches to pay to support those strategies (Mahoney, 1992, pp. 344–5; Schuster and Zingheim, 1992, pp. 3–26). As well as a process for linking pay to strategy, therefore, the new pay is used to refer to a portfolio of pay practices which are believed to be well matched to the requirements of leading-edge firms and which will spread to other organisations, including those in the public sector, in due course. The elements of this portfolio have been summarised repeatedly in the new pay literature (cf. Lawler, 1990; Palmer, 1996; Schuster and Zingheim, 1992; Wilson, 1995) and embrace changes in payment systems, payment structures, benefit provision and pay procedures.

With regard to payment systems, it is axiomatic for new pay writers that pay be variable and contingent on performance if it is to function as a strategic tool. It is by offering incentives to employees to assume the necessary roles or display the required behaviours that the new pay can contribute to the implementation of strategy. The central recommendation for pay system design, therefore, is that the proportion of pay which is contingent on performance should increase to a high level. Schuster and Zingheim (1992, p. 154) stress the need for variable pay to replace base salary and that organisations should pay 'moderately competitive' base salaries in order to leave plenty of scope for additional, non-consolidated payments which are contingent on performance (see also Lawler, 1995, p. 18; Palmer, 1996, p. 14). While expanding the scope of variable pay is the main recommendation, employers are also urged to alter the types of incentive they use and new pay writers are often very critical of traditional incentive schemes (Lawler, 1990; Schuster and Zingheim, 1992). Their proposals include the need to use multiple systems which link pay to individual, group and organisational performance, to identify new performance measures which reflect changing determinants of business success and, in particular, tie rewards to quality indicators, to use novel types of reward such as prizes and recognition and to use group rewards which reinforce team-based forms of organisation.

With regard to payment structure, new pay writers make two main recommendations. The first is that pay should be 'person' as opposed to job based, such that the position of individuals within the pay structure is determined less by the formal description of their role and more by the attributes, competencies and performance which they bring to that role. Lawler (1990) for instance, is a sharp critic of traditional job evaluation and an enthusiast for skill-based pay (see also Mahoney, 1992). The second recommendation is that the structure itself should be flat and comprised of relatively few broad salary bands. A broad-banded pay structure of this kind, it is claimed, can reinforce flexible and team-based forms of organisation while affording line managers ample scope to reward skill acquisition and performance (Armstrong, 1996, pp. 224–6).

Recommendations for benefit provision also have at their core a proposal for greater differentiation through the introduction of benefit flexibility and cafeteria plans. These provide for an element of individual choice over the form of remuneration and, according to Lawler (1990, p. 217), accommodate the diverse needs of a more differentiated workforce while simultaneously fostering an ethos of partnership and self-reliance. Benefit flexibility, however, can also further the cause of variable pay because these systems make it easier to transfer an element of benefit costs to employees and so can reduce the proportion of unproductive 'indirect pay' in the total remuneration package (Schuster and Zingheim, 1992, pp. 223–40).

The final area in which new pay writers recommend change is that of pay procedures and the processes through which pay is managed. Schuster and Zingheim (1992) and Lawler (1990; 1995) stress the value of employee involvement in the processes of designing and operating the new pay and tend also to emphasise the role of new pay systems in promoting employee identification with the company and its goals. Running alongside this theme of involvement, however, is a competing emphasis on flexibility in reward procedures and the need for line managers to manage pay without excessive restriction. Ledford (1995) for instance, advocates 'nimble reward systems', by which he means continually evolving reward policies, which contain a minimum of formal rules and which can be applied with minimum cost by line managers in devolved business units (see also Smith, 1992a).

This tension between 'soft' involvement and 'hard' management control is apparent within the wider literature on human resource management (HRM) and, indeed, the new pay can be viewed as an attempt to transpose themes which have general currency to the specific field of reward. Thus, the objectives of the new pay are the same as those which appear in accepted models of HRM (Guest, 1989; Storey, 1995), including organisational flexibility, competition through quality and responsiveness to customers and high levels of employee commitment, and its core recommendations, for strategic integration, internal coherence, employee involvement and line management autonomy, contain a similar echo. It follows from this connection that the weaknesses of HRM are likely to be reproduced within the new pay and vice versa and that the ethical critique of the new pay to which we now turn is equally applicable to more general prescriptive writing on human resource management.

Risk

While there may be much of value in the new pay model, one of its most prob-lematic features is the intention to increase employee risk, a characteristic which it shares with other management practices such as outsourcing, competitive tendering and reliance on contingent contracts. The new pay generates risk in a number of ways. First, and most obviously, it does so by seeking to increase the proportion of pay which is contingent on assessments of individual, group or organisational performance. This implies that the links between pay and working time or between pay and seniority, which render earnings more predictable for employees, will be progressively attenuated. It also implies that the amount of total remuneration made up of consolidated base salary and guaranteed benefits will decline in favour of bonuses and other 'at risk' payments which are contingent on measures of employee competence and outputs. The defining feature of the variable pay systems proposed by new pay writers is that payments are not consolidated and have continually to be re-earned with the effect that total remuneration can 'go down as well as up in line with performance' (Palmer, 1996 p. 14).

A second contribution to risk is made by the type of payment system which new pay theorists propose. What characterises several of these is their use of 'soft' performance measures which are not directly controlled by employees. Thus, there is an emphasis on tying pay to team or group measures, to meas-ures of financial performance and customer satisfaction and to line manager ratings of employee performance or competencies. All of these measures generate uncertainty because they are either subjective or susceptible to influ-ences beyond the individual employee's control. Finally, risk is created through the emphasis on 'nimble reward management', on line managers making rapid but necessarily rough and ready judgements about employee entitlement to reward. The deregulation of reward within the firm, therefore, in order to maximise managers' scope for flexibility, can further add to uncertainty as the basis of decisions becomes more opaque from the perspective of employees.

This increase in employee risk can be considered undesirable on a number of ethical grounds. A utilitarian argument against the new pay, for instance, would suggest that variable and contingent systems of payment pose a threat to employee well-being essentially because they contradict the need of employees for a stable and secure income. Such a need is both economic – employees need to be able to guarantee their income to meet their financial commitments – and psychological – anxiety may result where income becomes unpredictable (Warr, 1987). Of course, like any utilitarian argument this is vulnerable to the counter-charge that the immediate costs to workers of the new pay are outweighed by longer term benefits or by gains which accrue to other relevant interests such as shareholders, tax payers or consumers. If implementing the new pay model leads to a sustained increase in levels of performance, therefore, any incidental increase in employee risk might be considered worthwhile. Despite the claims of its adherents, however, it is by no means certain that the new pay can or does make a significant contribution to performance. UK research on individual performance-related pay and profit-sharing schemes, two payment systems which are advocated by new pay theorists, suggest a variable but generally modest positive impact on worker behaviour which in at least some organis-ations is counterbalanced by the kind of perverse effect referred to above (see Baddon *et al.*, 1989; Dowling and Richardson, 1997; Dunn *et al.*, 1991; Heery, 1998; Kelly and Monks, 1998; Marsden and Richardson, 1994; Poole, 1988; Thompson, 1993). The performance pay and profit-sharing schemes which have been studied often place only a limited proportion of employee earnings at risk and so do not provide a strong test of the new pay, but they do at least suggest that a compensating boost to performance cannot be guaranteed from any decline in income security.

A second argument against the new pay can be derived from principles of procedural justice and the scope afforded for inconsistent and arbitrary treat-ment of employees. Running through the new pay is an emphasis on contin-gent reward and the need to tie earnings to measures of performance valued by managers. It can be argued that the implementation of these principles is likely to be characterised by actual and perceived injustice, both because pay is linked to performance measures which are only partially subject to employee control and because of the wide latitude allowed for management judgement. Research by Bevan and Thompson (1993) indicates that sex discrimination is particularly likely to arise where reward management is nimble and line managers are accorded substantial discretion in making pay awards (see also Dickens, 1998). Moreover, studies of performance pay based on individual appraisal indicate high levels of perceived unfairness among employees who claim managers are inconsistent in their application of payment scheme rules (Heery, 1998; Lewis, 1998; Marsden and Richardson, 1994).

A third argument against the new pay has to do with distributive justice as much as procedural fairness (that is, with the principle of 'fair shares' for contribution to economic activity). Not only does the new pay agenda imply an increase in employee risk but it also implies a transfer of risk from employers to workers. While interest in variable and contingent remuneration has grown, a desire to avoid hostile takeover has led firms to increase rates of return and offer improved guarantees to shareholders (Kay and Silberston, 1995). According to Hutton (1995), dividends as a share of national output doubled during the 1980s and carried on rising during the recession of the early 1990s. Over the period 1989–93 dividends grew by a cumulative 7 per cent in real terms, while profits reached a post-war peak of around 17 per cent of national output in 1994. For Schuster and Zingheim (1992, p. 154), variable pay enables employees to contribute 'when the organisation needs support as it relates to labour costs', but such support may be called on when other stake-holders are acting to diminish their risks.

The new pay has also been promulgated at a time when executive remu-neration has been rapidly increasing. A CBI survey of developments in reward (CBI, 1995, p. 13), however, indicated that executives are more likely than other employees to become subject to new pay practices and in partic-ular to receive remuneration in the form of variable, non-consolidated bonuses. It may be, however, that the new pay involves lower risks for execu-tives than for other employees. For instance, executive salaries have risen alongside bonuses and share options, some have been shielded from insecu-rity by rolling contracts, share options and bonuses have provided windfall gains and slack systems of corporate governance may have permitted some executives to influence their own remuneration (Conyon, 1995; Kay and Silberston, 1995).

While advocates of the new pay propose to increase risk for employees, therefore, other economic actors are seeking to reduce their risks or have the power to subvert or escape from threats to their security. This is regrettable because the bulk of employees are dependent on their remuneration, while executives and shareholders are in a position to spread their risks (Blair, 1995). Despite the rhetoric of partnership which flows through the new pay litera-ture, it is possible to discern a fairly hard-edged set of proposals for transfer-ring the risks inherent in economic activity from those who are powerful to those who are less able to bear them.

Representation

A second regrettable characteristic of the new pay is that it neglects the issue of employee rights and, in particular, affords little scope for the independent representation of employee interests. The new pay prescriptive model has been articulated and shaped management practice during a period of union decline in both the USA and UK and trade unions and collective bargaining do not feature prominently in new pay literature. When they are mentioned, they tend to be presented as of diminishing relevance, given the growth of direct communication with employees, or as impediments standing in the way of innovation (Schuster and Zingheim, 1992, p. 21). For Armstrong and Murlis (1994, p. 70), the 'performance oriented organisation' is characterised by 'individual performance bonuses... [with] some team elements... [and] employee equity participation' while its 'employee relations climate' is distinguished by the 'breakdown of a collective orientation [and] the management of individuals'. New pay writers also tend to be sceptical of the value of legal intervention to protect employee interests and some have expressed hostility to the legal enforcement of comparable worth or equal pay (Schuster and Zingheim, 1992, pp. 123–4).

This lack of concern with or opposition to representation, whether through unions or the law, arises from a number of deep-seated elements in the new pay model. The first element is the assumption that pay should be strategic and that policy should reflect, and be continually checked to ensure it reflects, the needs of the business. This prescription effectively squeezes out any alternative conception of pay as the meeting place for competing but equally legitimate interests. In a revealing passage, Wilson (1995, pp. 364–5) inveighs against 'entitlement systems... when people are automatically and regularly rewarded for not doing anything special'. Using the example of service-related benefits, he declares that employees do not have the 'right to receive [their] present level of benefits' and that 'each award should be fully earned', that is contingent on behaviour or performance which is of value to the employer. Lawler (1990, p. 278) makes a similar argument in opposition to comparable worth legislation, that law of this kind is undesirable not just because it tends to raise labour costs but because it limits the strategic choices available to managers and 'makes skill- or knowledge-based pay difficult or impossible to implement'.

A second element is the belief that shared interests can be fostered at the workplace through the adoption of new pay practices. Central to the new pay is the claim that incentives can not only motivate employees, they can also realign interests and foster a co-operative relationship between workers and employers. Provided the new pay is carefully designed and implemented and supported by parallel initiatives in other fields of human resource management, it can contribute to high commitment management. 'New pay links companies and people by means of economic partnership,' declare Zingheim and Schuster (1995), 'in which the results of successful company performance are shared with the people who make success a reality. Strategic alignment means people and organisations share goals and the rewards of success.' Essentially, this is a claim that the employer, through the careful design of reward practices, can act as the representative of employee interests and that consequently other representatives are not needed.

A third element is the attachment of new pay writers to the principle of employee involvement in the management of pay. For Lawler (1995, p. 20), the most important benefit of employee involvement is that employees' 'understanding and acceptance of the system tend to be quite high when they participate in designing it, allowing for a rapid start-up of the system and a commitment to its survival'. Other new pay writers (Ledford, 1995, p. 52; Zingheim and Schuster, 1995) emphasise the importance of involvement in eradicating 'misunderstandings' about the new pay and ensuring that the new basis for co-operation is clearly visible to employees. For Palmer (1996, p. 20), organisations pursuing a new pay agenda must secure 'the agreement and commitment of individual employee themselves' and this means 'moving away from the traditional approach by which the unions are the only communication channel'.

A series of arguments can be made against this set of claims and assumptions and simultaneously for the independent representation of employee interests in pay determination. The first and most glaringly obvious is that employees have separate and opposing interests regarding remuneration to those of employers and therefore require a representation channel to secure the expression of those interests. Conflict over pay may arise over the form of remuneration (for example, cash or credit transfer), the amount of pay, the distribution of pay and the system of pay, with employees seeking to base pay on criteria, such as comparability, which differ from those favoured by employers. Despite the decline in overall strike activity, it is worth remembering that the bulk of industrial disputes continues to arise over pay issues and that individual disputes over wages are the second most frequent category, after unfair dismissal, within the Employment Tribunal system (Davies, 1998; ACAS, 1997, p. 60). There is also longitudinal evidence from the British Social Attitudes Survey of rising employee disquiet at the growth of income inequality within firms (Kelly, 1997, p. 409).

Of course, shared interests in the field of remuneration also exist and it may well be that aspects of the new pay foster complementary interests. The overlap between employer and employee interests is unlikely ever to be complete, however, and even in the most well-managed firm the scope for friction is likely to remain. To provide an example, recent survey research on attitudes to pay among local government officers covered by performance pay schemes (Heery, 1996, p. 157) indicates that most endorse the principle of basing pay on individual performance, a core proposition of the new pay, but simultaneously retain their attachment to more traditional principles of reward, such as inflation proofing, fair comparisons and payment for service and qualifications. The latter would probably be classed as regrettable 'entitlements' by adherents of the new pay.

While some new pay initiatives may provide the basis for shared interests at work, empirical research on employee responses to the kinds of systems advocated by new pay writers suggests they can be as prone to conflict as more traditional systems of remuneration. According to Schuster and Zingheim (1992, p. 316), the new pay can promote a new relationship between employees and organisations and 'help us forget the labels of disenfranchised, adversarial and we versus them', but particular new pay techniques appear themselves often to become the object of workplace conflict. Studies of employee responses to individual performance-related pay, for instance, reveal widespread employee dissatisfaction with the application of schemes, which arises in part from the competing perspectives and interests which employees and managers bring to these systems (Dawson *et al.*, 1995; Kelly and Monks, 1998; Marsden and Richardson, 1994). There is also qualitative evidence of employees seeking to manipulate, subvert and defuse perform-ance pay schemes (Heery, 1998) and occasionally workers have taken indus-trial action to block the introduction or reform of performance pay or to secure changes in its operation. In 1997, for instance, previously quiescent employees at Barclays Bank took industrial action against a new performance pay scheme which, significantly, increased the proportion of variable pay and threatened to erode the value of base salaries (IRS, 1997; see also Gall, 1997).

Other new pay initiatives have not been so extensively studied and there is little information on how employees respond to or regard competency or team-based pay, broad banding or flexible benefits. Two case studies of skill-based pay, however, have been published by Clarke (1995) and Scott (1994). Both describe employee dissatisfaction with and resistance to the technique and its tendency, like traditional payment-by-results, to generate perverse effects. These two cases may be atypical, but they are based on the detailed examination of new pay practice within the workplace which is lacking in the upbeat, prescriptive writing of new pay theorists. What they and the studies of performance pay suggest is that, rather than fostering complementary worker–manager goals, the new pay, once implemented, can serve to divide interests and itself become the subject of conflict at work.

Another set of arguments concerns the effectiveness of employee involve-ment as a means for the representation of employee interests. It must be noted that effective representation is not really the purpose of employee involvement for new pay writers for whom it functions primarily as a means to draw upon employees' knowledge and ensure their commitment to management's goals. Its role has to do with the effective implementation of management strategy, therefore, rather than a means whereby the inde-pendent interests of employees can find expression in the system of pay management. From a deontological perspective (that is, one which assures that an action be taken because it is good in itself) such a motivation is in itself morally suspect because it compromises the principle of duty and regards employees instrumentally and teleologically rather than as ends-in-themselves (Legge, 1998, p. 24).

It is also mistaken to assume that involvement can serve as an effective alternative to other and stronger forms of employee participation based on independent representation. The latter may, in fact, be necessary to prompt managers into more ambitious experiments with employee involvement and ensure that they are maintained (Weiler, 1993, p. 92). Fragments of HRM have been found more frequently in unionised firms in Britain than in the 'bleak house' of non-unionism (Sisson, 1994) and there is evidence that a union presence can support some of the open and participative practices which some new pay writers believe are desirable. Research on the union response to performance-related pay indicates that, while unions do not generally favour such schemes, they typically press for more rigorous and transparent systems of performance review and the monitoring and audit of schemes. Additional research on performance pay in local government indicates that union involvement in scheme introduction is associated with a more formalised procedure for performance appraisal, a right of appeal, monitoring of the distribution of payments and greater investment in training and communication (Heery, 1997, pp. 216–19).

The final argument for independent representation is a democratic one and is grounded in a Rawlsian or stakeholder conception of a business ethics that is the view that companies should be responsive to the interests of all who have a 'stake' in their activities and success (Legge, 1998, p. 22). It has been suggested that employees possess separate and conflicting interests to those of employers and that those interests are unlikely to be satisfied by the application of the new pay model and the surrounding battery of techniques of involvement which are proposed by some of its adherents. In the previous section it was also suggested that employee interests in remuneration have high salience, that pay matters to people. Given these conditions, employees should have the right to representation and to influence the pay and benefit systems to which they are subject. A 'defining attribute of democracy is that all citizens have a right to participate in the making of decisions that affect their essential interests' (Adams, 1995, p. 28). The form, level, distribution and relationship to work performed of remuneration comprise one such interest and a final argument that can be made against the new pay is that its authors pay scant regard to the democratic rights of citizens in the field of employment.

Conclusion

This chapter has reviewed the new pay model which has come to dominate prescriptive writing on pay management in both the USA and the UK and which is increasingly influencing pay policy and practice on both sides of the Atlantic. There is considerable scepticism as to whether the new pay generates the benefits for organisations which its advocates claim but the purpose of the chapter has been to develop an ethical, as opposed to a managerial, critique. That critique has been made on three main grounds: that the new pay poses a threat to employee security and so is contrary to the principle of utility; that it is potentially unjust in both procedural and distributive senses;

and that it affords little scope for the exercise of democratic rights by citizens at the place of work.

If this critique is justified then what should be done about it? The new pay is problematic, in the first instance, because it seeks to place employee remuneration increasingly at risk. However, most would accept that it is neither feasible nor desirable for pay to be completely free of risk and, indeed, many employees endorse the principle of contingent pay, are the willing recipients of bonus payments and believe that it is right that they should share in the financial success of the enterprise (Kelly and Kelly, 1991, pp. 27–8). Arguably, what should be aimed at, therefore, is a situation of *acceptable risk*, in which the interest of the employer in contingent and variable pay is balanced against the interest of the employee in reasonably stable and predictable income. Table 10.1 displays a set of principles which could secure that balance.

TABLE 10.1   Principles of ethical pay management

- The use of variable pay as a supplement and not a replacement for a 'fair' base salary or wage
- Commitment to maintaining the value of employee benefits and particularly those that provide for economic security
- Basing contingent pay systems on rigorous measures of performance which are subject to employee control
- Regulation of management decision making about pay, supported by training, strict guidelines and review
- Transparency and full communication of pay system rules
- Regular monitoring and periodic audit of pay systems to ensure consistency of application and an absence of sex, race and other forms of discrimination
- Effective due process mechanisms for employees to appeal against management judgements
- Full involvement of employee representatives in the design, application and review of payment systems

Such a list is similar, in certain respects, to the codes of practice which have been issued by the European Commission and Equal Opportunities Commission to guard against sex discrimination in pay management (Commission of the European Communities, 1996; EOC, 1997). It also fits with the advice of some new pay writers (Lawler, 1990, pp. 40–3) that companies should have an explicit statement of pay philosophy to guide management action.

The problem with a list of this kind is that few organisations may choose freely to adopt it, particularly as some of its key suggestions are contrary to the dominant trends in remuneration practice. A second recommendation, therefore, is that there should be a legal right for employees to bargain their remuneration. A legal right is necessary because with rare exceptions employers are unwilling to cede joint decision making voluntarily and in most workplaces UK unions are too weak to compel bargaining without state assistance (Adams, 1995, p. 175). It is also necessary because of the social costs and often limited effectiveness of representation through individual statutory rights, like the right to equal pay. The latter are most effective where they are positively mediated by systems of representation in the workplace and, indeed, virtually all equal pay cases in Britain have originated in unionised environments (Dickens, 1989; Millward, 1995).

A legal right to bargain pay collectively (plus hours of work and holidays) via a statutory trade union recognition procedure was established in Britain following the publication of the government's White Paper, *Fairness at Work* (DTI, 1998). How effective this right will prove in supporting employee representation remains to be seen. In framing its proposals the government has been anxious that new rights for workers do not inhibit labour market flexibility, which seems very like the call for 'nimble reward management' writ large, and has signally failed to endorse worker participation through collective bargaining as its preferred means of regulating the employment relationship. The detailed proposals are also problematic and include a requirement that to secure recognition a union will need not just the majority of votes cast in a ballot but the votes of 40 per cent of those eligible to vote; a threshold which denies the right to collective representation to workers in firms with 20 or fewer employees; and a procedure for union derecognition which can be activated by employers. In the home of the new pay, the United States, similar 'certification' legislation has not failed to prevent the decline of collective bargaining to an historic post-war low and has come to be manipulated by employers to keep their workplaces 'union-free' (Adams, 1995). The true test of Labour's policy will be if this scenario is avoided and the proportion of employees who are covered by collective bargaining, and therefore have the right to shape their remuneration in accordance with their own definition of their interests, begins to rise.

Perhaps the most influential perspective among ethicists who are interested in the employment relationship is stakeholder theory, in which the enterprise is conducted on behalf of the separate interests of its various stakeholders who participate in decisions which affect their welfare. The weaknesses of stakeholder theories of justice, according to Legge (1998, p. 23), are that disparities in resources between stakeholders (for example, employers and workers) may lead only to 'pseudo-participation' and that the responsibility of management for maintaining the survival of the organisation, and therefore the long-term interests of all, might be used to justify repeated action against particular stakeholders (for example, individual workers or the workforce as a whole) in the short term. The promotion of effective trade unions through supportive legislation and other measures seems the most practicable response to each of these weaknesses. The evidence on union effects (Booth, 1995; Millward, 1994) demonstrates that unions make a difference to their members' pay and conditions of employment and to the processes through which they are managed and suggests that unions, even in a difficult environment, continue to articulate the distinct interests of employees and provide a means for genuine participation. To the extent that ethicists are committed to a stakeholder model of the enterprise and maintain an interest in the conditions under which employee interests are effectively represented, perhaps they should develop awareness of research and debate within, the similarly normative, but often neglected field of industrial relations.

Acknowledgement

Thanks to Peter Turnbull and the editors for helpful comments on an earlier draft.

Note

An earlier version of this chapter was published as an article 'Risk, Representation and the New Pay', in a special issue of *Personnel Review* (1996) on 'Business Ethics and Human Resource Management', **25**(6): 54–65.

References

ACAS (1997) *Annual Report 1996*, London: Advisory, Conciliation and Arbitration Service

Adams, R.J. (1995) *Industrial Relations under Liberal Democracy*, Columbia: University of South Carolina Press

Armstrong, M. (1996) *Employee Reward*, London: Institute for Personnel and Development

Armstrong, M. and Murlis, H. (1994*) Reward Management: a handbook of remuneration strategy and practice* (3rd edn), London: Kogan Page

Baddon, L., Hunter, L., Hyman, J., Leopold, J. and Ramsay, H. (1989) *People's Capitalism? A Critical Analysis of Profit Sharing and Employee Share Ownership*, London: Routledge

Bevan, A. and Thompson, M. (1993) *Merit Pay, Performance Appraisal and Attitudes to Women's Work*, Brighton: Institute for Manpower Studies (now Institute for Employment Studies, IES)

Blair, M. (1995) *Ownership and Control: Rethinking Corporate Governance for the Twenty First Century*, Washington DC: The Brookings Institute

Booth, A. (1995) *The Economics of the Trade Union*, Cambridge: Cambridge University Press

Brown, W. (1997) 'Bargaining for full employment' in Philpott, J. (ed.) *Working for Full Employment*, London: Routledge

CBI (1995) *Trends in Pay and Benefit Systems: 1995*, CBI/Hay Survey Results, London: Confederation of British Industry

Clarke, J. (1995) *Managing Innovation and Change: People, Technology and Strategy*, London: Sage

Commission of the European Communities (1996) *A Code of Practice on the Implementation of Equal Pay for Work of Equal Value for Women and Men*, Brussels: Commission of the European Communities

Conyon, M. (1995) 'Directors' pay in the privatised utilities' *British Journal of Industrial Relations*, 33(2): 159–71

Corbridge, M. and Pilbeam, S. (1998) *Employment Resourcing*, London: Financial Times Management

Davies, J. (1998) 'Labour disputes in 1997' *Labour Market Trends*, June: 299–311

Dawson, S., Winstanley, D., Mole, V. and Sherval, J. (1995) *Managing in the NHS: A Study of Senior Executives*, London: HMSO

Dickens, L. (1989) 'Women - a rediscovered resource?' *Industrial Relations Journal*, 20(3): 167–75

Dickens, L. (1998) 'What HRM means for gender equality' *Human Resource Management Journal*, 8(1): 23–40

Dowling, B. and Richardson, R. (1997) 'Evaluating performance-related pay for managers in the health service' *International Journal of Human Resource Management*, 8(3): 348–66

DTI (1998) *Fairness at Work*, London: Department of Trade and Industry

Dunn. S., Richardson, R. and Dewe, P. (1991) 'The impact of employee share ownership on worker attitudes' *Human Resource Management Journal*, 1(3): 1–17

EOC (1997) *Code of Practice on Equal Pay*, Manchester: Equal Opportunities Commission

Gall, G. (1997) 'Developments in trade unionism in the financial sector in Britain' *Work, Employment and Society*, 1(2): 219–35

Geary, J.F. (1992) 'Pay, control and commitment: linking appraisal and reward' *Human Resource Management Journal*, 2(4): 36–54

Guest, D. (1989) 'Human resource management: its implications for industrial relations and trade unions' in J. Storey (ed.) *New Perspectives on Human Resource Management*, London: Routledge

Heery, E. (1996) *Performance Related Pay in Local Government: A Case Study of the New Industrial Relations*. Doctoral thesis: University of London

Heery, E. (1997) 'Performance-related pay and trade union de-recognition' *Employee Relations*, 19(3): 208–21

Heery, E. (1998) 'A return to contract? Performance related pay in a public service' *Work, Employment and Society*, 12(1): 73–96

Hewitt Associates (1991) *Total Compensation Management: Reward Management Strategies for the 1990s*, Oxford: Blackwell

Hutton, W. (1995) *The State We're In*, London: Jonathan Cape

IPD (1998) IPD 1998 *Performance Pay Survey*, London: Institute for Personnel and Development

IRS (1997) 'Pay dispute at Barclays' *Pay and Benefits Bulletin*, 430: 11

Kay, J. and Silberston, A. (1995) 'Corporate governance' *National Institute Economic Review*, August: 84–97

Kelly, A. and Monks, K. (1998) 'View from the bridge and life on deck: contrasts and contradictions in performance-related pay' in Mabey, C., Skinner, D. and Clark, T. (eds) *Experiencing Human Resource Management*, London: Sage

Kelly, J. (1997) 'The future of trade unionism' *Employee Relations*, **19**(5): 400–14

Kelly, J. and Kelly, C. (1991) '"Them and us": social psychology and the new industrial relations' *British Journal of Industrial Relations*, **29**(1): 25–48

Lawler III, E.E. (1990) *Strategic Pay*, San Francisco: Jossey Bass

Lawler III, E.E. (1995) 'The new pay: a strategic approach' *Compensation and Benefits Review*, July–August: 14–22

Ledford, G.E. (1995) 'Designing nimble reward systems' *Compensation and Benefits Review*, July–August: 46–54

Legge, K. (1998) 'The morality of HRM' in Mabey, C., Skinner, D. and Clark, T. (eds) *Experiencing Human Resource Management*, London: Sage

Lewis, P. (1998) 'Managing performance-related pay based on evidence from the financial services sector' *Human Resource Management Journal*, **8**(2): 66–77

Mahoney, T. (1992) 'Multiple pay contingencies: strategic design of compensation' in Salaman, G. (ed.) *Human Resource Strategies*, London: Sage

Marsden. D. and Richardson, R. (1994) 'Performing for pay? The effects of merit pay on motivation in a public service' *British Journal of Industrial Relations*, **32**(2): 243–61

Millward, N. (1994) *The New Industrial Relations?* London: Policy Studies Institute

Millward, N. (1995) *Targeting Potential Discrimination*, Research Discussion Series, Manchester: Equal Opportunities Commission

Murlis, H. (ed.) (1996) *Pay at the Crossroads*, London: Institute for Personnel and Development

Palmer, S. (1996) 'Pay and the business agenda' in Murlis, H. (ed.) *Pay at the Crossroads*, London: Institute for Personnel and Development

Poole, M. (1988) 'How employees respond to profit sharing' *Personnel Management*, July: 30–4

Randle, K. and Rainnie, A. (1997) 'Managing creativity, maintaining control: a study in pharmaceutical research' *Human Resource Management Journal*, **7**(2): 32–46

Schuster, J.R. and Zingheim, P.K. (1992) *The New Pay: Linking Employee and Organizational Effectiveness*, New York: Lexington

Scott, A. (1994) *Willing Slaves? British Workers under Human Resource Management*, Cambridge: Cambridge University Press

Sisson, K. (1994) 'In search of HRM' *British Journal of Industrial Relations*, **31**(2): 201–10

Smith, A.W. (1992a) 'Structureless pay: a modest proposal' *Compensation and Benefits Review*, July–August: 22–5

Smith, I. (1992b) 'Reward management and HRM' in Blyton, P. and Turnbull, P. (eds) *Reassessing Human Resource Management*, London: Sage

Stevens, J. (1996) 'Pay at the crossroads' in Murlis, H. (ed.) *Pay at the Crossroads*, London: Institute for Personnel and Development

Storey, J. (1995) 'Human resource management: still marching on, or marching out?' in Storey, J. (ed.) *Human Resource Management: A Critical Text*, London: Routledge

Thompson, M. (1993) *Pay and Performance: the Employee Experience*, Brighton: Institute for Manpower Studies (now Institute for Employment Studies, IES)

Walsh, J. (1993) 'Internalization v. decentralization: an analysis of recent developments in pay bargaining' *British Journal of Industrial Relations*, 31(3): 409–32

Warr, P.B. (1987) *Work, Unemployment and Mental Health*, Oxford: Clarendon Press

Weiler, P. (1993) 'Governing the workplace: employee representation and the law' in Kaufman, B.E. and Kleiner, M.M. (eds) *Employee Representation: Alternatives and Future Direction*, Madison, WI: Industrial Relations Research Association

Wilson, T.B. (1995) *Innovative Reward Systems for the Changing Workplace*, New York: McGraw-Hill

Zingheim, P.K. and Schuster, J.R. (1995) 'Readiness assessment: benchmarking and piloting' *Compensation and Benefits Review*, July/August: 40–5

CHAPTER 11

Conditions of worth and the performance management paradox

Diana Winstanley

Introduction

In this chapter it is suggested that the mixing of fundamentally differing perspectives and theories related to the effective performance and healthy functioning of the individual leads to a performance management paradox. The performance management paradox lies at the heart of the contradictory nature of contemporary human resource management. Differing assumptions, for example embedded in McGregor's Theory X and Theory Y (McGregor, 1960), or in Fox's (1974) high-trust or low-trust management, spawn very different approaches to human resource management. Where these become mixed, practices can become confused and even counterproductive. Elsewhere the problems inherent in pursuing contradictory approaches to HRM, such as best fit and best practice, have been well documented. For example Legge (1995, pp. 66–9) documents the contradictions of the 'hard' model reflecting 'utilitarian instrumentalism' and the 'soft' model, reminiscent of 'developmental humanism'. She suggests, among other things, ambiguities to do with the conceptual language, for example over diverse meanings of 'integration' and 'flexibility', as well as deeper contradictions raised by capitalism itself.

At the nub of the performance management paradox is the pursuance of a dual and contradictory approach to performance management. Employees are treated as intrinsically valuable, self-actualising individuals and the organisation provides an arena in which their developmental potential can be realised. At the same time the organisation pursues conditions of worth approaches, which require constant evaluation, grading, classification and measurement and individuals are subjected to systems which constantly remind them of their contingent relationship with the organisation. The enactment of this paradox through contradictory processes for development and evaluation in performance management has been raised repeatedly in the literature as problematic and has dogged much practice through the difficulties of operating these processes in ways which are mutually supportive rather than counterproductive. The clash of these perspectives will be shown to raise contradictions for performance management.

Two related areas identify the crux of the paradox: conditional versus unconditional regard and evaluation versus self-actualisation. The opposing approaches are supported by very different psychological theories and paradigms on the nature of human health and well-being and their repercussions for organisational practices and effectiveness: on the one hand, the humanistic perspective as outlined by Rogers (1959, 1967), Maslow (1943, 1987) and, to some extent, McGregor (1960) and, on the other, the behaviourist perspective drawn by Skinner (1953). The rise and ultimate triumph of the behaviourist over the humanistic model in organisational psychology and the economic over the social model of the organisation in management has led to the contradiction being resolved in ways which are problematic for ethical HRM. It is suggested that a more ethical perspective would require a shift towards a more humanistic model of the organisation and its employees.

The critique of performance management given here will begin with the functionalist critique drawn from traditional managerialism which focuses on dysfunctional aspects and problems with operationalisation of performance management systems. From this view, the ethical concern is primarily to do with ethical instrumentalism and making the systems fairer and more functional. It is suggested that the managerialist perspective has attempted to address the problems of performance management by paying more attention to issues of evaluation. It is suggested that the centrality of evaluation in contemporary work on human resource management leads to a heightening of the performance management paradox and to other criticisms of performance management. The analysis then moves to more radical critiques of performance management based on labour process theory and postmodern perspectives. The labour process theoretical perspective focuses on the contradictory relationship between employer and employee and issues of control. Here ethical dilemmas are seen to be endemic to the employment relationship. The critique from more postmodern perspectives focus particularly on the nature of surveillance and the rhetoric of performance, and ethical concerns with relation to power and subjectivity. Finally, the critique is drawn from the humanistic perspective which places the contradiction provided by the behaviourist underpinnings of performance systems at odds with humanistic concerns for the individual and their self-esteem and ability to self-actualise. It is argued that this last area is perhaps the most under-theorised, and yet has the most relevance to the ethical focus of this book. It is proposed that debates about the nature of human beings from psychotherapeutic perspectives should be more part of the general debates over performance management.

The chapter concludes by identifying what a minimum floor of ethical principles could look like in the area of performance management and provides examples where attempts have been made to put this into practice. In summary the principles of respect for the individual, mutual respect, procedural fairness and transparency of decision making are highlighted, drawing on earlier work of Winstanley and Stuart-Smith (1996).

The functionalist critique of performance management

To understand the criticisms of performance management within the managerialist literature, it is important first to define it. Commonly, performance management systems revolve around an objective setting and evaluation process. Thus it has been labelled the MBO of the 1990s (Fowler, 1990). It is defined as a system for setting performance objectives, for managing and developing performance with relation to these objectives, and for measuring performance against these objectives, with a feedback loop to correct, build on and develop performance and to develop the objectives themselves. This process can go on at the organisational, the group and the individual level, and there is commonly a cascading link – a 'golden thread' between the organisational and the individual performance. These activities may be accompanied by a process of benchmarking, where both the performance objectives themselves, and the performance of the individual or organisation are benchmarked against others. For example, with relation to employees, they may have objectives which are set with relation to their own work and linked to organisational performance objectives, they may receive developmental support, and be subject to performance appraisal and review with relation to these objectives. A number of actions may arise as a result of the review process, such as new development plans, the distribution of performance-related pay, and even suggestions for career development and promotion.

Performance management is one of the most frequently criticised human resource management practices, usually in terms of technical effectiveness and motivational aspects. In a previous article (Winstanley and Stuart-Smith, 1996) we summarised some of these criticisms, which can be identified under three headings: problems in operationalisation, subjectivity and bias and performance management and effectiveness.

1. *Problems in operationalisation*

   It is commonly suggested that performance objectives should be SMART – Specific, (some refer to it as Stretching), Measurable, Achievable (some mention Agreed here), Results oriented (or possibly, Realistic or Relevant) and Time bound. However, in practice performance objectives and goals are notoriously difficult to design, they are often unable to reflect intangibles, they may lack flexibility to respond to change and they are difficult to apply to the whole of a person's job. Also in practice, the lack of time, the over-bureaucratisation of the process, emphasis on rewards and under-emphasis on development, can all cause problems. A discussion of such problems with goal setting can be found in Williams (1998, pp. 90–2).

2. *Subjectivity and bias*

   Much has been written of the lack of fairness arising from the subjectivity and bias of the appraiser or evaluator, as well as their lack of skill and the repercussions for equal opportunities, (for example see Bevan and Thompson, 1992b; Murphy, 1991; Townley, 1990; Wayne and Liden, 1995). Unfairness can be of two sorts: procedural unfairness, in terms of the methods used and outcome unfairness, in terms of the effects these have on people.

   Many of the criticisms from a functionalist and managerialist perspective are valid, but do tend to suggest that as long as we address these problems, the activity of performance management itself is desirable. However, a managerialist perspective has been developing which goes beyond assessing problems with the systems and how they work and questions whether or not the activity is worthwhile at all. These focus on issues to do with performance management and effectiveness.

3. *Performance management and effectiveness*

   Ongoing work evaluating performance management has raised questions as to whether performance management systems actually meet their objectives. In particular two are highlighted, whether they lead to improved performance and, equally important, whether or not they enhance employee motivation. In fact, there is no conclusive evidence that the use of performance management systems results in improved performance at all. Instead they can produce undesirable side effects, including demoralisation and demotivation on the one hand and an over-bureaucratisation on the other. The large-scale surveys and in-depth case studies commissioned by the IPD as part of an ongoing review of performance management (originally seen as appraisal) in the UK were unable to find any association between organisational performance and the presence of formal performance management systems (Bevan and Thompson, 1992a; Fletcher and Williams, 1992), despite the fact that organisational performance was the main reason for introducing performance management. The evidence against their success is particularly prominent when it is combined with performance related pay. A good example here is provided by Thompson (1993) in a study of the employees experience of pay and performance. The author's own research into the individual performance review process in the NHS and its link with performance-related pay for senior managers found many examples where performance-related pay was seen as a negative motivator (see Dawson *et al.*, 1995; Winstanley *et al.*, 1995).

Literature on performance and effectiveness has responded in two ways. It has raised the question as to whether the approaches to evaluation are adequate, leading to the creation of many more tools for evaluating effectiveness and methods for performance management and measurement. The second focus derives from a perceived need to generate data on the link between human resource management systems and organisational effectiveness. These are now discussed.

The rise of evaluation

The suggestion, that performance management tools have not been sufficiently well developed and that what is needed is more and better tools, has been fuelled by the rise of interest in quality and business excellence. This has led to a proliferation of performance management systems based around measures linking individual performance to organisational measures of success – 'the golden thread'. These cover a plethora of management by objectives systems supported by positive and negative reinforcements. Two examples demonstrate the percolation of quality and excellence practices into performance management – the EFQM excellence model and the balanced scorecard.

The EFQM business excellence model (see Figure 11.1), which evolved out of the European Foundation for Quality Management Quality Award (1992), is widely used by large organisations, in order to measure themselves, and enables comparison and benchmarking with other companies. The business excellence model measures enablers, including leadership (10 per cent), people management (9 per cent), policy and strategy (8 per cent), resources (9 per cent) and processes (14 per cent); and also results, including people satisfaction (9 per cent), customer satisfaction (20 per cent), impact on society (6 per cent) and business results (15 per cent). The experience of companies adopting this model, such as Nortel Northern Telecom, suggests that the process of application is every bit as important as the final scoring process and the ability to benchmark against a European standard. The process requires continuous improvement and the identification of opportunities for improvement and action plans, in an annual cycle of scoring, action planning, action and review, with the process being integrated with other management processes, including human resource management and performance management practices.

Likewise, literature on organisational performance has moved from models based on performance focusing purely on profit margins and financial indicators, to those which encompass a more multifaceted view of performance. For example, the balanced scorecard approach propounded by Kaplan and Norton (1992, 1993, 1996a, 1996b and see Figure 11.2), balances the indicators of

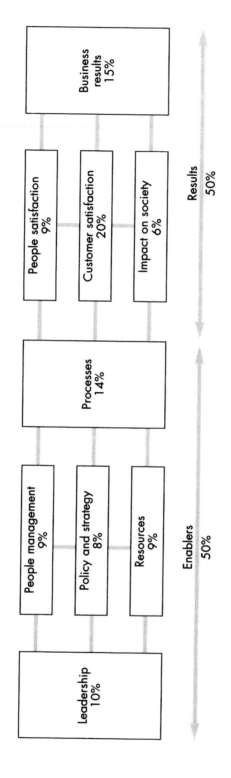

FIGURE 11.1   The EFQM Excellence Model 1999 (© EFQM)

(The EFQM Excellence Model is a registered trademark)

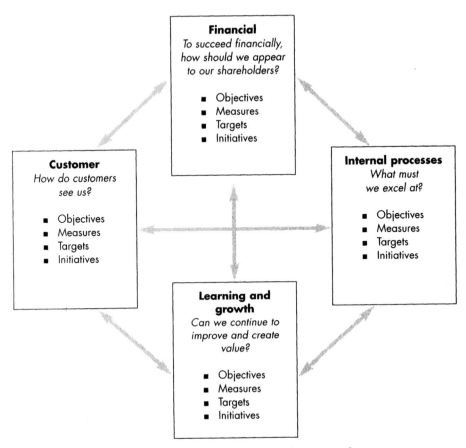

FIGURE 11.2   The balanced scorecard
(Adapted from Kaplan and Norton, 1992, p. 72)

performance around the financial perspective ('how do we look to share-holders?') with the customer perspective ('how do customers see us?'), the internal business perspective ('what must we excel at?') and the innovation and learning perspective ('can we continue to improve and create value?'). These also shift from a shareholder model of performance to more of a stakeholder-oriented one, although the employee perspective is not as prominent as that of customers and shareholders. It also requires active performance management, rather than merely measurement, incorporating the four processes of translating the vision, communicating and linking, business planning and feedback and learning. Thus, once again, performance measurement is linked with manage-ment and the processes of evaluation and development are fused. Research indicates that about 60 per cent of US companies have tried it and the number of European organisations using it is growing fast, and includes BT, BP Chemicals,

NatWest Retail Services, Coutts Bank, Citibank, the insurance group Skandia, the document company Xerox and the Spanish railway company Renfe.

This all may seem a long way away from performance management when related to people in the workplace, but these systems are being increasingly used as instruments for evaluating, managing and driving individual performance. Coutts Bank, for example, in using the balanced scorecard have produced systems of cascading scorecards, where each individual member of staff has their performance appraised according to individual scorecards, which link into group and organisational scorecards – a form of 'golden thread'.

The advantage of these approaches is the clear communication of top-down objectives to drive individual performance. They integrate systems for managing and measuring human resource capabilities with business strategy. Goal and performance oriented, they constitute a form of ethical instrumentalism, where maximising the ends, or performance of the organisation, justifies the means, the practice of managing people as resources in the workplace. Not only do they justify an emphasis on evaluation, they also widen evaluation to a form of 360 degree measurement, linking in measures and evaluation from managers, customers, peers, as well as self-evaluation and upward feedback. Ethically, these may be seen more compatible with stakeholding perspectives mentioned in Chapter 1 due to the inclusion of a wider constituency in the identification and measurement of performance. However, an alternative view could suggest that this leads to excessive evaluation which undermines healthy functioning of individuals, a point made in the critiques that follow.

Another trend in management literature has also drawn greater attention in human resource management to the process of evaluation, and that is the shift to a research focus on the link between specific human resource management practices and effectiveness. Research utilising correlations of human resource practices with measures of business success in the US has led to raging debates in the UK over desirable configurations of human resource practice. Thus for example, high performance work practices (HPWP) became associated with extensive employee training, compensation contingent on individual, work-group and overall firm performance, job-related and competency-based selection and employee participation and involvement (Tyson, 1997, pp. 176–7). This has led to a questioning as to whether there is an ideal type of human resource management that all organisations should follow – 'best practice', or whether different business requirements demand different human resource configurations – the 'best fit' approach. A number of studies utilised highly quantitative approaches to produce more statistically valid research on the association between certain human resource practices and particularly features of 'high performance' work teams, with organisational success. Huselid (1995) for example, found that a one standard deviation increase on the deployment of organisational HPWP was associated in

968 firms with decreased turnover, increased sales, increased firm market value and increased profits, confirming previous work. This approach has also been adopted in the UK with work by Guest and Peccei (1994) on the effectiveness of HR departments. Later work by Peccei (1997) has had mixed results using UK data on high performance work practices. In this they include aspects to do with performance-oriented appraisals, flexible job design, a strong integrated internal labour market, good downward communication, systematic training, contingent pay and sophisticated selection. They have also examined the standard universal hypothesis (that is, the best practice model where HPWP are associated with improved performance per se), the configurational model (where there is a congruant pattern of HR practices) and also the contingency 'external best fit' model where there is external fit between the dominant business strategy and the HR practices adopted.

Given the confusion over what high performance work systems should consist of, it becomes even harder then to suggest the most appropriate performance management system or approach to support it and this begs the question of what we actually mean by performance management. The emphasis on quality and excellence, the development of top-down 'best fit' models and the widening of evaluation in performance to '360 degree feedback' have all acted to develop the arena of performance management into a monster whose original purpose has become obscure. We now have many tools for performance management, and in particular for evaluation, but in this growth industry of measurement, have we lost sight of any humanistic notions of the individual at all?

Managerialist work on the shortcomings of performance management and measurement appear to miss the central point made in this chapter: that the performance management paradox itself (that is, the clash between evaluative and developmental cultures and practices) may be hampering both performance effectiveness and individual motivation and that not enough attention has been given to this in the literature. The way the literature has evolved on performance and effectiveness has short-circuited this viewpoint. It is as if the symptoms are noted but not the cause. Without clearly addressing the central paradox developed in the following, much of these actions act to mask rather than eradicate that paradox. The ethical approach implicit in much of this work is that of ethical instrumentalism – how can we fix these systems so that they do result in enhanced performance and how can we measure this to demonstrate that improvement is seen to be taking place? It is suggested in this chapter that from a different ethical perspective – that of ethical humanism – individuals continue to be seen as objects which are acted upon in the performance management process. Two critiques of performance management from the radical perspective raising issues of evaluation and control from a more critical perspective, demonstrate even more starkly the lack of humanism in performance management.

Radical critiques of performance management

Issues of control from a labour process perspective

One view of performance management suggests that it is a new form of 'Taylorism'. Control through the specification of performance objectives and measures, checks and evaluations to ensure that performance meets these, all suggest that performance management becomes a crucial tool for controlling the labour process. Performance management can be viewed as a form of 'boundary control' or 'arms' length regulation'. Behavioural selection criteria, appraisal, performance management systems and performance-related pay become part of the process for substituting direct with indirect forms of control (see for example Barlow 1989; Carter, 1989). A number of writers have suggested that Braverman and other labour process theorists have overly concentrated on direct forms of control and deskilling (see Noon and Blyton 1997, pp. 105–11 for a summary of Braverman's labour process thesis) and not paid enough attention to alternative strategies, such as of 'responsible autonomy' (Friedman, 1977) and other approaches that utilise more indirect methods for controlling the labour process. Elsewhere the author has outlined the use of recruitment (Winstanley, 1991), but the area of performance management affords similar opportunities for control. Is performance management an approach to managerial control more or less ethical than other forms? It could be argued that it enables more discretion over how the work gets done. From a labour process perspective, the interest in ethical approaches is largely irrelevant, but would suggest that the performance management paradox is inherent in the employment relationship and that attempts to humanise the relationship would mask rather than resolve it.

Power, control and surveillance from a postmodern perspective

A postmodern perspective also identifies issues of power and control, but goes further to link this to notions of surveillance and the metaphor of Foucault's prison. In the perception of the 'appraised', performance management can become akin to police surveillance, where control occurs through the collection of documentation and evidence, to build up a dossier on an individual. Instead of directly observing behaviour, supervision becomes more a matter of 'spying through keyholes'. Townley (1993), drawing on the work of Foucault (1977), views appraisal functions as equivalent to an 'information panopticon' using the Foucaultian metaphor of a prison, where:

The central tower was to house the administrative functions of management, the policing functions of surveillance, the economic functions of controlling and checking, the religious functions of encouraging obedience and work; from here all orders would come, all activities would be recorded, all offences, perceived and judged.

Barlow (1989) also examines some of the latent functions of appraisal in relation to the perpetuation of power. In Townley's schema, power, instead of descending (as in the framework of managerial control), ascends and becomes constructed and articulated, using bureaucratic and institutional processes to legitimate it as 'rational', 'neutral' and 'objective'.

The language of ethics and humanism may be one way of constructing a different type of performance management, but it would compete with rival and better established discourses of management, such as the 'discourse' of evaluation and effectiveness. From a postmodern perspective, paradox is the inevitable result of rival constructions of 'truth', as different subjectivities compete to become established as objective 'truth'. Therefore, the performance management paradox represents the clash between the discourse of control and evaluation, on the one hand, and the language of acceptance, development and self-actualisation, on the other.

The critique of performance management thus far has suggested that from the managerialist view problems of performance management are largely concerned with evaluation and motivation. Rather than seeing evaluation as problematic in itself, work has focused on providing more and better methods for evaluation. Radical writers have linked evaluation to issues of power and control, with problems arising from this being inherent in the employment relationship. However, one crucial building block in the notion of performance management is still needed and that is behaviourism. It is the combination of evaluation and behaviourism which together constitute the paradox when taking a humanistic perspective – the last critique which is very much bound up with ethical concerns in performance management.

Behaviourism and the conditions of worth organisation

Many concepts in contemporary performance management have a legacy within behaviourist assumptions about the nature of the individual and their effective performance. Much behavioural management theory is based around the work of Skinner (1953) on instrumental and operant conditioning and behaviour. He suggests that any behaviour that is rewarded or reinforced in some way will tend to be repeated in that context, and punished behaviour would likewise be reduced, so that positive reinforcement can be used to increase individual's adherence to those behaviours valued by the organisation and negative reinforcement to make less desirable behaviours less likely to achieve wanted outcomes. Objective-based systems identify those behaviours which are to be reinforced – the first part of the definition of performance management related to identifying these objectives. Likewise competency systems also provide the same function in identifying the behavioural competencies to be rewarded. Systems are then developed to evaluate and reward these valuable behaviours, for instance, through praise, performance pay and promotion. Undesirable behaviours are also negatively reinforced, through, say, disciplinary procedures or negative feedback. Performance management thus puts into practice behavioural management theory.

A number of problems with behavioural approaches to management remain to be addressed. It has been recognised that an over-focus on rewarding positive behaviour can lead to a more extrinsic form of motivation, and undermine intrinsic motivation (for example see Kohn, 1993). An employee who has, for example, derived considerable satisfaction from producing reports may find that introduction of performance measures on number and quality of reports produced, with performance-related pay attached to performance in these areas, removes their focus away from their intrinsic satisfaction so that they become more instrumental in their relationship with their work. Furthermore, subsequent removal of the performance measures and reward may lead to a loss of interest and motivation in this area of work altogether. More important, the contingent emphasis on the relationship may pose a problem for an individuals concept of self-worth.

The situation arrived at is:

1. Behaviourist theory has provided a paradigm that suggests positive and negative reinforcement can promote effective behaviour
2. Advances in quality and excellence literature have provided us with more tools to measure effectiveness, around which the reinforcements can be built
3. The activity of performance management has become an important way of enacting the cult of quality and excellence
4. The human resource management literature has targeted effectiveness and performance for the organisation as being of central concern.

All of these have put pressure on performance management to be an activity which is for the purpose of organisational effectiveness and requires measurement and evaluation of individuals and the use of contingent rewards to emphasise value in relation to those measures. However, an alternative argument could be built around the:

1. Need to treat individuals as valuable in themselves, with opportunities for development, growth and self-actualisation

2. Confusion over what exactly constitutes high performance
3. Utilisation of multiple sources of evaluation leading to excessive dysfunctional surveillance.

Is the focus on evaluation excessive and moreover does it lead to ethical concerns over autonomy, dignity, self-esteem and privacy? If one wanted to try and lead performance management back to a more humanistic model what would this look like?

Humanistic psychology suggests that excessive conditions of worth can be detrimental to organisational health and individual well-being. What is meant by 'conditions of worth'? Carl Rogers (Kirschenbaum and Henderson, 1990; Rogers, 1959, 1967), in his theory of therapy, personality and interpersonal relationships, discusses an individual's development in terms of the splitting of the self-concept from the existential, experiential self. The experiential self is one's fully felt experiences, feeling and emotions which have a tendency towards self-actualisation and growth in a fulfilling and resourceful life. The self-concept on the contrary develops as we experience from significant others conditions of worth and conditions for the receipt of their positive regard. In childhood these may be ' be good', 'good girls aren't bossy', 'good boys don't cry'. These conditions are also evident in organisational life, and notions of the good employee who should be 'flexible', 'committed', 'competent' and so on. The pressure to conform to these conditions of worth are strong, for these are what leads to positive regard from others.

However, Rogerian theory would suggest that too much contingent positive feedback, too many conditions of worth, can produce a splitting of the self-concept from the experiential self, to the extent that we can start to deny some aspects of our true self, and believe we are those things which others would like us to be. Why may this become unhealthy for our development? First, our unacknowledged selves may cause us much sadness and pain, as we cannot seem to realise fulfilment and self-awareness because we have lost access to significant parts of ourselves. Our self-concept may lead us to take on work and roles which we may find boring, frustrating and intolerable, but we see as necessary to maintain our self-concept. The self-concept can become a barrier to interpersonal contact, as we act a life or part which prevents us from expressing authentic feelings and emotions. Our yearning to throw off aspects of the self-concept may create a lack of internal judgement and locus of control in our lives, as we lose touch with what we really want and feel, we may lose confidence in our own intrinsic sense of worth.

Rogers (1959, 1967) and Maslow (1943, 1987) are both strong adherents to a humanistic model of social relationships in general. As Rogers suggests, his assumptions about personality and human relationships apply to all areas of life, they are 'a way of being' (1967, part 6 and 7) which he has advocated for therapy, education and the work context. Maslow (1987) and, to some extent, McGregor (1960) have applied them more explicitly to management in suggesting work systems which promote the self-actualising and developmental potential of individuals. The core assumptions are optimistic. They assume that individuals, given support, will grow in a positive and socially beneficial way – a point which is emphasised in the ethics of care literature mentioned in Chapter 1.

The performance management paradox suggests that it is contradictory to pursue both a behaviourist and a humanistic model with relation to performance management, to reward individuals contingently, and at the same time suggest they are accepted unconditionally, to positively reinforce desired behaviours, but to emphasise the intrinsic worth and regard held for each unique individual in totality.

A humanistic model of performance management

Is it possible to develop an alternative approach to performance management which is not so at odds with humanistic principles? In a previous article (Winstanley and Stuart-Smith, 1996) some of the ethical frameworks outlined in Chapter 1 were used to enable an approach to performance management which took the emphasis away from a process which is 'done to' the individual, to develop one which was enabling individuals to have more of an active role in developing themselves and the organisation. Any more humanistic model of performance management would need to have procedural fairness to limit adverse impact on individuals. This should be backed up by opportunities to scrutinise the basis for decision making and an appeal against those decisions which are believed to be unfair. For this transparency to be effective, those criteria used for performance evaluation need to be clearly communicated. However, building in fairness and transparency in the performance management process still maintains a fairly passive role for the 'appraisees', whereby they can check that the system works fairly, but not question the fundamental design of the system per se. Performance management is still something which is largely 'done to' the individual.

Another ethical appraisal of performance management would concern itself with the rights of the individual, or its effects on the individual. In Kantian terms, there is the question as to whether individuals in the process are treated as 'ends in themselves', or merely 'means to other ends'. One of the problems that has dogged performance management systems is that they have generally led individuals to feel that the latter is the reality.

Using a rights framework, it is possible to identify individual rights in performance management, the right to privacy over some personal information and the right to comment on the appraisal review findings, the right for more transparency of the process and also to maintain individual dignity and self-esteem. Using a contractarian view of rights, performance management processes are a basis for identifying a person's institutional duties, with objective setting the outline of duties, and appraisal the evaluation of whether the contractual duties have been met. This does not go far enough in protecting individual rights and ignores the right to participate in the design of the management process.

The use of performance systems and practices which reinforce modes of intrusive control and lead to passive or resistant roles for the individual were noted earlier. From an ethical viewpoint, the desirability of utilising systems which incorporate stakeholders in their design and not merely in the execution leads to a wider role for the individual as a 'creator' rather than 'victim' of performance management. The discussion of stakeholding approaches to HRM in Chapter 1 identifies the endemic pluralism in organisations. In this case, it may not be possible for all parties to agree on what performance measures would be appropriate and how such systems should operate. This requires some mechanisms to ensure that it is not just the power holders whose voice is heard and to ensure that where consensus exists it can be built upon, but where it does not, dissenters are not silenced. Again, procedural fairness is needed for there to be effective mediation between competing claims and information provision is needed to explain the reasons for those which cannot be addressed. If we view the organisation as a community of interests, more akin to Aristotelian views of the organisation, then we need to examine the basis for an ethics based on virtue and Solomon proposes six ingredients: community, excellence, role identity, holism, integrity and judgement. Through community, we find identity and meaning and this assumes a more bottom-up socially constituted, rather than top-down economics-driven, view. However, this is still predominantly unitarist in perspective and it is necessary to go further into the concept of organisations as communities of interests to address the pluralist concerns by utilising the stakeholder concept.

Goodpaster (1993) makes a critical distinction between stakeholder analysis and stakeholder synthesis: 'The strategic approach uses stakeholder analysis to pay attention to stakeholders as to factors that might affect economic interests', whereas a 'multi-fiduciary stakeholder synthesis' goes beyond an assessment of their effect on strategic implementation to incorporate their view in the strategic intent of the organisation. An approach using stakeholder synthesis to involve key stakeholders in the development of performance objectives would be one possible way of developing a more humanistic approach to performance management. The vignette that follows (Exhibit 11.1), drawn from Winstanley and Stuart-Smith (1996), is an example of this.

EXHIBIT 11.1

THE BRITISH SCHOOL OF OSTEOPATHY'S APPROACH TO DEVELOPING PERFORMANCE INDICATORS

In this example (reported in Winstanley and Stuart-Smith, 1996), a stakeholder approach was used to identify performance objectives at the British School of Osteopathy Clinic. The British School of Osteopathy (BSO) is both the oldest and largest osteopathic teaching establishment in the UK. The Clinic is a central part of the school's teaching of osteopathy and comprises 39 treatment rooms , with upwards of 700 patients treated per week, by students who are supervised by registered osteopaths.

Phase 1 required identifying the key stakeholders, who were the senior management team, the clinic tutors, clinic reception staff, students and patients.

Phase 2 utilised semi-structured interviews with senior stakeholders to agree strategic objectives of the organisation.

Phase 3 used the Delphi technique to identify consensus and conflict among employees. Statements made by interviewees in Phase 2 were listed, unattributed, on a sheet, which asked all respondents to score their agreement or disagreement with the statements on a scale of one to five. This was given to all the initial interviewees and to a wider sample of employees involved in the clinic.

Phase 4 utilised focus group interviews with clinic tutors and customers (students), who as well as filling in the questionnaires from Phase 3, explored issues of what they felt to be important about the clinic and what made it or would make it successful. Three groups of students were interviewed to establish the extent to which the school was satisfying their needs, where the school's objectives matched their own and where they saw improvements could be made.

Phase 5 used a patient questionnaire and depth interviews with customers (patients). The patient profile of the school was assessed and the patient questionnaire used to devise systematic data about their experience of the BSO. As well as data from 23 patients, 5 patients were selected to take part in unstructured depth interviews.

Phase 6 established performance measures. At each stage there was an inductive process whereby the performance measures each group felt to be appropriate were discussed. The findings were fed back to senior management to establish a consensus about the performance measures which should be adopted. This activity enabled the organisation to produce a number of key objectives, each-with them. of which had identifiable actions and measures associated with them.

Surprisingly it was found that there was much more consensus than had been expected and the process revealed considerable agreement about what the school ought to achieve, in terms of shared values and objectives. The project not only clarified which objectives the stakeholders felt the school should be pursuing and what priority they attached to them, but also the extent to which they believed it already achieved those objectives. This provided an invaluable guide to the management of the school. In addition, each stakeholder group identified their pre-eminent concerns, for which appropriate measurements were agreed.

Three humanistic and ethical principles are illustrated in the vignette. These are respect for the individual, mutual respect and procedural fairness and transparency of decision making. Stakeholders were given voice in the process and their views were incorporated in the organisational objectives and strategy. As a result, individuals were better informed, having access to more reliable information and improved communication and had a chance for that to be upward and not just downward. Although there was a plurality of interests, the approach tried to encapsulate a principal of mutual respect by establishing communities of interest and by reconciling conflicts which were a product of poor communication. Procedural fairness was seen to be one way of dealing with genuinely different interests and the openness of the approach helped this process. The performance management process became not a prison for capturing dissenters but a vehicle for expressing their views. However, using a stakeholding approach to performance management can only go so far in addressing the performance management paradox. Individuals may have greater say in the process and the process has more developmental potential, but the process still has as its focus the identification of performance measures, which inevitably have strong evaluative overtones.

This leaves the question of whether the performance management paradox can be eliminated. Labour process writers would suggest that this is an inherent contradiction in the employment relationship. It is here suggested that although it may remain, the current obsession of human resource management writers with evaluation and behaviourism does not serve us well. A reconsideration of the values of ethical humanism may spawn more ethical practice and at least tip the balance away from evaluation, towards a more developmental and accepting view of individuals. Given the changing structure of employment, with more and more work in professional and knowledge-based areas, where individuals are more likely to be motivated by autonomy, development and the opportunity to self-actualise, this seems sensible.

Note

An earlier version of this chapter was published as an article by Winstanley, D. and Stuart-Smith, K. 'Policing performance: the ethics of performance management', in a special issue of *Personnel Review* (1996) on 'Business Ethics and Human Resource Management', **25**(6): 66–84.

References

Barlow, G. (1989) 'Deficiencies and the Perpetuation of Power: latent functions in management appraisal' *Journal of Management Studies*, **26**(5): 499–517

Bevan, S. and Thompson, M. (1992a) 'An Overview of Policy and Practice' *Performance Management in the UK: An Analysis of the Issues*, London: IPM (now IPD)

Bevan, S. and Thompson, M. (1992b) 'Merit Pay, Performance Appraisal and Attitudes to Women's Work', Institute of Manpower Studies (now Institute of Employment Studies, Report 234, Brighton: IMS [IES])

Carter, N. (1989) 'Performance Indicators: backseat driving or hands off control?' *Policy and Politics*, **17**(2): 131–8

Dawson, S., Winstanley, D., Mole, V. and Sherval, J. (1995) *Managing in the NHS: A Study of Senior Executives*, London: HMSO, Chapter 5

European Foundation for Quality Management (1992) *Total Quality Management: European model for self-appraisal*, Brussels: EFQM

Fletcher, C. and Williams, R. (1992) 'Organisational Experience' *Performance Management in the UK: An Analysis of the Issues*, London: IPM (now IPD)

Foucault, M. (1977) *Discipline and Punish: The Birth of the Prison*, London: Allen Lane

Fowler, A. (1990) 'Performance Management: the MBO of the 90s' *Personnel Management*, **22**(7): 48–51

Fox, A. (1974) *Man Mismanagement*, London: Hutchinson

Friedman, A. (1977) 'Responsible Autonomy Versus Direct Control Over the Labour Process' *Capital and Class*, 1: 43–57

Goodpaster, K. (1993) 'Business Ethics and Stakeholder Analysis' in Winkler, E.R. and Coombs, J.R. *Applied Ethics: A Reader*, Cambridge, MA: Blackwell

Guest, D. and Peccei, R (1994) 'The Nature and Causes of Effective Human Resource Management' *British Journal of Industrial Relations*, **32**(2): 219–42

Huselid, M.A. (1995) 'The Impact of Human Resource Management Practices on Turnover, Productivity, and Corporate Financial Performance' *Academy of Management Journal*, **38**: 635–72

Kaplan, R.S. and Norton, D.P. (1992) 'The Balanced Scorecard: measures that drive performance' *Harvard Business Review*, January–February: 71–9

Kaplan, R.S. and Norton, D.P. (1993) 'Putting the Balanced Scorecard To Work' *Harvard Business Review*, September–October: 134–42

Kaplan, R.S. and Norton, D.P. (1996a) *The Balanced Scorecard*, Boston, MA: Harvard Business School Press

Kaplan, R.S. and Norton, D.P. (1996b) 'Strategic Learning and the Balanced Scorecard' *Strategy and Leadership,* September: 19–24

Kirschenbaum, H. and Henderson, V. (eds) (1990) *The Carl Rogers Reader,* London: Constable

Kohn, A. (1993) *Punished By Rewards,* Boston, MA: Mittlin

Legge, K. (1995) *Human Resource Management: Rhetorics and Realities,* Basingstoke: Macmillan

McGregor, D. (1960) *The Human Side of Enterprise,* New York: McGraw-Hill

Maslow, A. (1943) 'A Theory of Human Motivation' *Psychological Review,* **50**(4): 370–96

Maslow, A. (1987) *Motivation and Personality* (3rd edn), New York: Harper & Row

Murphy, K.R. (1991) 'Criterion Issues in Performance Appraisal Research' *Organization Behavior and Human Decision Processes,* **50**(2): 22

Noon, M. and Blyton, P. (1997) *The Realities of Work,* Basingstoke: Macmillan

Peccei, R. (1997) 'HRM and Organisational Effectiveness'. Paper given at King's College, London, 12 November

Rogers, C. (1959) 'A Theory of Therapy, Personality, and Interpersonal Relationships, as Developed in the Client-Centred Framework' in Koch, S. *Pyschology: A Study of a Science,* Volume 3, New York: McGraw-Hill, pp. 184–253

Rogers, C. (1967) *On Becoming a Person: A therapist's view of psychotherapy,* London: Constable

Skinner, B.F. (1953) *Science and Human Behavior,* New York: Macmillan

Thompson, M. (1993) 'Pay and Performance: the employee experience', Falmer, Sussex: Institute of Manpower Studies (now Institute of Employment Studies)

Townley, B. (1990) 'A Discriminating Approach To Appraisal' *Personnel Management,* **22**(12): 34–7

Townley, B. (1993) 'Performance Appraisal and the Emergence of Management' *Journal of Management Studies,* **30**(2): 221–38

Tyson, S. (1997) *The Practice of Human Resource Strategy,* London: Pitman

Wayne, S.J. and Liden, R.C. (1995) 'Effects of Impression Management on Performance Ratings: a longitudinal study' *The Academy of Management Journal,* **38**(1): 232–60

Williams, S. (1998) *Performance Management: Perspectives on Employee Performance,* London: International Thompson Business Press

Winstanley, D. (1991) 'Recruitment Strategies and Managerial Control of Technological Staff' in Smith, C., Knights, D. and Willmott, H. *White Collar Work,* Basingstoke: Macmillan, pp. 163–87

Winstanley, D. and Stuart-Smith, K. (1996) 'Policing Performance: the Ethics of Performance Management' *Personnel Review,* **25**(6): 66–84

Winstanley, D., Dawson, S., Mole, V. and Sherval, J. (1995) 'Under the Microscope: performance management and review for senior managers in the NHS'. Paper given at the BUIRA Annual Conference, Durham University, 30 June –2 July

CHAPTER 12

Employee participation and involvement

Tim Claydon

Introduction: contemporary approaches to employee participation

Recognition that the employment relationship is characterised by a structured antagonism (Edwards, 1995) needs to be the starting point for any discussion of the ethics of human resource management. The fact that management needs to be able to control and dispose of labour as if it were a commodified object while at the same time requiring the active co-operation of workers as willing subjects creates a contradiction at the heart of the employment relationship. While the interests of capital and labour cannot be expressed in terms of a simple conflict of interests, neither can they be seen as in unity. The contradictory needs of management set limits to trust and co-operation and at the same time allow employees to mobilise power resources in resistance to contested aspects of the managerial prerogative. The contradictory nature of capital's demands on labour are masked to varying degrees by labour's success in establishing rights and protections at work, by management policies aimed at retaining valued employees and generating a basis for enhanced co-operation in the workplace and by discursive devices that encourage employees to internalise the pressures that are imposed upon them by external agencies such as management. These discursive devices have always contained an implied ethic whether it be duty, loyalty, responsibility or self-interest. Any discussion of ethics in relation to employment issues has to recognise that ethical discourse does not offer an escape from or a solution to the contradictions of the employment relation, but may in fact reproduce them.

The aim of this chapter is to examine the ethical basis for the 'new' employee involvement and evaluate it in the light of ethical theory. Although a variety of types of employee involvement and participation are mentioned, the chapter focuses on employee empowerment programmes. It will be argued that egoism is the predominant ethic within business. Ethical theorists rightly regard ethical egoism as a flawed theory of ethics (de George, 1990), yet it is highly consistent with the competitive individualism that characterises western variants of capitalism, especially in Britain and the United States. The point is that while a variety of ethical glosses ranging from utilitarianism to virtue ethics has been put on contemporary approaches to employee involvement and participation, the underlying ethic is in reality an increasingly individualistic form of ethical egoism. The other ethical stances that are incorporated into the new managerialist discourse of employee involvement can be seen as discursive attempts to mask the tensions and contradictions generated by individualistic egoism as the ethical basis for the management of the employment relationship.

Any discussion of employee participation is bedevilled by problems of definition. Some definitions include collective bargaining as a form of participation (Fox, 1985); others distinguish between the two (Marchington *et al.*, 1992). Similarly some writers have treated employee participation and industrial democracy as synonymous (Schuller, 1985); others have drawn a distinction between them (Elliott, 1978). The relative meanings of employee participation and employee involvement are also open to question since employee involvement may or may not extend to participation in decision making (Marchington *et al.*, 1992). The definitional complexities surrounding the concept are largely explained by its divergent roots in different paradigms such as quality of working life, human resource management, industrial relations, and labour process theory (Marchington *et al.*, 1992).

Since the early 1980s the practical focus of employee participation has shifted from the maintenance of organisational stability to the initiation and management of organisational change through employee commitment. At the same time, the assumption of common interests has increasingly provided the underlying ethos for new patterns of employee participation and involvement (Marchington *et al.*, 1992). The new forms favour the direct involvement of individual workers over indirect involvement through collective representation, such as via trade unions. They are management initiatives that owe little or nothing to pressure from employees or trade unions and they are not concerned with altering the structure of authority 'by giving employees a right to share in decision making with management' (ibid. p. 6). To some observers, particularly those in the labour process tradition, many of these initiatives are examples of 'pseudo-participation' – 'techniques used to persuade employees to accept decisions which have already been taken by management' and which are aimed at achieving the fuller exploitation of labour (Delbridge and Turnbull, 1992; Parker and Slaughter, 1988; Pateman, 1970 p. 70; Sewell and Wilkinson 1992).

Trade union pressure for employee participation however, has not been entirely absent. The 1990s have seen growing advocacy of union and management 'partnership'. Strongly supported by the TUC and the Involvement and Participation Association (IPA), partnership has been defined in terms of union acceptance of new working practices in return for employment security, fair financial rewards, investment in training and employee voice in company decision making (Coupar and Stevens, 1998). Effective employee voice is seen in terms of information provision and effective arrangements for consultation between management and employee representatives (Monks, 1998). The emphasis on employee voice in decision making differentiates the partnership concept from the more individualised approaches to participation and involvement of recent years. However, what it appears to share with them is an emphasis on 'working together towards a common, shared goal' and moving away from 'adversarial' industrial relations (Monks, 1998, p. 175).

The majority of management-led employee involvement initiatives have drawn selectively and pragmatically on a set of techniques that includes direct management communication with employees, employee training programmes intended to educate employees into greater awareness of the business, elements of discretion and autonomy at the level of the work task and some involvement in problem solving and production planning at the level of the task. These techniques have been linked to the discursive construction of the 'enterprise culture' and the 'culture of the customer' (Du Gay and Salaman, 1992; Heery, 1993). They have helped to promulgate a new and increasingly explicit set of moral obligations for employees; the duty to search for excellence and in so doing, to develop the 'project' that is the self. In turn this means accepting a greater degree of personal accountability and an increased share of the risks of employment (Du Gay, 1996).

Explaining the interest in ethics

The explicit use of ethical frameworks to evaluate new management initiatives in employment is a relatively recent development in Britain, as is the growth of interest in business ethics in general. We might ask why this is the case. One answer might be that the growing concern with the ethics of employee participation and involvement reflects a degree of unease over certain aspects of the changes that have been witnessed in recent years (Winstanley *et al.*, 1996a, 1996b). These include the long-term decline of trade union membership and influence; evidence of growing casualisation and low pay in certain sectors of the economy coupled with widely publicised salary increases for 'fat cat' bosses. There is also evidence of growing polarisation in the labour market between 'primary' and 'secondary' workers (Gregg and

Wadsworth, 1993). Against this backdrop, and in parallel with the growth of interest in commitment and in generating forms of employee involvement, complaints from workers about bullying managers, the unreasonable exercise of managerial prerogative, work intensification and work-related stress have become increasingly common. It seems plausible to argue therefore, that the growth of interest in ethical issues is rooted partly in concerns raised by the extension of managerial prerogative and the ease with which it may be abused.

From this perspective, ethical concerns relating to employee participation and involvement are based on an awareness of the inherently conflictual nature of the employment relationship. The weakening of collective organisations of labour is seen to have increased the likelihood of unfair exploitation and there is scepticism concerning the motives and outcomes of managerially led employee involvement initiatives. A number of ethical concerns relating to the contemporary forms of employee participation and involvement may be identified. Are managerial policies that seek to elicit individual commitment actually undermining collective organisation among employees and if so, what is the effect on workers' ability to exercise a degree of influence and control over their employment situation? Are the benefits from employee 'empowerment' such as enhanced autonomy and scope for self-development offset by the effects of work intensification, close performance monitoring and associated stress (Ojeifo and Winstanley, 1999; Sewell and Wilkinson, 1992)? What, if any, limits are there to what employers can properly demand of employees in terms of commitment? How ethical is the withdrawal of employers' commitment to provide structured training and career paths in the name of empowering employees to take responsibility for their own development (Herriot, 1998)? How does making a degree of employment security conditional on workers' acceptance of extended managerial control over effort levels and work organisation affect the basis for trust between management and workforce?

Ethical theory and employee participation: rights, duties, virtues or egos?

Deontological approaches, rights and duties

Employee participation at work has been advocated many times in various contexts since at least the turn of the century. Ojeifo and Winstanley (1999) have made a distinction in perspectives to employee participation and empowerment on the basis of those deontologists who argue it is good in itself, and those teleologists and consequentialists who see it as a form of enlightened self-interest, in that it brings greater efficiency, productivity and organisational well-being.

Those adopting a deontological approach to ethics argue that there are basic moral duties and rights that we have to observe, irrespective of the consequences of so doing. The deontological position is taken from Kantian philosophy. Kant argued that through the exercise of reason it was possible to identify moral principles that could and should be held by all. Such principles could be identified on the basis of whether they could be consistently universalised; that is, if adopted by all they would not lead to their own demise. Kant argued that this criterion, the categorical imperative, could be restated in terms of the principle that one should always treat others as ends and not means. MacIntyre (1985) interprets this as giving people reasons for following a particular course of action that they can then evaluate independently as opposed to using non-rational means of persuasion. It means treating another person:

> as a rational will, worthy of the same respect as is due to myself, for in offering him reasons I offer him an impersonal consideration for him to evaluate... By contrast an attempt at non-rational persuasion embodies an attempt to make the agent a mere instrument of my will, without any regard for his rationality. (MacIntyre, 1985, p. 46)

In addition to the general moral obligations that each has to all, there are also 'special obligations'. These are 'special' in the sense that they are incurred when entering into certain relationships (such as marriage), taking certain actions (such as making promises) or taking on certain roles (such as manager or trade union representative) and are specific to those relationships, actions and roles (de George, 1990). However, special obligations are based on the same categorical imperative as general moral duties; to treat others as ends rather than as means.

How are we to characterise the ethics of the 'new employee involvement'? There is much in the language and rhetoric of 'excellence' and 'empowerment' that is suggestive of a deontological ethic. This can be expressed as the duty of organisations to recognise the needs of employees for and the right to self-development and self-actualisation through involvement and participation at work (Legge, 1996; Maslow, 1954). However, it is increasingly the case that self-development is being represented as a responsibility of the employee if they are to maintain their employability as organisations restructure their operations and re-organise their workforces. While this concept of involvement can be presented with a deontological gloss, it is apparent that much of its force stems from the threat of job loss. Employees, in being required to demonstrate their employability through their involvement and commitment at work, are being treated as means rather than ends, even in those cases where this is expressed in relatively enlightened and supportive terms by management.

The difficulty of applying a deontologically based ethic to business relationships has been well rehearsed (Collier, 1995; de George, 1990; McCracken *et al.*, 1998). What does one do when duties and rights conflict with each other? To see the real difficulties here it is worth turning to stakeholding and duty of care approaches.

Stakeholding and duty of care approaches

'Stakeholder' and 'duty of care' approaches to ethics in employment also have deontological roots to their claim that employing organisations have 'special obligations' to employees which they must honour if they are to be regarded as behaving ethically (Legge, 1996; Winstanley, Woodall and Heery, 1996a). Such obligations would normally be seen as including provision for various employee communication and 'voice' mechanisms (Legge, 1998). However, these approaches tend to be relatively weak on the issue of power, downplay the importance of conflict in employment and assume a basic consensus of values and goals within organisations.

For example, if we adopt a stakeholder approach to organisational relationships, what are the limits to the special obligations owed by the organisation to employees as stakeholders? How are their claims upon the organisation to be ranked against those of other stakeholders? These problems are compounded by the fact that business relationships are typically seen as means–ends relationships; individuals are valued, not for themselves, but for how well they conform to externally determined performance standards; they are valued as means rather than ends. Decision making is dominated by the more powerful within organisations.

Nevertheless, the case for employee participation has often been made in deontological terms that recognise the issues of power and conflict. To assert the *right* of workers to information, consultation or negotiation on matters affecting their employment is to imply that, in order for workers to be treated as ends rather than simply as means, employers and management have a special obligation to involve employees in decision making. This was articulated by the Trades Union Congress in its evidence to the Donovan Commission in 1967 when it stated: 'If all decisions are made unilaterally by the employer there can be no basis of mutual respect' (Trades Union Congress, 1967, para 106). Related arguments in favour of participation appeal to the need to extend democratic rights which reflect 'fundamental human values which are commonly held and officially sanctioned in most industrial countries' (Poole, 1986, p. 3). Here there is recognition of inequalities of power in the employment relationship and an assertion that in the interests of justice as fairness (Rawls, 1971), employees or their representatives have to be able to exercise some control over decisions that affect their lives. Deontologically based appeals for ethical behaviour from employers and managers demand unrealistic degrees of altruism from the powerful unless they are accompanied by countervailing power from trade unions and/or the state.

Utilitarianism, consequentialism and ethical egoism

Consequentialist ethical theories take *outcomes* as the criteria for judging whether an action or a maxim is ethical. Utilitarianism, following Bentham and Mill, holds that the main ethical principle should be the achievement of the greatest good for the greatest number. Contrary to Kantian ethics, the utilitarian principle permits the use of people as ends if this increases the total sum of human happiness. Employee participation has frequently been justified in utilitarian terms.

A utilitarian case has been made for employee participation on the grounds that it mitigates the undesirable social consequences arising from the concentration of decision-making power into a few hands (Poole, 1986). This recognises inequalities of power and the potential for conflicts of interest between social groups and implies that rights to participation by employees may have to be imposed upon otherwise unwilling employers, for example through legislation. A rather different line of utilitarian reasoning is that employee participation generates better employee relations, increased job satisfaction, higher productivity and hence better economic performance and enhanced prosperity. Here the emphasis is on shared rather than conflicting interests.

Another consequentialist theory of ethics is ethical egoism. Ethical egoism is a theory of enlightened self-interest that judges the worth of actions on the basis of whether they are in the long-term interests of the individual. The use of others as ends is justified if it furthers one's own *long-term* interests. Thus seeking short-term gains through dishonest and cynical behaviour towards others is unethical because it may harm one's long-term interests, for example through loss of reputation. Ethical egoism therefore 'enjoins prudence as well as self-seeking on individuals' (Claydon and Doyle, 1996, p. 15). Ethical egoism can be applied to organisations; as group egoism, it demands conformity to organisational requirements on the grounds that individuals' interests are best served by serving those of the organisation (Green, 1994).

From the ethical egoist standpoint, employee participation is seen as a way of increasing the commitment of employees to the employer and drawing on the expertise of employees to enhance productive efficiency. This is also in the long-term interests of employees since they benefit from organisational success in terms of employment security and rewards. Again, there is an assumption of a coincidence of interests between managers and the managed.

The utilitarian case for the new involvement would be that it raises overall productivity, economic performance and prosperity. However, this argument takes a narrow view of 'utility'. It confines the concept largely to income levels and discounts the costs that might be associated with new forms of involvement such as work intensification and the heightened sense of insecurity and guilt which frequently results from the transfer of risk and pressures to supply increased effort (Casey, 1995). Moreover, this line of ethical reasoning is not at the forefront of the contemporary managerialist discourse of involvement, although it underlies statements by government and trade unions in favour of 'partnership'. This may be because managers realise that an appeal to 'the greatest good of the greatest number' is not necessarily one that coheres well with their attempts to develop more individualised cultures which privilege membership of the organisation over that of broader social categories such as occupation or class.

This rhetoric of individualism is manifest in the contemporary emphasis on enterprise culture and the search for 'excellence' that encourages us to see our own lives as 'enterprises of self' in which we 'consume' our jobs as part of the project of self-development (Du Gay, 1996). In 'empowering' employees by giving them increased authority and responsibility, the new involvement provides an opportunity for employees to develop the project of their own lives.

Virtue ethics

Virtue ethics has its origins in Aristotelean philosophy. As expounded by MacIntyre (1985) virtue ethics is concerned, not with establishing moral rules for judging particular actions, but with the question of what is a good life. Virtues are those dispositions in our character that enable us to live a good life. Virtue is exercised in the search for excellence in 'practices' that result in 'goods internal to that form of activity', *viz* the extension of 'human powers to achieve excellence and human conception of the ends and goods involved' in the good life. The good life, therefore, 'is the life spent in seeking the good life for man and the virtues necessary for the seeking are those which will enable us to understand what more and what else the good life for man is' (MacIntyre, 1985, pp. 187, 219).

Contrary to the spirit of liberal individualism however, individuals are not free 'to pursue their own self-chosen conception of the good life'. In demonstrating virtue individuals are expressing and affirming their identity as members of a particular community and as bearers of its history and tradition and the common view of what the search for the good life is. However, this should not be understood in terms of an irrational attachment to the past, or as an acceptance of 'the moral limitations of the particularity of those forms of community', but as a continuity of discourse and debate concerning the practice of the 'good' (MacIntyre, 1985, pp. 221–2).

A number of recent writings have attempted to apply virtue ethics to modern organisational life. These have sought to discover virtue in the concept of business 'excellence' (McCracken *et al.*, 1998; Solomon, 1992). Collier (1995) has referred to the concept of excellence in her attempt to outline the characteristics of the 'virtuous organisation' in quasi-Aristotelian terms, asserting that:

> Companies with employment policies which attempt to add value to employee skills, which encourage employees to take initiatives, which take consultation seriously, are exercising virtue... The essence of the practice of management then becomes the shaping of a 'culture' in which people feel it possible to find meaning and fulfilment in excellence as defined in performance terms. This in turn will involve not just the management of diversity, but the management of dilemmas between competing and conflicting values. (Collier, 1995, p. 147)

Similarly, Karen Legge has interpreted virtue ethics in terms of providing scope for individual 'self-actualisation' through work (Legge, 1996 p. 35).

It may be, however, that the appropriation of virtue ethics by management theorists is misleading. There is a rather facile elision of business excellence, individual virtue and social good which begs a number of theoretical and empirical questions. MacIntyre, for example, argues forcefully that virtue cannot be exercised in the context of an individualistic, acquisitive culture in which 'the concept of a practice with goods internal to itself... is... removed to the margins of our lives' (MacIntyre, 1985 p. 227). Modern bureaucratic management is, in the view of MacIntyre, largely concerned with 'the manipulation of human beings into compliant patterns of behaviour' (MacIntyre, 1985 p. 74).

Concerns have been raised over managers' attempts to establish high-involvement, high-performance organisational cultures centred discursively on the concepts of 'enterprise', 'excellence' and 'the customer'. However, the promoters of these cultures have put their own ethical gloss upon their advocacy. For example, a central line of argument within the increasingly dominant discourse of 'enterprise' is that employees have in the past become too 'dependent' on employers providing stable, patterned careers and absolving them from personal responsibility for their own self-development. Consequently employees have been urged to become more self-reliant and enterprising and to take more responsibility for their own development to ensure their continued employability (Holbeche, 1995; Kanter, 1990). Moreover, this is increasingly presented, not as a painful necessity but as a life-affirming opportunity. This has become an increasingly central feature of the contemporary rhetoric of employee involvement and empowerment. As Du Gay has stated, 'these programmes of organisational reform characterise employment not as a painful obligation imposed on individuals, nor as an activity undertaken to meet instrumental needs, but rather as a means to self-responsibility and hence self-optimisation' (Du Gay, 1996 p. 182). They represent work as providing employees with the opportunity to contribute, 'not only to the success of the company for which they work, *but also to the enterprise of their own lives*' (ibid., p. 60, emphasis in original). According to Du Gay '(t)his autonomisation and responsibilization makes paid work (no matter how objectively alienated, de-skilled or degraded it may appear to social scientists) an essential element in the path to individual virtue and self-fulfilment' (ibid., p. 182). This 'discourse of enterprise' clearly operates from a unitarist perspective based on an assertion that the employment relationship is founded on common interests.

Du Gay argues that it is of little use to attempt to submit the managerial discourse of enterprise to logical critique by exposing its contradictions since 'discourse/ideology doesn't work in a logical intellectual fashion' (ibid., p. 67). However, it is surely possible to examine critically the implicit ethic that provides this particular discourse with its moral authority and from this to mount an ethically based critique of the discourse itself.

The notion of duty to oneself that is contained within the concept of the self as a project to be optimised and fulfilled might plausibly be seen as embodying the ethics of virtue. The 'end' of the self as one who has attained an understanding of what it is to live a 'good life' is achieved increasingly through the search for excellence in one's work, a search that both requires and develops the predisposition to search for excellence and to achieve the goods that are 'internal' to that practice, such as an increased awareness of one's own abilities and potential and how they can be used to develop one's own life. Organisations that encourage the exercise of virtue by providing employees with opportunities to participate in decision making and take responsibility for their actions are demonstrating virtue by establishing internal cultures that encourage the pursuit of excellence and the living of a 'good life' (Collier, 1995).

This ethical interpretation of employee involvement built upon the discourse of excellence is, however, problematic. It is by no means certain that ethical theorists would accept the validity of this appropriation of 'virtue' by management theorists. As shown already, MacIntyre (1985) argues that the concept of virtue is incompatible with the principle of acquisitive individualism. He also argues, as we have seen, that in a society that is governed by such a principle, there are few practices which have goods internal to themselves and these are not to be found in the world of modern business. Despite the growing preoccupation with the management of culture there is evidence that managers are still mainly concerned with instrumental outcomes and securing behavioural compliance rather than with the moral involvement that is central to the search for understanding virtue and the nature of the good life (Ogbonna, 1992).

As subjects, members of the virtuous community debate the purposes of the community itself and what constitutes the good life within and for it, yet within the enterprise the new employee involvement and the management of organisational culture keep employee voice within well-set limits. Employees are 'involved' in the 'mission' as defined by senior management and are 'empowered' to carry out tasks in service of the mission, yet to question the mission is to risk partial or total exclusion from the 'enterprise community' (see Casey, 1995, pp. 122–3). It is usually the case that the main aim (and outcome) of new forms of work organisation and employee involvement is behavioural compliance with more demanding work standards (Ogbonna, 1992; Rees, 1998).

Another problem with proposing a relationship between involvement and virtue is that the effects of high-involvement, high-performance cultures on some groups of employees are arguably the opposite of those that are associated with the development and exercise of virtue. Casey (1995) describes the effects of high-involvement, empowered organisational culture on employees in a high-technology American corporation. These included 'juvenile sibling competitiveness', 'neurotic anxiety displacements and obsessive-compulsive behaviour' (Casey, 1995, pp. 158–9). To the extent that the new involvement succeeds in reconstituting the 'subject worker' as a devoted member of the enterprise community, it involves workers participating voluntarily in 'the processes of truncation of self, of delimited possibilities for psychic development and awareness and a social life delimited by production. These are the outcomes of the corporate colonisation of the self' (Casey, 1995, p. 149).

This is not to condemn all employee involvement practices merely as cynical attempts to manipulate and exploit employees. There is clear evidence from some recent studies that new forms of work organisation and more participative management styles have been perceived by some employees as improving their working lives and in some cases raising their self-confidence and self-esteem (Glover and Fitzgerald-Moore, 1998). Moreover, Casey points out that Haephestus Corporation workers perceived the new culture as 'credible, attractive, apparently social, and… desirable' and that employees 'derive a good enough meaningfulness from its busyness and routines' (Casey, 1995, p. 149). What is being argued here, however, is that this has nothing to do with virtue in its Aristotelean sense.

Ethical egoism? The ethics of contemporary employment participation

From the discussion so far it seems evident that the ethical theory that can be linked most directly to new approaches to employee involvement is ethical egoism. Employee involvement and participation are aimed at raising employee commitment and performance and rallying managers and managed employees in support for 'organisational' goals of restructuring, flexibility and quality improvement. The rhetoric of empowerment, excellence and enterprise provides the discursive dimension of such projects. Within this rhetoric the themes of employability and the self as project, with their 'tough love' overtones, are entirely consistent with ethical egoism. In serving the interests of the organisation, the individual also serves their own self-interest but can only maintain membership of the organisation by continually demonstrating their worth to it. It is in this way that the new employee involvement aims to elicit the engagement of employees with management goals and policies. Engagement is expressed in employees' acceptance of management's mission and values for the organisation, their participation in problem-solving groups and project teams, their eagerness to undergo training and development and to accept greater degrees of responsibility and accountability in their jobs. It is claimed to serve not only the organisation but also the employees themselves by enabling them to demonstrate their current worth to the organisation and enhance future labour market opportunities should it no longer be able to employ them.

Egoism therefore, is also represented as being the basis for employees' consent to such initiatives. Basic material self-interest encourages the search for a measure of employment security, higher earnings and future employment advantages. Individual egoism and narcissism, together with the feelings of insecurity that they generate (Sturdy, 1992), encourage us to demonstrate competence and raise our esteem in the eyes of co-workers and managers.

Ethical egoism may be expressed in ways that correspond to soft and hard HRM. The 'soft' expression of group egoism is paternalistic and protective of employees and is based on long-term, stable employment relationships and structured internal labour markets in return for consummate performance and willing co-operation with management. This form of group egoism, with its effect of masking the commodity status of labour and representing the employment relationship in terms of 'status' rather than 'contract', has been in retreat in recent years. It has been replaced by a harder, more demanding approach to employees that offers less job security and demands greater effort and responsibility. This may well have weakened the moral basis for the co-operation between workers and management that the new employee involvement seeks to generate and upon which it relies. Widespread downsizing and delayering may have had substantial negative effects on employees' organisational commitment, undermining the foundations of group egoism (Cappelli, 1995).

If this argument is correct it raises the possibility that the new discourse of employee involvement, with its emphasis on the responsibility of the individual to secure their own future, is a recognition that appeals to group egoism are less plausible than they used to be. The appeal to a more individualistic expression of ethical egoism is in tune with the sense of competition, striving and survival of the fittest that is bound up with the enterprise culture and the language of excellence.

This more individualistic appeal to ethical egoism, however, raises questions of its own. We might ask whether the contradictory nature of the employment relationship is not becoming more starkly revealed. Pressures on management to cut costs and redistribute costs from shareholders to employees have made the commodity status of labour more obvious in recent years. At the same time, however, the conditions of modern competition have led to an emphasis on 'quality' and the 'customer' that demands employee co-operation with management. Is an approach to employee involvement that is founded in ethical egoism of an increasingly individualistic type likely to be effective in managing this contradiction and is it one that should be supported? Ethical egoism is commonly rejected as an adequate theory of ethics because it provides no explanation for why an individual who can injure others in the pursuit of his or her self-interest without harm to himself or herself should not do so. Such a situation might be enjoyed by those who have the power to impose their will on others and evade or prevent retaliation. Similarly, if someone values short-term gains over long-term harm ethical egoism provides no argument why they should not pursue short-term gains even if this is injurious in the long run. The willingness of managers to discount the long-term costs of work intensification such as stress and 'burnout' to themselves and others may be matched by increased opportunism among employees.

These tensions may help to explain why, in recent managerialist discourse, including academic writings, a rather different ethical gloss has been put upon attempts to generate high-involvement, high-performance work cultures. Notions of duty, obligation and the pursuit of the 'good' through the practice of virtue can be seen as discursive devices aimed at maintaining and enhancing self-disciplined behaviour among employees. They are also therefore, attempts to deal with the basic weakness of the ethical egoist position and curb the tendency to opportunistic pursuit of immediate gains by workers at the expense of long-term costs. However, as long as ethical egoism remains as the underlying ethic of business organisation, there is the likelihood that while management may be assiduous in trying to minimise unethical opportunistic behaviour by workers, they will be less so with respect to their own actions.

The ethical egoism that underlies business practice and business relationships is qualified to an extent by legal enactments, institutional arrangements for expressing the interests of employees and other parties affected by the actions of organisations and also by the moral decisions of individual managers and employees in specific instances. To the extent that these generate more humanised work relations and help people to feel valued for their own sake, they must be welcomed. At the same time, we need to be aware and critical of aspects of the new employee involvement that represent work intensification and the transfer of risk to the employee as 'duties' from which employees have been absolved wrongly in the past, or as opportunities for the pursuit of 'virtue'.

Conclusion

The ethical contradictions contained within the contemporary discourse of employee involvement should occasion no surprise. They mirror the contradictory nature of the employment relationship, that is, the need of management to be able to treat labour as an objectified commodity but at the same time to call upon the active co-operation of workers as subjects. As already stated, being aware of this does not imply complete dismissal of initiatives that aim to secure employee co-operation with management where these can claim to be generating 'good' outcomes such as better employment conditions and security and opportunities for a greater degree of self-fulfilment through work. However, the ethical position favoured here is as follows. We cannot assume a unity of interests between employer and employee, manager and managed. However, imputing pre-existing 'interests' to managers and managed employees is also problematic (Knights, 1990) since interests are constituted discursively as well as materially and so are, to a degree, malleable. On this basis we would advocate the necessity of treating employees as far as possible as 'rational wills' (MacIntyre, 1985) and involving them in discussion, not only of how best to achieve organisational goals, but also the nature of those goals. However, given that the potential for conflict is inherent within the employment relationship, an ethically based appeal to management to treat workers as ends rather than as means in this way would be naive, however much such an appeal was dressed up in the language of 'stakeholding'. The conflictual element inherent in the employment relationship, together with the issues of distributive power that it generates, need to be recognised. This entails support for independent employee voice mechanisms and acceptance that co-operation between managers and managed can only and should only be negotiated, partial and qualified.

References

Cappelli, P. (1995) 'Rethinking Employment' *British Journal of Industrial Relations*, 33(4): 563–602

Casey, C. (1995) *Work, Self and Society After Industrialism*, London: Routledge

Claydon, T and Doyle, M. (1996) 'Trusting Me, Trusting You? The ethics of employee empowerment' *Personnel Review*, 25(6): 13–25

Collier, J. (1995) 'The Virtuous Organization' *Business Ethics. A European Review*, 4(3): 43–9

Coupar, W. and Stevens, B. (1998) 'Towards A Model of Industrial Partnership: beyond the "HRM versus industrial relations" argument' in Sparrow, P. and Marchington, M.

(eds) *Human Resource Management: The New Agenda*, London: Financial Times/Pitman Publishing, pp. 145–59

de George, R.T. (1990) *Business Ethics* (3rd edn), New York: Macmillan

Delbridge, R. and Turnbull, P. (1992) 'Human Resource Maximization: The management of labour under just-in-time manufacturing systems' in Blyton, P. and Turnbull P. (eds) *Reassessing Human Resource Management*, London: Sage, pp. 56–73

Du Gay, P. (1996) *Consumption and Identity at Work*, London: Sage

Du Gay, P. and Salaman, G. (1992) 'The Cult[ure] of the Customer' *Journal of Management Studies*, **29**(5): 615–33

Edwards, P. (1995) 'The Employment Relationship' in Edwards, P. (ed.) *Industrial Relations: Theory and Practice in Britain*, Oxford: Blackwell, pp. 3–26

Elliott, J. (1978) *Conflict or Cooperation? The Growth of Industrial Democracy*, London: Kogan Page

Fox, A. (1985) *History and Heritage*, London: George Allen & Unwin

Glover, L. and Fitzgerald-Moore, D. (1998) 'Total Quality Management: Shop floor perspectives' in Mabey, C., Skinner, D. and Clark, T. (eds) *Experiencing Human Resource Management*, London: Sage, pp. 54–72

Green, R.M. (1994) *The Ethical Manager: A New Method for Business Ethics*, London: Macmillan

Gregg, P. and Wadsworth, J. (1993) 'A Short History of Labour Turnover, Job Tenure, and Job Security, 1975–93' *Oxford Review of Economic Policy*, **11**(1): 73–90

Heery, E. (1993) 'Industrial Relations and the Customer' *Industrial Relations Journal*, **24**(4): 284–95

Herriot, P. (1998) 'The Role of the HR Function in Building a New Proposition for Staff', in Sparrow, P. and Marchington, M. (eds) *Human Resource Management: The New Agenda*, London: *Financial Times*/Pitman, pp. 106–16

Holbeche, L. (1995) 'Peering into the Future of Careers' *People Management*, **1**(11): 26–31

Kanter, R.M. (1990) *When Giants Learn to Dance*, London: Unwin Hyman

Knights, D. (1990) 'Subjectivity, Power and the Labour Process' in Knights, D. and Willmott, H. (eds), *Labour Process Theory*, Basingstoke: Macmillan, pp. 297–335

Legge, K. (1996) 'Morality Bound' *People Management*, **2**(25): 34–6

Legge, K. (1998) 'The Morality of HRM', in Mabey, C., Skinner, D. and Clark, T. (eds) *Experiencing Human Resource Management*, London: Sage, pp. 14–30

MacIntyre, A. (1985) *After Virtue. An Essay in Moral Theory*, (2nd edn), London: Duckworth

Marchington, M., Goodman, J.,Wilkinson, A. and Ackers, P. (1992*) New Developments in Employee Involvement*, London: Employment Department

Maslow, A.H. (1954) *Motivation and Human Personality*, New York: Harper & Row

McCracken, J., Martin, W. and Shaw, B. (1998) 'Virtue Ethics and the Parable of the Sadhu' *Journal of Business Ethics*, **17**: 25–38

Monks, J. (1998) 'Trade Unions, Enterprise, and the Future' in Sparrow, P. and Marchington, M. (eds) *Human Resource Management: The New Agenda*, London: Financial Times/Pitman, Chapter 11, pp. 171–9

Ogbonna, E. (1992) 'Organizational Culture and Human Resource Management: Dilemmas and Contradictions' in Blyton, P. and Turnbull P. (eds) *Reassessing Human Resource Management*, London: Sage, pp. 74–96

Ojeifo, E. and Winstanley, D. (1999) 'Negotiated Reality: The meaning of empowerment' in Quinn, J. and Davies, P. (eds) *Ethics and Empowerment*, Basingstoke: Macmillan

Parker, M. and Slaughter, J. (1988) *Choosing Sides: Unions and The Team Concept*, Boston, MA: South End Press

Pateman, C. (1970) *Participation and Democratic Theory*, Cambridge: Cambridge University Press

Poole, M. (1986) *Towards a New Industrial Democracy. Workers' Participation in Industry*, London: Routledge & Kegan Paul

Rawls, J. (1971) *A Theory of Justice*, Oxford: Oxford University Press

Rees, C. (1998) 'Empowerment Through Quality Management: Employee accounts from inside a bank, a hotel and two factories' in Mabey, C. Skinner, D. and Clark, T. (eds) *Experiencing Human Resource Management*, London: Sage, pp. 33–53

Schuller, T. (1985) *Democracy at Work*, Oxford: Oxford University Press

Sewell, G. and Wilkinson, B. (1992) 'Empowerment or Emasculation? Shopfloor surveillance in a total quality organization' in Blyton, P. and Turnbull, P. (eds) *Reassessing Human Resource Management*, London: Sage, pp. 97–115

Solomon, R.C. (1992) *Ethics and Excellence. Cooperation and Integrity in Business*, New York: Oxford University Press

Sturdy, A. (1992) 'Clerical consent: 'shifting' work in the insurance office' in Sturdy, A., Knights, D. and Willmott, H. (eds) *Skill and Consent. Contemporary Studies in the Labour Process*, London: Routledge

Trades Union Congress (1967) *Trade Unionism*, (2nd edn), London: Trades Union Congress

Winstanley, D., Woodall, J. and Heery, E. (1996a) 'Business Ethics and Human Resource Management: themes and issues' *Personnel Review*, 25(6): 5–12

Winstanley, D., Woodall, J. and Heery, E. (1996b) 'The agenda for ethics in human resource management' *Business Ethics. A European Review*, 5(4): 187–94

PART III

ETHICAL INTERVENTIONS IN PRACTICE

CHAPTER 13

Conducting a social audit: lessons from The Body Shop experience

Maria Sillanpää and Charles Jackson

Introduction

There is some evidence that companies which are run with a view to the long-term interests of their key stakeholders are more likely to prosper than those which take a short-term, 'shareholder first' approach (Centre for Tomorrow's Company, 1998; Wheeler and Sillanpää, 1997). For example, Collins and Porras (1995) in tracking the commercial performance and organisational resilience of 18 US companies with 50–100-year successful track records found that not only did these companies invest heavily in employee training, knowledge transfer and alignment of organisational values, but they also outperformed the stock market by an average of 15 times. Similarly, Kotter and Heskett (1992) found that over an 11-year period, large established US companies which gave equal priority to employees, customers and share-holders delivered sales growth of four times and employment growth of eight times that of 'shareholder first' companies. Put simply, companies need to listen, to process and to respond constructively to the values and needs of their stakeholders, most especially their employees, customers and investors. Failure to do this will reduce long-term commercial viability and increase the risk of corporate demise.

While there is considerable interest in stakeholding as a management philosophy, there is less certainty about how best to operationalise it in practice. The debate has philosophical as well as practical aspects. How do we judge whether a company is managed in a stakeholder inclusive way? Can we develop a methodology that is sufficiently transparent but also robust enough to convince sceptics? What factors are crucial to the ethical integrity of such a methodology? In this chapter we set out the approach developed at The Body Shop to measure its performance as a stakeholder corporation (The Body Shop, 1996a). This includes the development of an audit methodology that allows the company to involve stakeholders in the design process and then to collect information about the company's performance as it affects different stakeholder groups. It also includes a process of external verification, so that the end result is verified in a similar way to a set of financial accounts.

The Body Shop had, by 1998, conducted two social audits and published the results in its *Values Reports* (The Body Shop 1996b; 1998). While such documents present findings for external audiences and provide a benchmark against which future performance can be judged, the results also have to be used within the organisation to shape its policies and practices. A key stakeholder group in any organisation is its employees. Using findings from both social audits, we illustrate the challenge that conducting a social audit implies for management and HR practitioners in particular. The Body Shop experience shows that publishing a social statement (a verified report on the outcomes of a social audit process distributed to each stakeholder group) is only the start of a process of involvement which may have risks as well as benefits. It can raise expectations that are hard to meet and is not some quick fix that will miraculously raise morale or improve productivity. In practice this means that what happens after the publication of a social statement is equally, if not more, important, than the process leading to the statement. The processes by which improvement targets are agreed and implemented need to be given just as much attention as the social audit process itself. Only in such circumstances will an organisation honestly be able to call itself a stakeholder corporation.

Two basic principles of stakeholder inclusion

If stakeholder inclusion is to become the norm in business, how may successful stakeholder-inclusive experience be captured and systematised? Wheeler and Sillanpää (1997) suggest that two basic principles of stakeholder inclusion are common to many successful corporations in North America, Europe and Japan (for example, IBM, Hewlett-Packard, Motorola, S C Johnson, BT, Daimler-Benz, Matsushita and Sony). These principles are alignment of values and establishing a dialogue based on empowerment. At their heart is a commitment to listen and respond to stakeholder needs and beliefs.

These principles are linked to one another and have been successfully applied over many years but not necessarily in the overt way as proposed by the emerging practice of social auditing.

Alignment of values

Alignment of values is a key theme of quality management. The literature on quality management is littered with examples of companies which have rescued themselves from mediocrity by establishing a reputation for superior product quality (see for example, Oakland, 1996). Similarly value chain alignment has been achieved in the retail sector where exceptional service is twinned with guarantees on product quality. Wal-Mart (US) and Tesco (UK) are exemplars of this approach, outperforming companies which have concentrated more traditionally on product value for money.

'Value' as perceived by customers or other stakeholders may go well beyond what is conventionally understood by the physical attributes of products. Other, less tangible values can be offered for stakeholders to unite around. For the Co-operative Bank in the UK and Levi Strauss social responsibility forms part of the brand equation for customers. For The Body Shop and Ben & Jerry's Homemade, public political campaigns on environment, animal welfare and human rights provide a unifying force. For purveyors of branded drinks the 'value' may be as much to do with lifestyle and personal image as flavour. In summary, aligning values requires two active commitments:

  i. a commitment to share perspectives via active dialogue
 ii. a willingness to allow collective values to develop and evolve, again via dialogue. Values which are articulated top-down are by definition non-inclusive and will inevitably become ossified.

Dialogue-based empowered relationships

In recent years there has been a deluge of management literature explaining how to deal with the accelerating pace of change in business (for example Cannon, 1996; Peters, 1992; White *et al.*, 1996). The rapidly globalising economy only adds to the complexity and uncertainty (for example, Bryan and Farrell, 1996). One way to make sense of chaos is to base decisions on the maximum amount of available information. The only sure way to secure information is to actively request it. In the case of relationships with key stakeholders this means regular conversations, focus groups and surveys. The firm must also organise itself to be receptive to inputs of opinion especially from its own employees. Table 13.1 sets out some trends in organisational behaviour which are being driven largely by macro-economic and technological factors. The best companies are embracing both these forces and actively nurture organisational behaviours needed to harness them. Nearly all are predicated on inclusive, dialogue-based interactions between the firm, its managers and its employees.

TABLE 13.1   Trends observed

Employer-directed companies	Usual trend	Employee-inclusive companies
Organisational goals emerge from leadership	=>	Organisational goals are articulated through language of shared values and vision
Authority derives from position	=>	Authority derives from behaviour and intellect
Influence increases with seniority	=>	Influence increases with knowledge
Organisational structure dictates work relationships	=>	Organisational structure liberates and encourages team working
Work systems linear and technical	=>	Work systems cyclical and organic
Style formal or uniform	=>	Style informal or diverse
Responsibility devolved vertically	=>	Responsibility shared laterally
Corporate objectives agreed by leadership and cascaded	=>	Corporate, team and individual objectives aligned through dialogue

(Wheeler and Sillanpää, 1997)

As a result of a study of 580 UK companies, the Industrial Society concluded:

> It is becoming a competitive disadvantage not to be moving significantly towards empowerment, although there will always be organisations that manage to survive with the 'command and control' approach. But you can only empower people when everyone shares a very strong vision of what the organisation needs to be like. That usually means you have to be explicit about the organisation's values. (Industrial Society, 1995).

A dialogue-driven approach is needed to nurture empowered relationships and the good news is that this can be systematised using relatively simple techniques of information capture and communication.

Social audit – a practical tool for stakeholder inclusion

The first attempts at social auditing in the 1960s were largely concerned with expanding conventional financial reporting to include information on 'corporate social expenditure' in response to intensifying criticism by the general public. By the late 1970s the majority of Fortune 500 companies in the US included a page or two in their annual reports to inform readers of their 'social expenditure' or to provide information on equal opportunities or community relations, for example. In the 1980s a second type of social auditing developed essentially driven by the consumer movement and the ethical investment community who were keen to build up and publish profiles of corporate social performance. Although not referred to as social audits, that was very much what they were trying to do, to measure and communicate how companies rated against certain sets of ethical criteria. A number of these investigations became instant bestsellers in the late 1980s and early 1990s, for instance, *Shopping For A Better World* (Hollister *et al.*, 1994) and *The 100 Best Companies to Work for in America* (Levering and Moskowitz, 1993).

The 1990s have seen the beginning of a third wave in social auditing driven by companies which have adopted an active ethical stance. Social auditing is no longer a process imposed from the outside; it is driven by the organisation itself. In 1991, Traidcraft Plc, a UK-based fair trading organisation, joined forces with the not-for-profit research organisation, the New Economics Foundation (NEF), to develop an internally driven, systematic approach to social auditing based on a mix of participative research and organisational development techniques. This initiative was a pioneering effort to advance more rigorous approaches to social auditing based on the 'stakeholder approach'. The early 1990s also saw the emergence of the 'ethical accounting' approach adopted by Sbn Bank, a regional Danish bank. A number of Scandinavian organisations, ranging from small companies to hospitals and schools, have now adopted this method. Like the method developed by NEF and Traidcraft, ethical accounting involves a consultation process with the organisation's key stakeholders. Beyond this, the approach encourages stakeholders to propose practical changes to the organisation's operational practices, for example, customer services or product development. Unlike the NEF/Traidcraft approach, however, the published statement is not externally verified. Another example is the approach adopted by the American ice-cream manufacturer, Ben & Jerry's Homemade. The main feature of Ben & Jerry's

TABLE 13.2   Key principles of social audit

Inclusivity
The principle of inclusivity means that any auditing process must reflect the views of all stakeholders, not only those who have historically had the most influence over the evolution of the organisation's formal mission. What this means is that the assessment cannot be based on a single set of values or objectives.

Comparability
Social audit should offer a means whereby the organisation can compare its own performance over time, make comparisons with other organisations engaged in similar work, and relate their performance to appropriate norms drawn from external benchmarks, statutory regulations or non-statutory norms.

Completeness
The principle of completeness means that no area of the company's activities can be deliberately and systematically excluded from the assessment The principle of no 'malicious exclusion' is the key criterion within any one audit cycle.

Regular and evolutionary
Social audit should be regular and its scope evolutionary in that all significant aspects of the organisation's 'social footprint' are addressed over time. The approach must demonstrate 'learning' and continual change.

Management policies and systems – embeddedness
It is essential for any systematic process that the organisation develops clear policies covering each accounting area and systems and procedures that allow the accounting process to be regularised and the organisation's awareness and operationalisation of policies to be assessed through an audit.

Disclosure
For social audit to have the most constructive effect, the results of the process need to be disclosed to the stakeholders who have been implicated by the process. Internal and external disclosure adds value to the process by ensuring that it can be used as a means to contribute to organisational learning and dialogue culture as well as in strengthening the company's public legitimacy via increased transparency and accountability.

External verification
Social accounts, especially if aimed at increased organisational legitimacy, should be verified by an independent agent who has no vested interests in the results.

Continuous improvement
The ultimate aim of social auditing must be to facilitate progress rather than merely reflect past performance. That is, any relevant system must be able to identify whether the organisation's performance has improved over time in relation to its articulated values, mission and targets set by the organisation as well as those established through broader norms.

(Adapted from Zadek, Pruzan and Evans, 1997)

approach was to invite a high-profile advocate of corporate social responsibility to spend time each year exploring any aspect of the company's activities that he or she might deem important. The idea being that the external commentator has free access to the company's internal records and a freedom to consult the company's stakeholders. Based on this process the person then writes a personal evaluation or 'social statement'.

As Zadek *et al.* (1997) point out, a comparison of the various emerging approaches is not straightforward, since the circumstances of different processes are often critical in determining the design. However, they suggest that there are clear signs of a convergence of standards and emergence of consensus about what constitutes good practice. In particular, the establishment of the Institute of Social and Ethical Accountability in 1996 has encouraged the emergence of a professional approach with agreed standards not only in the method, but also in the quality of practice. The key principles of social auditing advocated by the Institute are shown in Table 13.2 (Zadek *et al.*, 1997). These have been adopted by The Body Shop for the development of its methodology and process of implementation.

The Body Shop social audit methodology

The development of the social audit methodology used by The Body Shop commenced in 1993 and was formalised for the first audit cycle of 1994/95. The methodology was developed collaboratively with NEF with the aim of synthesising aspects of environmental auditing, quality management and the existing tradition of academic and practical work in social auditing. The framework shown in Figure 13.1 outlines the ten key components of the ongoing audit cycle as they are implemented by the company. These are now described in more detail.

Commitment and leadership

The Body Shop committed itself to a formal social audit process following publication of Anita Roddick's autobiography in 1991 in which she wrote:

> I would love it if every shareholder of every company wrote a letter every time they received a company's annual report and accounts. I would like them to say something like, 'OK that's fine, very good. But where are the details of our environmental audit? Where are the details of your accounting to the community? Where is your social audit?' (Roddick, 1991)

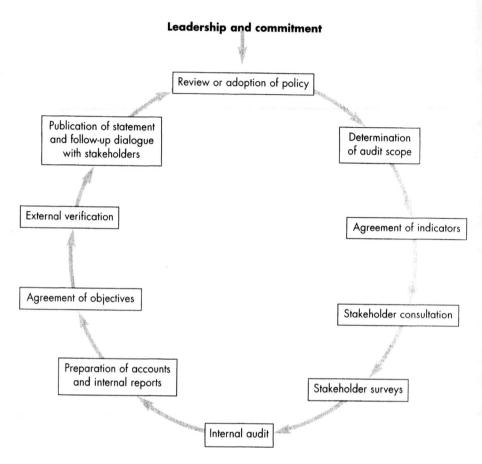

FIGURE 13.1   Framework for social auditing at The Body Shop
(The Body Shop, 1996a)

Without the commitment of the founders and the development of an 'accountability ethos' within The Body Shop in the early 1990s, the company would not have been in a position to publish a statement of its social performance in 1996. As with environmental auditing, clear leadership is probably the most important single factor in driving a process of social auditing to a successful conclusion.

Policy review

In every company a variety of policies prescribe the organisation's intentions with respect to its stakeholders. These range from occupational safety and health (usually very well documented) to customer service (frequently expressed more through a company's culture than through any formalised system). There may be dividend policies for shareholders, payment terms for suppliers, codes of ethics for company representatives working overseas, and so on. Clear policies help provide a framework for assessing the quality of a company's relationships with its stakeholders. Before any assessment or audit of social relationships, a company should be aware of its explicit and implicit intentions with respect to each stakeholder group.

For The Body Shop's first social audit, the main policies against which performance was assessed were the company's Mission Statement and Trading Charter. More specific policies existed, for instance, for health and safety, human resources and fair trade.

Determination of audit scope

Because parallel systems exist at The Body Shop for auditing with respect to animal protection and the environment, the subject area of the social audit was restricted to people: human stakeholders who may affect or be affected by The Body Shop. As the number of individual stakeholder groups could theoretically be quite large, a decision had to be taken as to which groups should be included in the first audit cycle. The Body Shop took the view that in the first cycle, the net should be cast as wide and as deep as possible. But inevitably some groups and sub-groups could not be reached for practical reasons.

An important factor in scoping a social audit is the question of geography. For instance, where a company has wholly or majority-owned operations in different countries, a decision has to be taken as to whether one or all countries are to be covered in each cycle. For The Body Shop this meant choosing not to include US stakeholders in any great depth in the first year but to concentrate mostly on UK-based groups.

The stakeholder groups for The Body Shop's first social audit included:

- Staff directly employed by The Body Shop International
- International head franchisees
- UK and US local franchisees
- UK and US customers
- Suppliers

- Community trade suppliers shareholders
- Local community (Littlehampton)
- UK non-governmental organisations
- Foundation applicants.

Agreement of performance indicators

There are three types of performance measurement in The Body Shop's approach to social auditing.

1. Performance against standards (performance indicators)

These reflect national and international best practice for activities that relate to the organisation's social performance. Quantitative and qualitative data are submitted by relevant departments and validated by the audit and verification processes. Departments are also encouraged to set internal targets relating to individual standards, and to collate information on external benchmarks. Therefore, the ideal set of reported information relating to individual standards should evolve towards the format shown in Table 13.3.

TABLE 13.3   Ideal format for reporting performance indicators

Standard	Performance indicator	Internal benchmark/ target	External benchmark
For example employee turnover	Based on ongoing internal monitoring; data and monitoring process subject to internal audit and verification	Based on target setting by relevant department or company	Based on publicly available data (for example industry performance)

Examples of employee-related performance indicators reported by The Body Shop in its first two *Values Reports* are provided in Table 13.4.

TABLE 13.4 Examples of quantitative employee-related performance indicators in *Values Report* 1995 and 1997

Performance indicators

- Equal opportunities monitoring data (for example gender, age, ethnicity and disability-breakdown by salary banding)
- Employee stability rate
- Identification of exit reasons

- Overall pay increase

- Pay ratio between lowest and highest 10 per cent
- Pension scheme breakdown (for example company contributions, membership)
- Executive benefits

- Appraisal completion
- Number of company-sponsored professional qualifications gained
- Number of employee welfare assistance clients
- Grievances and disciplinaries
- Accident incident rates

- Work station assessments

- Average employee turnover

- Redundancies and terminations
- Summary of job bands and salary levels
- Pay differential between median pay in lowest salary band (Band 1) and median pay in highest salary band (Band 8)
- Pay ratio to market

- Flexible benefits (take-up levels)

- Examples of pay levels with comparisons to market data
- Internal promotions
- Number of career counselling clients

- Industrial tribunals

- Sickness/absence rates
- Health and safely endorsement actions taken by authorities
- Lifestyle and health assessments ('Lifescan')

(The Body Shop, 1996a, 1998)

2. Stakeholder perceptions of performance against core values

Each stakeholder group is invited to assess how closely it perceives the organisation is performing against its stated aspirations, as defined by the Body Shop Mission Statement and Trading Charter.

3. Stakeholder perception of performance against specific needs of stakeholders

These needs are particular to individual stakeholder groups. They are identified as salient through consultation with stakeholders and measured in surveys of opinion.

Stakeholder consultation and dialogue

Perceptions are arguably the most important barometer of human relationships. An employee who feels he or she is treated fairly may tolerate quite severe challenges in the workplace but retain his or her loyalty and commitment. For effective stakeholder inclusion, perceptions *are* reality.

Few major companies eschew market research with customers; indeed for many it is their most significant investment in stakeholder inclusion. In order to measure systematically the perceived quality of relationships between other stakeholders and the firm, techniques similar to market research need to be deployed. In our experience, large-scale confidential surveys, where focus groups with stakeholder representatives co-design the questionnaires, can be applied to almost any relationship.

Engaging stakeholders in direct dialogue is one of the most important and sensitive processes in social auditing. The Body Shop's first social audit engaged stakeholders in focus groups to explore specific needs and to allow views and concerns to be expressed. To ensure open dialogue in the discussion, it was considered important, especially for the initial stages of the process, that the external verifiers had access to the process as observers. Following the focus groups, questionnaires were designed that were intended to capture perceptions of the company's performance against both stakeholder-specific issues and core values articulated by the company. Professional assistance was sought in finalising the questionnaires to avoid inadvertent introduction of bias. Space was also allowed on the questionnaires themselves for open-ended comments about the company's performance. Surveys were done using the largest manageable sample size; respondents completed the questionnaires anonymously and returned them to an independent organisation for confidential analysis. Only summary information and lists of comments were submitted to The Body Shop for inclusion in the audit process and the social statement.

The internal management systems audit

There were three main sources of information for the first audit process:

i. the results of the focus groups and surveys
ii. the documentary information from departments which had agreed performance indicators
iii. the output from confidential face-to-face interviews with individual managers and members of staff. This latter source of information was based on the 'management systems' audit process used in environmental and quality management. Specific checklists were developed for the interviews and results used to build up a dynamic picture of departmental handling and knowledge of issues and company policies relevant to social performance.

The audits result in departmental action plans prioritising recommendations for proposed improvements. The internal audit reports as well as documentation relating to the auditing procedures are made available to external verifiers. The management systems audits are conducted by a semi-independent audit team which reports direct to the executive committee.

Preparation of accounts – the social statement

The Body Shop's first social statement gave each stakeholder group its own section within the report. An introductory section gave a general explanation about the scope of the audit and how the information had been compiled and what assumptions were used. The company founders also gave their overview in a foreword, thereby setting a tone to the document.

Each stakeholder section then followed a common format:

1. The basis for the company's approach and aims for each stakeholder group (with reference to relevant policies and similar documents) as well as basic information about the stakeholder group (for example, size, structural/contractual relationship to the company)
2. The methodology used for each consultation process (that is what combination of focus groups and surveys were used to capture stakeholder perceptions)
3. The outcomes of consultation with survey results described in as neutral a way as possible so as to avoid premature interpretation, together with direct quotations from stakeholders selected in an independent fashion
4. Quantitative and qualitative performance indicators where these existed

5. A company response from a senior manager setting out their reaction to the audit results as well as specific targets ('Next Steps') for future improvements.

This format was based on the assumption that setting out the statement in this way would promote the post-publication dialogue process and allow stakeholders to take a view on the adequacy or otherwise of the company response. The final components of the first social statement were a verification statement from NEF and a summary chapter on those stakeholders not included in the cycle, but who should be in future cycles.

The social statement was published as a part of a larger document called the *Values Report 1995*. In addition to the social statement, this consisted of the company's fourth environmental statement and its first animal protection statement. In an attempt to develop greater integration, the *Values Report 1997* is a single document, structured throughout in a stakeholder-driven way, each stakeholder section reporting on those aspects of environmental, animal protection and social/stakeholder performance most salient to a particular stakeholder group.

Agreement of strategic and local objectives

As with environmental auditing, a crucial part of the process is to set strategic objectives for the business to help clarify priorities for improvement. Setting strategic objectives and placing these in the public domain require a significant amount of internal discussion, management commitment and senior authorisation and support.

Target setting provides a key leverage for continuous improvement in any auditing and public reporting context. The Body Shop has had a formal target-setting programme within its environmental management system since 1992. Both local and strategic targets have been set, based on audit findings and progress reported on in public statements. Similar target-setting programmes were established for animal protection and stakeholder-related performance when audit methodologies were established for these during 1994/95. Strategic objectives must also be underpinned by localised objectives. These are in some ways simpler to negotiate because they involve fewer decision makers at the corporate level. However, the endorsement and support of the company board and central management committee are essential if more localised objectives are to be executed and kept in line with wider business goals.

As mentioned earlier, the Social Statement 1995 included a response from the relevant board member or senior manager to each stakeholder section. All in all, 89 specific 'Next Step' commitments were made together with seven company-wide strategic targets. The *Values Report 1997* reports on progress towards these targets. The external verifiers assessed the company's claims towards these targets. The 1997 statement includes 97 new targets relating to the company's stakeholder/social performance as well as ten integrated targets where stakeholder/social performance forms a component part.

Verification

Independent verification is now accepted practice in financial accounting and environmental and quality management. Based on our experience it is also of enormous value in assessing and improving the quality of relationships with stakeholders. Organisations such as NEF have pioneered techniques of 'social audit' verification with some success (Zadek *et al.*, 1997). It involves, for instance, documentation review, testing the veracity of numerical accounts, examining the integrity of internal management and audit systems and, ultimately, signing off on the accuracy of published reports as 'true and fair' accounts. It has also proven useful for the verifiers to convene advisory panels of experts in particular stakeholder perspectives to comment on the methodology, scope and tone of the draft statement.

Publication of statement

The social statement needs to be a true and fair picture of the social impacts of the organisation, insofar as the defined scope of the audit allows. It needs to be comprehensive and systematic, but above all to be understood. Because of the variety of stakeholder needs for information, The Body Shop has adopted a multi-tier approach to its public reporting. First, the full statement is published based on the approved, verified accounts and actively disseminated to targeted groups of key stakeholders. The full statement is also made available on the Internet. In addition, more detailed information is provided, for instance, to employees and franchisees on specific results relevant to them. A summary document is produced for wider scale distribution alongside even briefer material appropriate for customers and other large audiences. In each case readers are made aware of how they can obtain more detailed information.

Follow-up dialogue

Following publication of the company's first social audit, stakeholders were invited to engage in follow-up dialogue in order to obtain feedback on how they reacted to the findings. The aim of this process is to help shape future audit cycles, enable indicators and data presentation to be fine-tuned and help set priorities for future action by the company. The departments responsible for specific stakeholder relations were encouraged to enter into direct dialogue with stakeholder representatives. In some cases this dialogue has been facilitated and/or attended by the internal audit team. The *Values Report 1997* includes details of this process as well as key actions taken as a result.

Learning and development at The Body Shop

We have chosen to focus on learning and development because of its clear relevance to HR professionals. Learning and development is also seen as a key focus for increasing the competitiveness of UK businesses. Investors in People, for example, provides a framework for best practice for employers and is widely viewed as a principal tool for increasing workforce training and development.

The context

In 1995 The Body Shop was coming to the end of a period of rapid expansion. Employee numbers had increased considerably from 1900 in 1992 to 2199 at the time of the first social audit in 1995, a 16 per cent increase. In contrast employee numbers were virtually unchanged at 2282 at the time of the second social audit in 1997, an increase of under 4 per cent.

Shortly before the 1995 social audit commenced, a formal unit responsible for learning and development activities across all head office divisions had been established. The intention was to develop a more cohesive approach to learning and development activities across the business and toward that end a new strategy for learning and development was launched. This included three learning resource centres, a scheme to support personal development open to all employees (the LOVE scheme – Learning is Of Value to Everyone) a range of development programmes for managers and supervisors and a new policy on sponsorship in further education.

The results from the first social audit can be considered as a baseline from which the impact of the new strategy for learning and development can be measured. Thus targets were set in the *Values Report 1995* for learning and development:

- the launch of a new learning and development strategy with a wider range of provision and more flexible delivery
- a strategy to develop departmental and individual learning plans with a revised appraisal system
- the establishment of a framework for management skills development programmes
- the provision of a range of business-focused learning events
- the review of the company's policy and practices on support for professional and vocational qualifications and the provision of work experience opportunities.

In reviewing the attitudinal and factual data from the two surveys, it is possible to identify several areas where progress has been made, such as appraisal, attitudes towards encouraging learning and obtaining qualifications, and others where initiatives have yet to take effect, such as satisfaction with learning provision and time spent on learning and development. We review each of these areas in turn.

Appraisal

In the 1995 Social Audit, 49 per cent of respondents said they had had an appraisal in the last 12 months, although HR records indicated that only 20 per cent of employees had had their completed appraisal documentation logged with human resources.

A new appraisal system was introduced in the second half of 1995. Under the new system employees have the right to an annual appraisal which should include a personal learning and development plan. Seventy-two per cent of all respondents to the 1997 survey reported that they had had an appraisal in the last 12 months and 38 per cent that they had a personal learning and development plan in place. However, HR records indicate that only 47 per cent of employees had logged completed appraisal documentation, considerably fewer than the 85 per cent target set as an internal benchmark by HR. Although these divergent results suggest some degree of uncertainty in the overall rate at which appraisals are being carried out, they do indicate that the number of appraisals being carried out has increased considerably over the last two years.

However, the 1997 results demonstrate that it is not just whether respondents have had an appraisal that influenced learning and development but also the quality of the appraisal itself. Key findings from the employee survey highlight the benefits of appraisal as a stimulus for learning and development activity. Respondents who had had an appraisal were:

- *More likely to have a personal learning and development plan.* Fifty per cent of those who had had an appraisal in the last 12 months had a personal learning and development plan compared to 9 per cent of those who had not had an appraisal in that time
- *More likely to have reviewed their personal learning and development plan in the last 6 months.* Sixty-three per cent of those with a plan who had had an appraisal in the last 12 months had reviewed their personal learning and development plan in the last six months compared to 24 per cent of those with a plan who had not had an appraisal.

Having a personal learning and development plan also had a considerable impact. Respondents with a personal learning and development plan were:

- *More likely to have initiated learning and development activities in the last 12 months.* Sixty-nine per cent of those with a plan had initiated personal learning and development activities in the last 12 months compared to 38 per cent of those without a plan
- *Significantly more satisfied that The Body Shop encourages learning and with The Body Shop's learning provision and more satisfied with their appraisal.*

The survey also found attitudinal differences among respondents who had had an appraisal:

- Seventy-five per cent of those with an agreed personal learning and development plan were 'quite' or 'very' satisfied with the way the appraisal was carried out compared to 55 per cent of those without an agreed plan
- Seventy-five per cent of those with an agreed personal learning and development plan were 'quite' or 'very' satisfied with the outcome of their appraisal compared to 51 per cent of those without an agreed plan.

Encouraging learning

While analysis of the Social Audit showed that average scores on the fivepoint scale of 1 to 5 had increased from 2.71 in 1995 to 2.87 in 1997, average scores remained below the mid-point, 3, indicating an overall measure of dissatisfaction. In the latest Social Audit respondents with a learning and development plan were significantly more satisfied ($t=10.38$, $p<.001$) with The Body Shop's efforts to encourage learning than respondents without such a plan. Respondents with a plan had an average score of 3.13 on this scale compared to 2.70 for those without a plan.

Obtaining qualifications

The 1997 Social Audit found that 17 per cent of respondents reported they had professional qualifications up from 11 per cent in 1995. In addition, 21 per cent of respondents were currently studying for a qualification and roughly half of this group were studying for a work-related qualification. The largest increase in satisfaction was on the attitude statement, 'The Body Shop encourages me to obtain qualifications', up from 14 per cent very or quite satisfied in 1995 to 24 per cent in 1997.

Satisfaction with learning provision

Scores on the learning provision scale declined from an average of 3.28 in 1995 to 3.17 in 1997. Although this indicates that respondents remain satisfied on balance with The Body Shop's performance in this area, it seems that the initiatives taken have not yet led to positive changes in attitudes. The decline in scores on this scale was mainly attributed to a decline in satisfaction with training on the environment, down from 41 per cent 'quite' or 'very' satisfied in 1995 to 30 per cent in 1997. Results from the 1997 Social Audit show that respondents with a learning and development plan were significantly more satisfied (t=4.04, p<.001) with learning provision than respondents without plans. Respondents with a learning and development plan had an average score of 3.27 on this scale compared to 3.10 for those without a plan.

Time spent on learning and development

Although a number of new initiatives had been launched and satisfaction with The Body Shop's efforts to encourage learning had increased, the actual amount of time respondents spent on learning and development activities was more or less unchanged. In fact the percentage of respondents who reported that they had not engaged in any learning and development activity in the last 12 months had actually increased slightly from 22 per cent in 1995 to 25 per cent in 1997.

New survey benchmarks

The social audit is constantly evolving. While new questions will be added to address new concerns, it is important that questions that allow us to benchmark from one survey to the next are retained. As far as learning and development are concerned, the new questions on satisfaction with the appraisal process will allow comparisons to be made in future surveys.

New targets

The Body Shop committed itself in its 1997 *Values Report* to a new range of targets for learning and development. These include achieving Investors in People certification by the end of 1999. The full list of targets is shown in Table 13.5.

Conclusion

The Body Shop's social auditing has led to an increased understanding of the company's identity, with massive votes of confidence by stakeholders in its values and mission. Greater understanding of stakeholders' needs and aspirations was already leading to improved communication and business decision making by those departments responsible for looking after individual stakeholder groups. The Body Shop also believed that, in the future, fewer mistakes would be made and less effort and resources expended on inappropriate business and HR initiatives. In short, social auditing is not just an ethically desirable activity, it is also a driver for improved effectiveness for the organisation and enhanced inclusion and thus support from stakeholders.

However, as we have seen from examining the results concerned with learning and development, real change does not happen without considerable effort on the part of relevant departments and managers. It is easy to raise expectations of change but not always so straightforward to deliver it. One strength of the social audit methodology is that it provides a clear process for

TABLE 13.5   **New targets from the 1997** *Values Report*

- *Global strategy:* We will implement a new global learning strategy, commencing at the end of 1997.

- *Individual/departmental learning plans:* During 1997/8 we will develop individual learning plans via the implementation of a revised appraisal system to facilitate greater role clarity, clearer objective settings and more detailed planning of job-related learning and personal development requirements.

- *Evaluation of management development:* During 1998 we will develop a system to measure business/management development programmes in terms of tangible returns in investment.

- *Business-focused learning:* We will continue to design and develop senior, middle and junior management development programmes during 1998 which focus on real business issues and in many cases lead to professional accreditation.

- *Secondments:* We will formulate a secondment policy during 1998 focused on local and global opportunities.

- *Investors in People:* We will commit to achieving the Investors in People certification by the end of 1999.

- *Standards for learning and development:* By the end of 1997 we will have explored options for setting a minimum standard with regard to time invested in learning and development activity per person, per year with a view to implementing this standard by the end of 1998.

- *Global performance management system:* We will explore the potential for a global performance management system during 1998.

- *Senior managers as role models:* We will work with senior managers at executive level to design and implement personal development programmes during 1998.

- *Coaching:* During 1998, we will deliver a coaching programme throughout the business and support the 'communication of understanding' to employees on what constitutes a learning activity.

- *This Is The Body Shop:* We will deliver the 'This Is The Body Shop' training and awareness programme to eight international markets during 1997/98.

- *Customer service philosophy:* We will put in place a system for exploring and developing a customer service philosophy in each division of the business during 1998 where the focus will be on value-added activity.

- *Purchasing training:* During 1997/8 we will repeat training on the ethical screening, rating and inspection of suppliers for all employees responsible for purchasing stock.

(The Body Shop, 1998)

TABLE 13.6   Seven dos and don'ts of social auditing and disclosure

DO	DON'T
• Ensure senior management commitment at the very outset of any plans for social auditing. As with environmental management and auditing, clear leadership is probably the most important single factor in driving a process of social auditing and disclosure to a successful conclusion.	• Launch into a social audit without talking to someone who has done one. It is a long-term commitment, so plan ahead at least two audit cycles.
• Consider joining the Institute for Social and Ethical Accountability – an important source of independent advice and experience.	• Forget the importance of training for social auditing: for managers and auditors. In its current form it is a new science and the principles and pitfalls need to be understood.
• Involve departments, managers and staff at every level, especially in deciding the scope for the audit. Key departments are those that have most to do with stakeholder groups, for example human resources, communications/PR, investor relations and so on.	• Forget to focus on the benefits and business case for social performance measurement and disclosure for all stakeholders. Good social auditing should make an organisation more responsive and efficient. There is a clear business case for social auditing.
• Set up an internal audit system or department and have it report to a main board director.	• Omit to publicise the role of the audit team and its purpose; people may feel more threatened by a social performance audit than by an environmental audit.
• Exercise real care in selecting an independent verifier; they will have access to the very soul of the organisation and their integrity is paramount. Always network to find verifiers with experience who are recommended by others.	• Forget that you may also need other sources of expert advice, for example on survey design and analysis.
• Allow plenty of time for drafting and finalising the social statement. Audited departments will be very keen to be involved in putting results in context and proposing priorities for improvement.	• Allow one stakeholder voice to outweigh others. Take into account minority views but don't let them take over; a good external verifier will act as wise counsel on the right balance to be struck.
• Report: formally and informally, publicly and internally. Stakeholder understanding is crucial to progress, as are targets and objectives for the future.	• Be afraid of including both good and bad aspects of social performance; better that you draw attention to your faults than your critics do.

achieving change as well as monitoring the way change is being delivered. This means that the company gets regular and clear feedback on the extent to which it is reaching the targets that it has set itself. An added value of public accountability is in the credibility it gives to the process for both internal and external audiences.

Finally, there are a number of practical and strategic points to bear in mind when considering whether or not a company should go ahead with social auditing. Table 13.6 lists a number of dos and don'ts based on The Body Shop's experience.

References

The Body Shop (1996a) *The Body Shop Approach to Ethical Auditing*, Littlehampton: The Body Shop

The Body Shop (1996b) *The Values Report 1995*, Littlehampton: The Body Shop

The Body Shop (1998) *The Values Report 1997*, Littlehampton: The Body Shop

Bryan, L. and Farrell, D. (1996) *Market Unbound: Unleashing Global Capitalism*, New York: John Wiley and Sons

Cannon, T. (1996) *Welcome to the Revolution: Managing Paradox in the 21st Century*, London: Pitman

Centre for Tomorrow's Company (1998) *The Inclusive Approach to Business Success: The Research Evidence*, London: Gower

Collins, J. C. and Porras J. I. (1995) *Built to Last: Successful Habits of Visionary Companies*, London: Century, Random House

Hollister, B., Will, R., Tepper-Marlin, A., Dyott, S., Kovacs, S. and Richardson, L. with Council on Economic Priorities (1994) *Shopping for a Better World*, San Francisco: Sierra Club Books

Industrial Society. (1995) *Empowerment: Managing Best Practice 8*, London: Industrial Society

Kotter, J. and Heskett, J. (1992) *Corporate Culture and Performance*, New York: Free Press

Levering, R. and Moskowitz, M. (1993) *The 100 Best Companies to Work for in America*, New York: Currency

Oakland, J. S. (1996) *Total Quality Management: Text with Cases*, Oxford: Butterworth-Heinemann

Peters, T. (1992) *Liberation Management: Necessary Disorganisation for the Nanosecond Nineties*, New York: Alfred & Knopf

Roddick, A. (1991) *Body and Soul*, London: Ebury Press

Wheeler, D. and Sillanpää, M. (1997) *The Stakeholder Corporation: A Blueprint for Maximising Stakeholder Value*, London: Pitman

White, R. P., Hodgson, P. and Crainer, S. (1996) *The Future of Leadership: A Whitewater Revolution*, London: Pitman

Zadek, S., Pruzan, P. and Evans, R. (1997) *Building Corporate Accountability: Emerging Practices in Social and Ethical Accounting, Auditing and Reporting*, London: Earthscan

Staff charters: a framework for employers and their staff

Paul Taylor and Peter Jones

Introduction

Human resource management is both about how organisations can best maximise the contributions of those at work, and helping individuals to gain satisfaction from where they spend a significant amount of their waking time. This is a difficult but an essential combination. The election of the UK Labour government in 1997 brought new interest in the concept of both rights and responsibilities at work and in the wider society. It widened the debate over stakeholders in a positive way to address the roles of individuals and families as stakeholders in their society. People had entitlement to some stake and influence in the community in which they lived and worked which went beyond just the formal political right to cast a democratic vote. People were expected to contribute to their own development and improvement, and also that of their society and workplace. The contribution earned rights, including the right to work, with the support where necessary of government initiatives. It was also justified in its own right as an element of our membership of the wider community. We give and we also receive. The UK government's New Deal approach to creating employment opportunities was its major commitment to this approach and those provided with work opportunities also had a responsibility to take advantage of what was offered.

It is at work that people spend a significant amount of their time and have the greatest opportunity to develop as stakeholders. As employees, they are part of an organisation that adapts and develops through internal initiatives and external pressures. They may well be encouraged to develop their own roles beyond the confines of one limited job. They are at the interface of all relationships with customers and are expected to co-operate with and support other employees. They may well be shareholders. They are very likely to be members of a pension scheme with its concerns about longer term investment. They may be customers too. Unlike other shareholders, they have made a full investment in the organisation for which they work; all their financial and skill eggs are in the one basket. And there is a reasonable basic assumption that everyone should contribute to the best of their abilities rather than seek to do the minimum necessary. That basic assumption, in itself, raises significant issues about what individuals should expect of themselves not only at work but also in the wider community in which they and their families live. It opens up issues about fulfilment as well as contribution.

The notion of employee charters fits in well with a stakeholder approach to elicit the rights and responsibilities of employers and staff in the workplace. In this chapter we explore some of the origins and related concepts to that of an employee charter and examine the key components that go to make up a charter. As well as identifying its benefits, we illustrate the process of introducing an employee charter and the perceived benefits to one organisation, a hospital, the Royal Brompton NHS Trust. It is argued that from an ethical stakeholding perspective, and to some extent drawing on an ethics of care approach, an employee charter is one way in which organisations can provide a clearer guide for the rights and responsibilities of its staff at work.

What are charters?

The stakeholder concept aims to describe and emphasise the reciprocal set of rights and responsibilities that exists between individuals and society. Individuals earn and deserve rights by recognising their personal responsibility to make appropriate contributions to society. This general concept is also applicable to employment. This is especially so in times of continual change where there is an obligation on individuals to promote necessary changes and an expectation that the employer will involve them in decisions about what needs to be achieved and not ride roughshod over them and their interests.

Many organisations have recognised some aspects of this stakeholder involvement with the preparation of mission and vision statements which describe their general aspirations, what they want to achieve and their relationships with their customers, suppliers and employees. They may even have used the word 'stakeholders' to recognise each of the parties, including but not just limited to shareholders, who have roles to play in achieving their plans and who will benefit from doing so. Visions seek to set the general map of why the organisation exists, what it does, how it plans to grow and develop. They lead, inevitably, to descriptions of the kinds of behaviours that individuals should aspire to and seek to develop, recognising (sometimes implicitly) that the organisation is a community which depends on positive behaviours to achieve its objectives and which will not do so if the behaviour of individuals is inappropriate.

Developing a general statement of the rights and responsibilities of stakeholders fits well with the development of organisational visions or charters.

So what is an employee charter? There are six defining features which set it apart from other similar instruments:

1. It develops a notion of partnership and *mutuality* within the organisation
2. Although there may be a plurality of interests, a framework of *reciprocity* is used to ensure that the different interests of employers and employees can be met
3. The charter outlines this reciprocal relationship through a series of *rights and responsibilities*
4. These rights and responsibilities relate to the *individual* employee and not just collective relationships at work
5. The charter of rights and responsibilities are agreed upon through a process of *consultation* with key stakeholders
6. The charter is *made explicit* and it is communicated and published throughout the organisation.

There are other instruments and processes which look very similar to a staff charter, but lack one or other of the six key features. For example 'new deals', psychological contracts, other types of charters and professional codes of conduct are all similar types of agreement between employers and staff to the staff charter, but all lack at least one of the defining features.

The 'new deal' is a familiar phrase used largely in manufacturing and the car industry to denote a formal collective agreement between management and employees over new working practices. A typical example would be the New Deal forged between Rover car manufacturers and employees (IRS, 1992). In exchange for improvements in production, flexibility, grading, bonus schemes and consultation, Rover staff negotiated with management for union recognition and improved job security (although later experience has shown that these agreements are never written in tablets of stone). These changes enabled the company to survive in a very competitive market. This type of agreement, however, tends to emphasise the more collective rather than individual aspects of work, and although it goes beyond the traditional collective bargaining arena to discuss a host of new aspects of employment, and does emphasise mutuality and reciprocity, it is not largely developed in a rights and responsibilities framework.

The second related contract is that of the 'psychological contract', which has received attention largely because of the perceived change in those industries where significant downsizing and delayering have been taking place, for example the public utilities and the financial sector (Herriot and Pemberton,

1995; Hiltrop, 1995; Sparrow, 1996). It is suggested that the older style psychological contract providing for job security, development, promotion and reasonable pay, in return for effort and commitment, has been replaced by a newer form. In this instance the employers have largely retreated from offering job security, instead providing employability and a less desirable set of conditions (Sparrow, 1996, pp. 75–92). Although there is a framework of reciprocity, this is seen to be becoming unbalanced in many organisations and rather than being a contract which is mutually agreed upon and explicit, they are more likely to be seen to be imposed by the employers and often not formalised or written down, but instead the expectations are those which are largely in the head of the employee.

The Citizen's Charter has led to the development of charters for a number of utility companies such as British Gas and British Telecom. These have specific standards or targets of achievement which lay down what consumers can expect. With the introduction of the Patient's Charter into the National Health Service in 1994 there was a general feeling among staff that they too could benefit from the introduction of a specific charter for staff. This could be seen as a contract between management and staff which would provide avenues for change and improvement and guarantee the right to equality and swift and fair redress if things go wrong. Although unlike the psychological contract, these are explicit, they are generally one-way rather than two-way expectations, that is they outline the responsibilities of staff to customers or patients, but not the responsibilities of the organisation to its staff. There is no reciprocity.

Likewise professional codes of conduct, which have been produced for most staff groups within the NHS and other professional organisations and groups (such as for lawyers), are similar to staff charters, but lack the element of two-way reciprocity. Also they do not cover all staff, cannot be reactive to local circumstances and are too limited in content to cover all the issues that may compose a staff charter. In the UKCC code of conduct for nursing staff the majority of the 16 criteria relate to professional issues with components covering health and safety, confidentiality and 'conflict of interest' issues.

This implies that there is quite wide-ranging content within staff charters, and that they embrace all staff and not just one or two professional groups, and arguably these could be added to the list of defining features. Before exploring the content and remit of staff charters, it is useful to turn to examine where they have been introduced.

Despite an exhaustive literature search only one published application of staff charters could be found. Drummond (1991) discusses the application of a staff charter to the Benefits Agency. Due to the pressures produced from increased workloads staff were feeling undervalued and overworked. Initially an efficiency drive designed to improve practices and motivate staff was implemented under the title 'Caring for Staff'. Responses to this initiative were initially less than enthusiastic which led to the proposal of a staff charter to consolidate the suggestions proposed in the Caring for Staff initiative and to set out a clear contract between staff and managers. The Benefits Agency staff charter was established to improve the staff-caring image of the organisation.

Features of this proposed staff charter included: management training for all levels of the staff structure, improvement in equal opportunities especially for women, introduction of job sharing and flexible working and a greater value placed on part-time workers. The possible benefits suggested as a result of this staff charter include improved communication and enhanced innovation by staff.

Therefore, in terms of the organisational case study presented here, namely, the Royal Brompton NHS Trust, developing a staff charter was a ground-breaking exercise. Not only was it a new concept for the organisation, but apparently it is a concept which is unfamiliar to most other organisations as well.

Staff charters – the benefits

In order to promote an organisational change which could lead to the development and implementation of a staff charter the benefits need to be clearly identified. Some of the potential benefits identified by the Royal Brompton Hospital were that it would:

- Consolidate the caring culture and image of the organisation
- Establish a set of values for the organisation
- Empower the individual to share responsibility for the aims of the organisation
- Assist in employee retention and recruitment
- Increase awareness of issues such as stress and health and safety
- Improve opportunities for training and development.

Many Trusts are keen to consolidate a caring culture, in the eyes of both patients and staff. Some of the changes that have taken place in the delivery of patient care and the increasing need to identify priorities, combined with the tough financial constraints placed upon NHS Trusts, have led Trusts such as the Royal Brompton to seek to communicate more effectively the need for a caring culture and find ways to get this embedded in the ethos and culture of patient care.

Associated with this, Trusts are also attempting to clarify a set of values which drive the organisation. A staff charter is one way of making these values clear at the point of recruitment and also for staff once they are within the organisation. The mutuality of the staff charter, highlights the shared responsibility the individual and the employer have to the achievement of the organisation's aims. The potential benefit of improved recruitment and retention was particularly important for the Royal Brompton. Professional staff shortages in hospitals can increase overall costs and compromise the quality of care.

A number of studies have been conducted into recruitment and retention of nursing staff. A Gallup survey of 900 nurses and midwives commissioned by the healthcare union, Unison, in 1995 demonstrated the recruitment crisis within the NHS. The main reasons for dissatisfaction were feeling undervalued (75 per cent), staff shortages leading to increased workloads (63 per cent) and the changing nature of the NHS itself (77 per cent).

In terms of retention, a report by Stolte and Myers (1995) demonstrated that salary, scheduling, opportunities for advancement, lack of recognition, lack of autonomy and problems with management have a major impact on nurse retention. These factors closely resemble those described by Smith and Discenza (1988) namely equity or fairness in pay, challenging work, periodic skill development, a voice in how work is undertaken and the formation of teams. Continuing education and training is also a key factor in the retention of staff. Williams and Cullen (1994) also suggest that any change in the working environment should be examined to determine its impact on retention. Leaders should also be developed who can inspire staff to contribute to the organisation's mission.

Responses to the shortage of specialist nursing staff have been reported in the national media with offers such as 'golden hellos – a signing on fee for new recruits who agree to stay for a set period, worth up to £2000'. This situation has been placed in perspective by Millar and Crail (1996), who in discussion with human resources directors outlined the poor success rates of financial incentives. They also stated that staff retention by such measures as improvements in staff facilities was as important an issue. This has been further illustrated by Millar (1996a) in a discussion on improvements in hospital accommodation.

A staff charter may be seen as one way of improving recruitment and retention, and addressing some of the problems which have been identified. For example the NHS Executive report (1996) outlines a section on good employee development which includes a major objective as follows:

> Recruitment and retention, which is central to achieving service delivery, should be improved through the spread of good employment practices which develop team work and respect individual as well as organisational needs.

Significant organisational changes, increased workloads caused by staff shortages and job insecurity have an effect on the motivation, morale and retention of staff. The resultant stress induced by excessive demands on the individual can lead to major short- and long-term behavioural, physical and emotional problems (Davies, 1995). The provision of adequate counselling services may lead to an alleviation of the effects of stress and other potential results may be reduced absenteeism rates. Any provision of counselling services must be seen to be confidential and may in some cases need to be provided off-site.

In a survey of safety representatives it was noted that concerns about significant stress levels were noted in 71 per cent of NHS establishments. The 1994 case of *Walker* v. *Northumberland County Council*, which resulted in an award of £175,000 to the employee, demonstrated that employers should make provision for the prevention of stress-related ill health. It should not be acceptable especially in the NHS for the work and the environment to create stressful conditions. A staff charter can go some of the way to make explicit the employer's commitment to reducing stress and unhealthy workloads.

Training and development increases opportunities for staff to develop their careers through a structure of qualifications thus creating a more positive atmosphere in the workplace. In order to promote the uptake of training courses there needs to be adequate staffing levels in order to provide time for education and training to take place. A staff charter can make clear the organisation's policy and approach to training and development, and can incorporate its support for continuing professional education and development.

A number of professional groups represented within the NHS have continuing development schemes. Only one of these groups, that responsible for nursing, has a scheme which is mandatory, that for human resources staff is a requirement for upgrading of membership of the IPD (Institute of Personnel and Development), and the remainder are currently voluntary. Continuing professional development (CPD) for members of the IBMS (Institute of Biomedical Sciences) may however, as a result of the review of the Professions Supplementary to Medicine Act (*Biomedical Scientist*, 1996), become a requirement for continued registration. This would obviously have an impact on other healthcare professionals included within the Act, such as radiographers and dieticians. Professional groups outside of the NHS including lawyers, chartered surveyors and teachers also have mandatory schemes which have allowed for improved control over primarily professional and accreditation issues. The benefits of voluntary continuing development schemes could be summarised as a mixture of enhanced personal development, morale and job satisfaction. It is likely that within the next five years all professional groups will have mandatory schemes.

Continuing professional development (CPD) is not only limited to professional bodies, but may also be used to assist staff within an organisation to achieve their own objectives through a set of core competencies (Arkin, 1992). A similar perspective was outlined for a health service setting by Owen and Leon (1993) who demonstrated both advancement of nursing practice as well as improvements in staff retention. It seems sensible, then, for the organisation's responsibilities towards CPD, and an individual's rights to engage in development activities to be enshrined within a staff charter.

Although there has been much enthusiastic discussion about the application of staff charters to specific organisations there has been little implementation. The main stumbling block seems to be that the interface between employer and employee is more often reactive to a given set of circumstances rather than being proactive to change. Hospitals exist to provide services to the community but are also part of that community and therefore have duties to both employees as well as the people which they serve. These duties could be placed on a more formal footing by the adoption of a staff charter especially in an organisation such as the Royal Brompton Hospital that has the oft-quoted aim:

> to develop commitment and enterprise and be known as an organisation which cares about its staff.

The content of a staff charter

Although some of these issues concerning staff charters are discussed by Drummond (1991) there is insufficient detail to establish the core content of a staff charter. In some cases the rights of staff have been the sole component of staff charters for specific groups. This was the case for the charter of rights produced in 1995 for nursing healthcare assistants and nursing auxiliaries and assistants. Designed to promote a team approach there are ten points in this charter which simplify a number of the rights and for example offer 'dismissal is only used as a sanction of last resort' in return for 'the right to job security'. The aim of a reasonable staff charter should be to involve all employees and hence improve awareness and commitment.

The most comprehensive outline of the possible content of a staff charter is that provided by Peter Jones produced in association with David Bell and the Amici group of HR professionals and consultants (Jones and Bell, 1996). Their work was distributed to and discussed widely by branches of the IPD. The model proposed the rights and responsibilities outlined in Exhibit 14.1.

Introducing a staff charter; the process

Stage 1: Setting the agenda for the organisation

During a management training course at Imperial College, one of the authors, Paul Taylor, assimilated some of the potential benefits of a staff charter and as part of the course project decided to investigate its implementation into the Royal Brompton Hospital. He also utilised the content framework provided by the other author, Peter Jones, discussed earlier and outlined in Exhibit 14.1, as a basis for formulating questions for inclusion in a questionnaire of staff at the Royal Brompton.

Most hospitals have a joint staff consultative committee (JSC) composed of staff-side members (from unions and staff organisations) and management side members which includes representatives from different management levels including human resources. Such committees provide a suitable inter-face for staff from a cross-section of the hospital to develop proactive measures such as a staff charter. The viewpoints in such a group as the JSC could however polarise with the staff side taking a keener interests in issues that could be regarded as rights and the management side preferring the issues of responsibilities.

In order to introduce the concept of a staff charter to the Trust a question-naire was sent to a cross-section of 19 staff. The rights and responsibilities outlined in Exhibit 14.1 were tabulated and used to discuss the content of a staff charter with key stakeholders within the Human Resources Department and members of the JSC. The questionnaire itself was copied on to both sides of paper in order to separate the rights and responsibilities and avoid comparison. It was hoped that each of the rights and responsibilities would be closely examined if individuals were asked to rank each of the items in terms of importance.

The mean ranking score was used as a guide as to the position of the sub-headings in the proposal for a staff charter, starting with those seen to be most important. It was recognised that such prioritisation is dependent on both local and personal attitudes and should only be taken as a guide.

Although the issues of rights and responsibilities were initially separated in order to prevent a trade-off situation it was decided, wherever possible, to combine them under specific sub-headings in order to take the staff charter concept to a wider group within the Trust.

A suggestion for valuing staff was added as a possible introduction to the staff charter:

> The Royal Brompton Hospital Trust values all its employees on the basis of equi-table rights and is committed to the health and welfare of all staff. The following

principles which are included in the Staff Charter have always been those that have been practised within the organisation. As a result of its commitment to this Staff Charter, further improvements will result so that this Trust will be recognised as an organisation that respects, protects, values and develops its staff.

Staff should be provided with the essential resources required to carry out their work and in return organise themselves well and work to their full capacity.

Stage 2: Draft staff charter content

Exhibit 14.2 outlines the draft staff charter content, with items ranked in order of priority. Issues of pay were perceived by all staff to be the most important feature of a staff charter.

With relation to education and training, a number of problems have arisen as a result of inadequate cover for staff to attend internal courses. In some cases this had resulted in meetings having to be cancelled at short notice. The draft staff charter could also feasibly encourage the potential incorporation of continuing education schemes for professional groups into local courses in order to improve uptake. There was seen to be a disparity between different staff groups in the requirements of continuing education schemes. A universal minimum standard allowance for all staff could be agreed and included in a study leave policy.

The Health and Safety committee for the Trust had been reformed with a new constitution and suggested improvements for the implementation of policies and could be one vehicle for ensuring that charter commitments on health and safety are met. It was decided that the Trust's Health at Work Group would examine the issue of stress from awareness, prevention and treatment perspectives, to support the claims in the staff charter.

Information flow within the Trust, which is a prelude to consultation, has been generally found to be good; and there was a suggestion to improve the regular team-briefing sessions by the incorporation of a hospital newsletter which was to be considered.

There were some comments in the questionnaire responses on the issues of dismissal, for example with relation to the level of the 'offence.' This issue was found to be covered in the Trust's disciplinary procedure.

The system of individual performance review (IPR) had not been applied at all levels of the Trust but was believed to work well in some areas. It was suggested that this process should be reviewed for the Trust as a whole to support the charter's commitment to development and performance review.

The charter content on ethics was probably seen as the most difficult area to include. 'Whistleblowing' clauses need to be dealt with sensitively within the context of a NHS setting and there is a case for the NHS Code of Openness to be applied in this case.

Stage 3: Agreement of staff and management

The above criteria for a staff charter which were developed as a result of consensus responses to a questionnaire were discussed at the joint staff consultative committee. The concept received the assent of all present, including the chief executive and the balance between rights and responsibilities was agreed as the best route to maximising the benefits of a staff charter. A small working group was established from JSC with the following terms of reference to:

- prepare a final policy statement for presentation to the Executive Group
- formulate an annual action plan to ensure the detail of such a policy is put into practice within the Trust
- establish an audit tool for continued monitoring of the charter.

Stage 4: The final implementation

By late 1998 the process had not yet been completed, but it was expected that the charter would be adopted as corporate policy. The policy would be issued to all new staff so that the culture of the organisation changes, developing a mechanism that allows concerns of employees to be aired. Finally it was intended that a system to monitor compliance with the charter would be set up. Any proposed changes to the charter would be openly debated so that change and improvement would be an ongoing process. One of the key issues of empowering staff by the development of a staff charter should also include an examination of information flow in the organisation.

The charter was discussed by 22 senior managers within the Trust who completed a separate questionnaire to evaluate the current status of these rights and responsibilities within the Trust. An analysis of the extent to which the Trust currently achieved these criteria from answers given in this questionnaire is given in Figure 14.1. The two highest medians were demonstrated for employment rights and ethics responsibilities. The three lowest medians are for consultation rights and development rights and responsibilities. It was therefore intended that these three areas should be the targets for the first year of introduction of the staff charter.

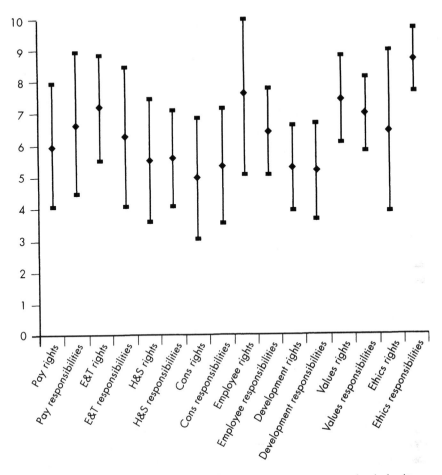

Note: Respondents were requested to score each staff charter issue on current level of achievement for the Trust, a score of ten being the highest. Results were analysed by the Astute statistics package running in Microsoft Excel. The mean for each issue is a measure of the central location of the data; the standard deviation is a measure of dispersion for these data.

FIGURE 14.1 Mean and standard deviation plot of questionnaire response to 'How does this Trust respond to the rights and responsibilities in the Staff Charter?'

The Royal Brompton Hospital merged with Harefield Hospital on 1 April 1998 creating the Royal Brompton NHS Trust. The single Trust on two sites created a period of uncertainty for staff and so it was hoped that the introduction of a staff charter would go some way to alleviating this. At that time staff generally felt that the charter could help support them through these changes and provide a reassurance that they are valued. Senior managers within the Trust have observed that a staff charter will set the foundation on which future staff relations can be constructed.

Exhibit 14.1

Jones and Bell's (1996) proposed outline of rights and responsibilities

Responsibilities

- *Commitment*
  Accepting positively a duty to contribute to the best of one's abilities to the achievement of the organisation's goals through an individual's own work and through an understanding of the organisation's aims and environment. It does not mean an unthinking commitment which demands long and unsocial hours and placing the organisation ahead of personal considerations. The key issue is getting the balance right.
- *Performance*
  Being prepared to perform appropriately and flexibly without unnecessary restrictions and demarcations, using skills to the full to contribute to the business's needs.
- *Learning*
  Taking personal responsibility for developing skills and competencies to increase effectiveness at work, seeking opportunities to do so both individually and with the support of employers. Both parties, employees and employers, have an obligation (and also a basic necessity), to develop organisational and personal capacity.
- *Coaching*
  Giving appropriate feedback to others, to help improve performance and relationships and seeking and welcoming such feedback about one's own performance and contribution. This requires a willingness to listen to and offer helpful comments and suggestions, to ask others for help, to acknowledge areas of weakness and a recognition that improvement is possible, and attainable, even just step by step.
- *Respect*
  Working with and helping each other at work on the basis of positive co-operation and mutual respect, valuing the different approaches offered by diversity and avoiding prejudiced discrimination based on subjective factors rather than objective commitment and performance.

- *Well-being*
  Protecting the health and safety of themselves and of others in physical, mental and emotional terms. This will mean a willingness to care for others and their well-being rather than merely ensuring that safety standards are maintained. Fear and stress are inappropriate features of any working environment.
- *Leadership*
  For those in leadership roles, accepting that they provide a model for the behaviour of others adds a special responsibility for the appropriateness of their personal behaviour and performance, in words and deeds.
- *Management*
  For those who manage others, recognising their particular obligation to develop those who report to them, to communicate effectively with them and to explain and justify actions which affect them.

Rights

- *Employees being treated as individuals*
  People being seen as an individual, and not just members of a group or team, who are able to contribute positively and effectively, and are given the means to do this, through full communication of the expectations of the organisation and their particular role and through the provision of adequate and appropriate facilities for training and development. Responding to their particular needs and wishes, rather than enforcing some conformity.
- *Performance feedback*
  Feedback on performance and contribution being given appropriately with the opportunity to improve their skills and overcome any shortcomings with the employer's support.
- *Dismissal being a last resort*
  All practicable steps being taken to ensure that dismissal is used only as a final last resort and that adequate as well as fair procedures are followed to ensure the fairness of decisions, from the first day of employment.
- *Objective employment choices*
  The use of objective and open criteria to make decisions between people about appointment, promotion, pay increase and all other employment matters, whether before or during employment, with criteria that are open and transparent. Recognising the individual's right to honest feedback where the decision may not be in the their favour.
- *Consultation and combination*
  People given the right to be consulted, and to combine together if they wish, in order to have an effective voice in representing their views to their employers.

- *Fair pay*
  The right of people to be paid at a fair and equitable level in relation to their skills and responsibilities and also to the external labour market. To share in the financial success of their employers in recognition of their contribution to that success.
- *Public involvement*
  Encouragement rather than restriction of employees in their rights as citizens to contribute to public debate on matters of interest or concern, with no kind of penalty on them for such contributions when these refer to their employer's business but are made for the public good. Encouraging people to take part in activities that are for the benefit of society, such as being magistrates or councillors.
- *Well-being*
  Taking all practicable steps to protect the health and safety of employees, including the positive avoidance of unreasonable or unnecessary stressful work demands whether in terms of hours worked or workload.
- *Personal life*
  Recognition and support for the right of employees to a reasonable personal life outside work and not intruding upon the privacy of their home life nor making excessive work demands which deprive them of time for it.

Exhibit 14.2

Draft staff charter content for Royal Brompton NHS Trust

1. *Pay*
   Staff have the right to fair and equitable pay in relation to their skills and responsibilities. Promotion or pay increases will be made on the basis of objective criteria.
   Staff have the responsibility to contribute to the achievement of the organisation's goals.
2. *Education and training*
   Staff have a right to the provision of and access to facilities for training and development relevant to their employment.
   Staff are responsible for improving and developing their skills.
3. *Health and safety*
   Staff have the right to expect that all practicable steps will be taken to protect their health and safety and that this will include the avoidance of unreasonable stressful work demands.
   Staff have the responsibility to ensure the health and safety of themselves and of others.

4. *Consultation*

Staff have the right to be consulted on their views by their employer.

Staff have the responsibility to adopt an attitude of positive co-operation, valuing diversity.

5. *Employment*

Staff have the right to expect that dismissal will only be used as a sanction of last resort.

Staff have the responsibility to work flexibly.

6. *Development*

Leaders will provide an appropriate role model of behaviour for good management practice.

Staff are responsible for giving and receiving appropriate feedback in order to improve performance and develop each other's skills.

7. *Values*

Staff have the right to a reasonable personal life outside work and their employers shall not make excessive demands which deprive them of time for it.

Staff have the responsibility to organise themselves well and work to their full capacity.

8. *Ethics*

Staff have the right to take part in activities which are of benefit to society e.g. councillors, magistrates. Staff have the right to raise local issues in public debate within the confines of patient confidentiality.

Staff have the responsibility to maintain patient confidentiality at all times.

References

Arkin, A. (1992) 'Professional updating: the employer's role' *Professional Management*, 24: 36–8

Biomedical Scientist (1996) 'Revolution in regulation of the professions' *Biomedical Scientist*, 40: 454–6

Communication World (1995) 'Survey says top executives should devote one third of time to staff issues' *Communication World*, 12: 11–12

Davies, O. (1995) *Stress in the NHS Health Manager*, 6: 8–9

Drummond, G. (1991) 'A charter to benefit staff' *Personnel Today*, 8 October: 18–19

Herriot, P. and Pemberton, C. (1995) 'A new deal for middle managers' *People Management*, 15 June: 32–4

Hiltrop, J.-M. (1995) 'The changing psychological contract: the human resource challenge of the 1990s' *European Management Journal*, 13: 286– 93

IRS (1992) 'Lean production – and Rover's "new deal"' *IRS Employment Trends*, p. 514

Jones, P. and Bell, D. (1996) 'Stakeholders at work: the responsibilities and rights of employees'. Paper given at the first UK conference on 'Ethical Issues in Contemporary HRM' held at Imperial College Management School, April

Millar, B. (1996a) 'Room service' *Health Service Journal*, 21 March: 24–5

Millar, B. (1996b) 'Mouths all mighty' *Health Service Journal*, 2 May: 14

Millar, B. and Crail, M. (1996) 'Bone of contention ' *Health Service Journal*, 18 January: 14–5

NHS Executive (1996) Priorities and planning guidance for the NHS 1997/1998

Owen, J. and Leon, C. (1993) 'Career development: a vehicle for retention' *Nursing Management*, **24**: 59–60

Smith, H.L. and Discenza, R. (1989) 'Developing a framework for retaining health care employees: a challenge to traditional thinking' *Hospital Topics*, **67**(3): 26–32

Sparrow, P. (1996) 'Transitions in the psychological contract: Some evidence from the banking sector' *Human Resource Management Journal*, **6**(4): 75–92

Stolte, K. and Myers, S.T. (1995) 'Reflections on recruitment and retention at the unit level' *Health Care Supervisor*, **13**: 36–44

Williams, M.B. and Cullen, K.V. (1994) 'Nurses shortages needn't be inevitable' *Modern Healthcare*, **24**: 36

CHAPTER 15

Whistleblowing

David Lewis

Introduction

The increasing attention to whistleblowing can be explained by a number of factors, including recent health and safety disasters and financial scandals, the work of the Nolan (now Neill) Committee on Standards in Public Life, the debate about so-called 'gagging clauses' and the enactment of the Public Interest Disclosure Act 1998. This Act amends the Employment Rights Act 1996 (ERA 1996) in order to provide protection for individuals who make certain disclosures in the public interest (known as 'protected disclosures').

This chapter looks at various definitions of whistleblowing, considers some of the implications of internal and external reporting, and then provides an overview of the current legal situation. Finally, the author provides an ethical and good business case approach to whistleblowing by suggesting ways in which employers should go about establishing and communicating reporting procedures.

A broad definition of whistleblowing would encompass disclosure by employees and former employees of malpractice, as well as illegal acts or omissions at work. The charity Public Concern at Work (PCAW) offers help and free legal advice to people who have 'a concern that something seems to be seriously wrong, illegal or dangerous which threatens the public interest'. The recent changes to the ERA 1996 in the Public Interest Disclosure Act 1998, build on this notion of public interest by affording protection only to those who make a 'qualifying disclosure'. According to Section 43B(1) of ERA 1996, a 'qualifying disclosure' is one which a worker reasonably believes tends to show one or more of the following: a criminal offence; a failure to comply with any legal obligation; a miscarriage of justice; danger to the health and safety of any individual; damage to the environment; the deliberate concealment of information tending to show any of the matters listed above.

Given the lack of consensus as to what amounts to malpractice, it is hardly surprising that Parliament has failed to offer succour to those who merely identify some wrongdoing at work. However, it is argued that both the 'moral rights' and 'enlightened self-interest' approaches require employers to take a broader view by introducing policies and procedures which encourage the reporting of malpractice generally.

Although in some situations it may be difficult to decide whether a particular incident amounts to internal or external whistleblowing, there are good reasons for drawing a distinction. Internal reporting offers advantages to both employer and employee. The employer is given the opportunity to deal with a problem without external pressures or publicity. From the employee's point of view, once a matter has been raised externally, they may be seen as an adversary and be more likely to suffer retaliation (Micelli and Near, 1992, p. 42). It should also be noted that the law provides support for internal rather than external disclosures in two ways. First, while internal reporting to higher management may be perceived by supervisors as disloyal, it cannot be treated as a breach of the employee's common law duty of confidence or fidelity (Lewis, 1995). Second, in determining whether there is a 'protected disclosure' within the meaning of Part IVA of the Employment Rights Act 1996, regard will be had to whether the worker complied with a procedure authorised by the employer.

Is whistleblowing ethical?

The conventional but simplistic view of whistleblowers is that they are troublemakers who deserve to be punished for disloyalty (see Sternberg, 1994). An alternative management approach is to treat them as dedicated individuals who provide a valuable safety net when other forms of regulation fail. Such an approach recognises that workers are often in the best position to know whether there is malpractice within an organisation. A moral rights view suggests that individuals have a moral right to raise ethical concerns, whereas the enlightened self-interest view supports whistleblowing when it seeks to favour the organisation by improving practices and ultimately the quality of work processes. More positively, there is the 'enlightened self-interest approach' which sees whistleblowers as benefiting their employers by offering solutions to work problems. Those who first contact their managers about malpractice give them the chance to correct it before the matter escalates. It is not simply a question of internal communication being preferable to external whistleblowing; there is also the desirability of avoiding work stoppages over employee concerns. Thus whistleblowing can also be viewed as part of a strategy to maintain and improve quality. No doubt some employers would resist the idea of providing rewards for ethical behaviour. However, viewed from this 'quality' perspective, it may well be appropriate to offer financial incentives to those who disclose malpractice. Arguably, those who report concerns about malpractice are in an analogous position to those who propose improvements in organisational efficiency through a suggestion scheme.

As regards the argument that whistleblowing poses a challenge to an organisation's authority structure, this may not be the case where disclosures are positively encouraged and a channel for reporting is available. If a mechanism for employees to raise their concerns is not provided, then either the problem will not be dealt with or the employee will feel obliged to air the matter externally. As Lord Borrie put it: 'The result can be that conscientious and loyal employees become aggrieved or disillusioned' (Public Concern at Work, 1993).

In some situations whistleblowing may be vital to preserve the health and safety of the workforce and the general public. For example, the investigation into the *Herald of Free Enterprise* disaster in 1987 found that employees had aired their concerns on five previous occasions about the ship sailing with its bow doors open. A member of staff had even suggested fitting lights to the bridge to indicate whether the doors were closed. The inquiry concluded: 'If this sensible suggestion... had received the serious consideration it deserved this disaster might well have been prevented' (Department of Transport, 1987). Thus, at its broadest, it can be argued that in a democracy employers cannot be left to their own devices when issues of public interest are at stake.

In the author's view, it is because whistleblowing is often in the interests of both the employer and wider society that adequate protection must be provided for those who are driven to it. However, from a 'moral rights' perspective, unless proper procedures are put in place, any obligation to disclose malpractice will continue to be in conflict with and overtaken by the worker's self-interest in retaining their job. Before outlining the possible contents of such procedures, we will discuss some of the factors which encourage or inhibit the reporting of concerns. In doing so we will also assess the impact of the recent amendments made to the ERA 1996 by the Public Interest Disclosure Act 1998.

Some constraints on disclosure

One potential constraint is the imposition of short- and fixed-term contracts. For example, in the offshore oil and gas industries many workers have been employed on two-week contracts. Given management's almost unfettered discretion whether or not to renew a contract, employees are likely to feel inhibited about making unauthorised disclosures of information. However,

Section 103A of the ERA 1998, which applies irrespective of a complainant's age or length of service, makes it automatically unfair to dismiss employees on the grounds that they have made a protected disclosure (that is a 'qualifying disclosure' which affords the individual protection as described in the introduction). For those employees on fixed-term contracts, the expiry of the contract 'without being renewed under the same contract' amounts to a dismissal for these purposes (Section 95 (1)(b) ERA 1996). Alternatively, workers who cannot claim unfair dismissal because they do not have a contract of employment can complain that they have been subjected to a detriment for making a protected disclosure and Section 43K ERA 1996 gives 'worker' an extended meaning for the purposes of Part IVA. In these circumstances the employer will have to show the grounds for non-renewal (Section 48 (2) ERA 1996). Of course, determined employers may try to invent potentially fair reasons for ending the relationship (for example, relating to conduct, capability, redundancy and so on) and much will depend on the vigilance of employment tribunals. However, there can be little doubt that it will no longer be enough simply to assert that those who have raised concerns are unsuitable for further employment.

Another inhibiting factor has been the widespread introduction of so-called 'gagging clauses' into work contracts. Such clauses expressly prohibit the disclosure of information acquired during employment and can cause confusion when placed alongside codes of conduct which encourage the internal reporting of malpractices. The recent introduction of Section 43J into the ERA 1996 is consistent with a 'moral rights' approach. This renders void any provision in an agreement which 'purports to preclude the worker from making a protected disclosure'. This section will impact on both work contracts and agreements to settle legal proceedings but will not apply to matters which fall outside the definition of a 'qualifying disclosure'. Thus a clause which prevented the disclosure of information about a type of wrongdoing which is not listed in Section 43B(1) ERA 1996 (that is, a qualifying disclosure; see introduction to this chapter) would still be enforceable. For example, an express term could restrain disclosures about gross mismanagement but not unlawful maladministration. Nevertheless it is to be hoped that the new law will make it easier for those who are bound by professional codes of practice (for example, health visitors, nurses, midwives and public service accountants) to reconcile their contractual and professional obligations.

The common law implied duty of fidelity prevents employees from disclosing information which has been acquired in confidence. However, the courts have permitted an exception where there is 'any misconduct of such a nature that it ought in the public interest to be disclosed to others' (see *Initial Services* v. *Putterill* [1968] 1, QB, 396). Such a disclosure must be to someone who has an interest in receiving it and the press might not always be an appropriate medium (see *Lion Laboratories* v. *Evans* [1985] QB, 526). Nevertheless, it is clear that the duty of confidence does not prevent a person disclosing to regulatory authorities matters which it was in the province of those authorities to investigate. This is so even if the disclosure might be motivated by malice (see Re A Company's Application [1989] IRLR 477 which involved the financial services sector).

Part IVA of the ERA 1996 impacts directly on the common law position by offering protection against dismissal or other forms of victimisation to workers who make a protected disclosure. However, it should be remembered that a disclosure will only be protected if the subject matter falls within Section 43B(1) ERA 1996 (see earlier) and the correct procedure is followed. Except where the disclosure is made in the course of obtaining legal advice, workers are required to act in good faith and have a reasonable belief that any allegations are substantially true. Certain categories are excluded from the protection afforded by Part IVA, for example, those who ordinarily work outside Great Britain, the security services, those who have a contract of service with the police and Crown employees who are subject to a certificate exempting them on grounds of national security. It should also be noted that a disclosure will not be protected if the person commits an offence by making it (Section 43B (3) ERA 1996). An obvious example here is a breach of the Official Secrets Act 1996.

Encouragement to disclose

Although workers in the UK have no constitutional right to whistleblow, Article 10 of the European Convention on Human Rights states that: 'Everyone has the right to freedom of expression. This right shall include freedom to hold opinions and to receive and impart information and ideas without interference by public authority and regardless of frontiers.' However, Article 10(2) refers to the necessity for restrictions on this freedom in order to prevent the disclosure of confidential information. The Human Rights Bill 1998 incorporates the convention into UK law. The provision of national remedies is designed to discourage citizens from seeking enforcement of their rights before the European Court of Human Rights. Turning from human rights to legal duties, whether employees have an obligation to report the misdemeanours of fellow workers to their employer depends on the individual contract and the circumstances. Thus the Court of Appeal has held that a senior executive in a multinational financial corporation had a duty to disclose the involvement of his colleagues in a serious fraud upon the employer, even if that required him to disclose his own misdeeds (see *Sybron Corporation* v. *Rochem Ltd* [1983] IRLR 253). In a survey of *The Times Top 500 UK Firms* (Lewis, 1996a), six of the 11 employers who had a whistleblowing procedure imposed a duty on their employees to report breaches of the organisation's code of ethics or business conduct. Since workers are less likely to report concerns if they fear retaliation, it is worth examining the circumstances in which the law has provided specific protection against victimisation.

Regulation 12 of the Management of Health and Safety at Work Regulations 1992 requires employees to inform *employers* of any work situation which could be reasonably considered to represent a serious and immediate danger to health and safety and of any shortcomings in the employer's protection arrangements which have not previously been reported. This duty is supported by Sections 44(1)(c) and 100(1)(c) of ERA 1996,which provide that, where there is no safety representative or it is not reasonably practicable to raise the matter through such a representative or a safety committee, it is unlawful to dismiss or to impose a detriment on employees who 'have brought to his employer's attention, by reasonable means, circumstances connected with his work which he reasonably believed were harmful or potentially harmful to health and safety'. These sections clearly deal with internal reporting. Those who feel compelled to take their concerns outside the organisation will be offered redress if they can show that they have made a 'protected disclosure' within the meaning of Part IVA of ERA 1996 (see earlier).

Section 104 ERA 1996 is relevant to external whistleblowing because it offers protection against dismissal to those who assert in good faith that their employer has infringed certain statutory rights. Similarly, both the Sex Discrimination Act 1975 and the Race Relations Act 1976 allow a complaint to be brought where discrimination takes place by reason that the person victimised has 'given evidence or information in connection with proceedings brought by any person against the discriminator or any other person' under this legislation, or has 'alleged that the discriminator or any other person has committed an act which… would amount to a contravention of' these statutes. In this context redress is not available if the allegation is false and not made in good faith. The protection afforded by these measures has been potentially widened by the introduction of Part IVA ERA 1996. Thus workers who reasonably believe that there has been a failure to comply with *any* legal obligation will be protected against dismissal or other detrimental treatment if they have made a 'protected disclosure'.

The implications for employers: producing codes of conduct and reporting procedures

According to the Nolan Committee on Standards in Public Life (Nolan, 1996) best practice includes:

- a clear statement that malpractice is taken seriously in the organisation and an indication of the sorts of matters regarded as malpractice
- respect for the confidentiality of staff raising concerns if they wish, and the opportunity to raise concerns outside the line management structure
- penalties for making false and malicious allegations
- an indication of the proper way in which concerns may be raised outside the organisation if necessary.

In relation to the first principle, the author recommends that employers should explain to their staff why the reporting of concerns is important and should define 'malpractice' in a way that both suits their needs and is acceptable to the workforce. Indeed, any whistleblowing procedure should be introduced only after full consultation with employees and their representatives. Unless careful consideration is given to the potential impact of whistleblowing on discipline, there may be a suspicion that the new arrangements could be used to monitor performance and investigate staff without their knowledge.

One positive way of encouraging a culture of openness and of involving employees would be to agree a code of conduct/ethics. For example, the British Airways Code of Conduct states that staff should:

> Be prepared to challenge if you believe that others are acting in an unethical way. Create the climate and opportunities for people to voice genuinely held concerns about behaviour or decisions that they perceive to be unprofessional or inappropriate. Do not tolerate any form of retribution against those who do speak up.

According to the Civil Service Management Code, if a civil servant:

> considers that he or she is being asked to act in a manner which appears to him or her to be improper, unethical... or to involve possible maladministration or to be otherwise inconsistent with the standards of conduct prescribed... the matter should be reported to a senior officer and, if appropriate, to the Permanent Head of the Department.

In the survey of *The Times Top 500 UK Firms* (Lewis, 1996a) six of the 11 with a written procedure referred to a code of ethical or business conduct. Such a code, which must be compatible with employees' contractual obligations, could also be used to provide guidance as to when and how the whistleblowing procedure should be invoked.

Employees can be made aware of the contents of a whistleblowing procedure by a variety of mechanisms. Both *The Times Top 500 UK Firms* (Lewis, 1996a) and the local authority surveys (Lewis, 1996b) reveal that the method most commonly used is employer handbooks. However, the report on local authorities suggests that the more personalised and diverse the ways the procedures were promoted, the more likely they were to be used by staff.

A whistleblowing procedure should specify the person or persons with whom employees should raise their concern initially and should indicate who should be approached if the individual continues to have concerns. In the local authority survey, 19 (40 per cent) of the procedures suggested more than one person with whom concerns should be raised initially and 25 authorities with a procedure (64 per cent) gave employees an option as to whom to approach if they continued to have concerns. The person ultimately responsible for ensuring that concerns are investigated should also be identified. Although such arrangements may mirror the contents of a grievance procedure, it should be noted that employees who are concerned about malpractice at work do not necessarily have a personal grievance. Thus it might be useful to state that the whistleblowing procedure is not designed to replace the grievance procedure but 'may lead to the use of other procedures, such as disciplinary and internal audit'. For example, see the procedure introduced by the London Borough of Lewisham, Social Services Department (IRS, 1995).

Additionally, the fact that whistleblowers may call into question the acts or omissions of their line managers emphasises the desirability of creating alternative channels of communication. This could be achieved internally by allowing direct access to the chief executive, an ombudsperson or by using a telephone 'hotline'. Many major American companies have established formal ombudsperson systems. Employers in both the public and private sector (together with trade unions who recruit in education and the health service) have introduced 'hotlines' in recent years. As a last resort employees may be advised to contact an external agency which can be trusted not to abuse confidential information, for example, an industry regulator or ombudsperson or Public Concern at Work. Although there is currently little evidence that employers encourage their staff to take concerns outside the management structure, it is clearly in the organisation's interest that any external scrutiny is conducted by a reputable body with investigatory powers rather than the general media.

Another principle endorsed by the Nolan Committee is that there should be respect for the confidentiality of staff raising concerns. Allied to this is the question of whether or not to permit anonymous reporting. The main argument in favour of anonymity is that it acknowledges the perceived vulnerability of whistleblowers. Unfortunately, it may not be very helpful to employers and it may also suggest that the discloser is doing something morally wrong. In the local authority survey, 28 (72 per cent) of the authorities who had a procedure stated that requests for confidentiality would be respected and 24 (64 per cent) allowed concerns to be raised anonymously. In *The Times Top 500 UK Firms* survey ten of the 11 organisations with a written procedure indicated that they allowed employees to preserve their anonymity.

Apart from problems of credibility and the fear of unjustified allegations (see section on possible disciplinary action that follows), anonymity may prevent an investigation of the issue which is causing concern. Indeed, even if an investigation is possible, there may be occasions when the identity of the discloser is revealed during the process. It follows that employees should be encouraged to seek advice at an early stage, either from a friend or representative internally or from a specialist outside agency, for example Public Concern at Work. No doubt such advisers will point out that Part IVA of the ERA 1996 is not designed to a protect those who report concerns anonymously.

Regarding discipline, procedures will need to emphasise that victimising or deterring employees from raising legitimate concerns is serious misconduct and could render the employer liable for any detrimental treatment imposed. Similarly, it may be appropriate to penalise staff for knowingly making false allegations. In the survey of *The Times Top 500 UK Firms*, five answered a question about employees suffering reprisals for raising their concerns; four referred to the possibility of disciplinary action and one stated that the procedure 'reassures that there won't be reprisals'. In the local authority survey, only eight councils (21 per cent of those with a procedure) indicated that their procedure provided for colleagues to be disciplined if they victimised a person who used it in good faith. By way of contrast, 16 authorities (41 per cent) stated that their procedure provided for action to be taken against those who acted maliciously in relation to unfounded allegations. Nine of these (23 per cent of those with a procedure) also indicated that action could be taken against employees who acted maliciously irrespective of whether their concerns were well founded.

Although Part IVA of ERA 1996 places great reliance on the notion of 'good faith', there are two main objections to looking at an employee's motive in this context. First, the possibility of a person's motive being examined might deter some important disclosures, for example, in relation to health and safety or serious crime. Second, there is the thorny issue of the burden of proof. Is it fair to require a discloser to prove good faith or should the employer have to show bad faith? In the author's opinion, if a person has reasonable grounds to believe that the information is true his or her motive for reporting should be irrelevant. To some extent malicious allegations could be deterred by making it a serious disciplinary offence to report a concern where there were no reasonable grounds for believing that the information supplied was accurate.

If staff are to be encouraged to 'do the right thing', employers might also consider imposing upon themselves the following obligations: to act promptly when allegations are made; to provide counselling and other forms of support; and to keep whistleblowers informed about any investigation which takes place and to report back on the outcome. Indeed, only ten organisations in the local authority survey (26 per cent of those with a procedure) provided for whistleblowers to be informed about the progress of any investigation. It would also be sensible for employers to commit themselves to monitor and review the operation of whistleblowing procedures on a regular basis. In the local authority survey, 21 of the councils with a procedure (54 per cent) said they had arrangements for monitoring or reviewing the procedure.

Summary

Employees are often the first to realise that there may be something seriously wrong within an organisation. However, they may not express their concerns because they feel that speaking up would be disloyal to their colleagues or to their employer. They may also fear harassment or victimisation. In these circumstances it may be easier to turn a blind eye rather than report what may just be a suspicion of malpractice. Thus in order to prevent problems being overlooked and to avoid legal pitfalls (the 'enlightened self-interest' approach), personnel practitioners should endeavour to devise procedures which both encourage and enable staff to report their concerns. Such a procedure should aim to:

- Define the types of concern that it covers. This definition may well be broader than the matters recognised as 'qualifying disclosures' by the ERA 1996
- Explain its relationship to other procedures. For example, that it does not replace harassment or grievance procedures but is intended to cover circumstances which fall outside their remit. It should also be made clear that the disciplinary procedure may be invoked if allegations are made which are both false and malicious
- Indicate how and with whom concerns should be raised and the advice and support that is available (both internally and externally)
- Allow staff to be accompanied by a representative of their choice at any meetings or interviews connected with the concerns raised
- Outline a target timetable for the employer's response and provide feedback on the outcome of any investigation and any action taken
- Indicate how staff can take the matter further if they are dissatisfied with the employer's response
- Reassure staff that they will be protected from possible reprisals or victimisation.

Despite all that has been said in this chapter, it could be argued that it is not the precise arrangements established by an organisation that are significant. What is essential, however, is that employers demonstrate commitment to ethical behaviour at the highest level, that procedures for handling concerns are agreed with employee representatives and communicated to the workforce and that staff are positively encouraged to use them when appropriate. Certainly those who have introduced whistleblowing procedures see them as contributing to their image as an ethical and efficient organisation. They may also be less likely to fall foul of the law.

References

Department of Transport (1987) *Court of Inquiry No. 8074*, London: HMSO

IRS *Employment Trends 590*, August 1995, pp. 5–8

Lewis, D. (1995) 'Whistleblowers and job security' *Modern Law Review*, **58**: 208

Lewis, D. (1996a) *Report on Whistleblowing Procedures in The Times Top 500 UK Firms*, London: Centre for Research in Industrial and Commercial Law

Lewis, D. (1996b) *Raising Concerns about Financial Malpractice and Probity: A survey of whistleblowing procedures in local authorities*, Middlesex University: Centre for Research in Industrial and Commercial Law

Lord Nolan (1996) *Second Report of the Nolan Committee on Standards in Public Life*, London: HMSO

Micelli, Z. and Near, J. (1992) *Blowing the Whistle*, New York: Lexington Books

Public Concern at Work (1993) *The Police*, London: Public Concern at Work

Sternberg, E. (1994) *Just Business: Business Ethics in Action*, London: Little, Brown

Concluding comments: ethical frameworks for action

Jean Woodall and Diana Winstanley

Summarising the ethical position of HRM

The individual contributions to this book have demonstrated that all areas of HRM policy and practice have an ethical dimension, but that there is no consensus either about what constitutes an appropriate ethical framework or about the possibility for ethical intervention. However, individual chapter contributors have shown how ethical frameworks can be used to analyse HRM practice and to advocate action in many different ways. Perhaps the most important point is that the practice of HRM must inevitably confront ethical dilemmas, and that some of these may be neither apparent nor easily resolved. In the introduction to this book we set out those ethical frameworks that we thought would be most illuminating for an exploration of contemporary HRM. The purpose of the first two parts has been to raise ethical awareness (the ability to discern ethical issues) and the capacity for ethical reasoning and analysis through an application of these frameworks to HRM. In the third part, we moved into the area of ethical action to explore the diverse ways in which the ethical side of organisational life can be revealed and promoted and in this final chapter we aim to provide an overview of ethical frameworks for action.

Realism and fatalism – is ethical HRM possible?

Before outlining some of the ways in which ethical action can be taken within HRM, it is important to ask the question of whether such action is feasible in the first place. Not all contributors (especially Karen Legge (Chapter 2) and Tim Claydon (Chapter 12)) would accept that the ethical treatment of employees within organisations is possible.

Running through the chapters there appear to be five main barriers to ethical action.

1. *The contradictory position of capital and labour relations*
   The first is the position taken by Tim Claydon (Chapter 12) which utilises the Marxist perspective on capital and labour relations. Claydon's pessimism is from a broadly economic deterministic stance when he argues that the fundamentally contradictory position of capital and labour renders any reformist liberal attempt to make working conditions more ethical a problematic exercise. He suggests that the use of the language of empowerment and enterprise is a form of deceit to mask the true nature of the employment relationship and contract.

2. *The limits of the global marketplace*
   Karen Legge is particularly strenuous in taking up the limits provided by economic forces with respect to the constraints placed upon ethical action by global capitalism and the difficulty of controlling ethics within the complex networks of organisations within a global marketplace. She indicates that the wider systemic factors inherent in a postmodern world make the ethical treatment of employees at work highly problematic. Behind this assertion lie the assumptions that a search for ethical consensus is elusive in a world that 'celebrates relativism and deconstruction', within a global context. Perhaps her pessimistic stance is arrived at because the remit of her chapter was to place organisations within the broader global competitive context. She shows how difficult ethical intervention becomes when products and services are delivered through a global value chain, and where employment practices in overseas subsidiaries and partners may be strongly influenced by local labour markets, the efficacy of government regulation, and national cultures.

   The problem with this argument is that such pessimism leads to fatalism – the scope for ethical advocacy is limited and nothing can be done anyway. Taken to its logical conclusion it ultimately implies that the practice and the study of HRM is a waste of time. Legge is obviously aware of this, but suggests that there is a possibility that some core labour market employees may receive more ethical treatment. She thus suggests that the nature of the employment contract or labour market position is the primary determinant of ethical treatment. At the most some socially conscious businesses and not-for-profit organisations might view the ethical treatment of employees as important as meeting their financial targets. The more likely case is that employers will justify the more favourable treatment of their permanent core workforce when they are perceived as making a key contribution to successful organisational performance – the enlightened self-interest perspective. This all too common use of a consequentialist/ utilitarian ethic makes it more likely that the recipients of ethical HRM will be found in the core workforce, rather than among sub-contracted and agency workers.

3. *The changing nature of labour markets and the employment contract*
Other chapter authors have explored the contractual basis of employment in greater detail, and have also demonstrated the unethical basis of much current practice as it shifts the burden of risk from employers on to employees, be they contingent workers (Stanworth, Chapter 8) or even managers who themselves might be part of the core workforce (Simpson, Chapter 9). Heery (Chapter 10) also shows how the 'new pay' ideas have been used for the same purpose. Stanworth argues that contingent forms of employment (part-time working, self-employment, temporary work, and teleworking) are not 'inevitable', and that the consequentialist/utilitarian logic used to justify their existence is in fact self-defeating. Presenting flexible working as a means to the end of wider business 'competitiveness' is to ignore the longer term adverse repercussions to organisations of more limited commitment, skills shortages and the wider social consequences of economic insecurity and risk. So, while it is possible to raise ethical awareness around these long-term issues, it is very difficult to find means of intervention that do not have repercussions for short-term profitability.

4. *The primacy of the profit motive*
Although these writers have largely lamented the difficulty of ethical action, another set of writers more from the right, have normatively pursued a minimalist ethical position, on the grounds that employers should put the profit motive first, and this argument was touched on in Chapter 1 with our discussion of the Friedman (1962) and Sternberg (1994, 1997) position on stakeholding, which equally applies to other areas of ethical action. Unless ethical action can be seen as in the interests of the organisation – the enlightened self-interest argument – it should not be pursued at all. These arguments have been discussed elsewhere (for example, see Winstanley and Stoney, 1997, 1999) in their explicit form. However, in contemporary human resource management they tend to take more of an implicit nature and are revealed through debates over human resource management and its relationship with performance and

effectiveness and with relation to strategic human resource management and best fit and best practice models.

5. *Best fit and best practice human resource management*
The focus of attention in HRM has recently homed in on the relationship between human resource management and organisational effectiveness and performance, leading to discussion of 'best fit' and 'best practice' approaches to HRM (Tyson and Doherty, 1997, 1999). By its nature this debate prioritises organisational effectiveness over individual well-being, unless the latter can be seen to lead to the former. Not only does this deflect attention from ethical issues, but it also poses obstacles to action for the promotion of ethical practices. Although it may be possible to identify best practice approaches which have an ethical component, the value of having invariable and unambiguous standards is questionable. More difficult an obstacle is in relation to 'best fit' models of human resource management, where effectiveness is achieved through 'strategic fit'. If the business strategy adopted is cost reduction, how far can costly ethical standards be seen to be complementary with such an approach? This makes the ethical treatment of employees a matter of contingency.

In this book we have shown how the primacy of best fit and best practice models reinforce further the contingent relationship of the employee with the organisation and how combined with the economic constraints provided by models which emphasise the workings of the market have all led to a lack of concern with ethics. Chapter 11 suggests that management writers have further pushed an emphasis on behaviourism and evaluation, to the extent that it has led to conditions of worth organisations which are at odds with the humanistic model. The humanistic model we believe has much to offer in developing ethical approaches to human resource management and much of this literature has been ignored or over-simplified.

If we felt that these barriers prevented any ethical action at all, we probably would not have bothered to write this book. Although clearly there are constraints to ethical action, we believe that it is possible to construct ethical action through a range of different processes. There are academics, policy makers and practitioners who construct ethical action in a number of different ways and these are discussed now.

Statutory intervention

The impasse mentioned earlier draws attention to whether one way to deal with ethical problems in the employment relationship is by means of statutory intervention. However, this is often met by the common rejoinder that excessive government regulation will drive global businesses to withdraw their investment and activity to more 'favourable' overseas destinations. For example, this is the current government's justification for only limited action to reverse the worst insecurities and injustices associated with the growth of labour market flexibility within the UK since 1980. Nonetheless, governments can and do often take action to ensure ethical treatment of employees within organisations. Legislation to equalise the rights of employees on non-standard contracts of employment with those of the permanent core workforce, on health and safety issues, on arrangements for handling redundancy, transfer of undertakings and so on, has crept slowly on to the UK statute book, albeit largely as a result of the obligations consequent upon membership of the European Union and in the wake of the 1997 Labour government's agenda for 'fairness at work'.

However, there is the question of how far this legislation keeps pace with other 'innovative' HR practice of a dubious ethical nature. For example, Heery (Chapter 10) shows how the new pay incorporates greater risk into the remuneration of employees and also marks a departure from employee representation in the determination of reward systems. He argues that employees must be able to retain a legal right to collective bargaining over remuneration, as there is overwhelming evidence that without this employers are unwilling to concede voluntarily to joint decision making. Similarly, Lewis (Chapter 15) shows the necessity for a legal framework to support public interest disclosure, in order that 'whistleblowers' might be protected when taking action within their own organisations. During the course of preparing the manuscript for this book, the Public Interest Disclosure Act 1998 became law, which outlined a statutory obligation on employers to make arrangements to encourage responsible whistleblowing. It remains to be seen whether such statutory intervention does make a difference, or whether interest groups such as Public Concern at Work will still find that a large amount of individual case work comes their way.

Legislative intervention may also be needed at the international level if the worst excesses of flexible employment practices are to be avoided (Stanworth, Chapter 8). If flexible working practices, and the transfer of risk on to the employee are acknowledged as ethically contentious, as opposed to inevitable, then strong concerted action is needed. However, given the limited scope and sanctions to date of international law in relation to employment, achieving international agreement and regulation is likely to be a very slow process. There are of course limits to statutory intervention. It tends to be reactive rather than anticipatory in nature, and is often the outcome of a long, protracted and costly process of lobbying. It can also inculcate an employer response seeking to attain only the minimum action necessary for compliance and sometimes encourages evasive behaviour. By itself the law does not change attitudes and does not always promote awareness.

Regulation and codes of practice

For these reasons, regulatory bodies are needed to promote ethical behaviour. Regulatory bodies such as the Equal Opportunities Commission (EOC) and the Commission for Racial Equality (CRE) and professional organisations such as the Institute for Personnel and Development (IPD) and the British Psychological Society (BPS) often seek to promote legal compliance and ethical behaviour by reference to a code of practice.

In the UK the IPD has a code of conduct (IPD, 1997) which is rather general in nature and focuses on professional conduct and complaints procedures. There are numerous other codes of practice relating to HRM – such as those of the Advisory, Conciliation and Arbitration Service (ACAS) and the British Psychological Society (BPS) – which set standards of behaviour in a variety of areas. Codes of practice are an important means of institutionalising ethics within HRM practice. Their limitations centre around compliance: organisations can easily be tempted into an unthinking automatic adoption of codes in the hope that they will provide a 'magic shield', without realising that this does not dispense with the need for ethical judgement. For example, Baker and Cooper (Chapter 4) demonstrate both the strengths and shortcomings of this approach in relation to psychological testing. They show that there can be a marked discrepancy between espoused ethical values in testing, as embodied in both the BPS and IPD codes, and the reported ethical practice of those using tests which often departs quite significantly from the ethical values. Taylor and Jones (Chapter 14) also discuss the role of professional codes as a means to make the case for employee rights within a staff charter. However, codes of practice are limited. They too often do little more than induce a mechanical compliance, are great at dealing with routine and predictable issues, but come unstuck with exceptional cases.

Another area where codes of practice appear to have a limited role in supporting ethical HRM is in employee development. This is not usually seen as an important area for ethical concern. However, as Woodall and Douglas (Chapter 7) demonstrate, the emergence of strategically focused HRD has changed the situation. In particular the emphasis upon aligning individual and organisational values implies that culture management and personal development processes are increasingly used by organisations that are not always respectful of human dignity, autonomy and self-esteem. Woodall and Douglas show how specific personal development interventions such as outdoor management development, neuro-linguistic programming (NLP), and Gestalt-based organisational development can all vary in the extent to which they value and support individual psychological safety and in the ethical awareness with which they are practiced. Woodall and Douglas argue that adopting codes of practice that relate solely to the conduct of the intervention processes may not be ethically sufficient, the substance of the intervention is also a matter for ethical concern. Ethical development requires considerable respect for individual privacy, self-esteem, dignity and autonomy. This is where reference to virtue ethics and the ethics of care is very important. Without a sense of ethical agency on the part of the HRD practitioner, it is unlikely that codes of practice can ever be 'live' ethical instruments. Too often they can end up as a 'life raft' to which organisations may cling without scrutinising their own practices and outcomes.

Voluntary ethical action – a focus upon processes

A formalistic ethical approach to HRM that relies upon the law and codes of practice needs to be supplemented with action that focuses upon ethical interventions, ethical policies and procedures and more importantly ethical processes. Liff and Dickens (Chapter 5) and Doherty and Tyson (Chapter 6) highlight two areas where organisations have devised interventions, policies and procedures to promote greater equal opportunities and employee well-being respectively. Likewise Spence's discussion of selection interviewing (Chapter 3), Heery's chapter on pay (Chapter 10) and Winstanley's outline of performance management (Chapter 11) identify three areas where there has been much debate over how to achieve greater fairness and objectivity in the process. Stakeholding, dialogue and discourse frameworks of ethics are becoming important tools for informing such interventions. For example Winstanley (Chapter 11) shows how a 'stakeholder synthesis' approach might be used to develop a performance management system responsive to professional needs and, similarly, Liff and Dickens (Chapter 5) indicate that a stakeholder approach linked to an ethic of care could be used to integrate competing claims in equality management, in order that the false dichotomies can be overcome, such as business interest versus social justice and distribution of rewards according to merit versus diversity.

Part III of this book has gone beyond a consideration of promoting ethical procedures and processes within the traditional areas of human resource management, to raise the possibility of instituting new processes which promote and secure better communication and feedback overall, as a way of either protecting or promoting the ethical treatment of employees. All of the interventions described in Part III (social auditing, Chapter 13, staff charters, Chapter 14, whistleblowing procedures, Chapter 15) are examples of this.

For example, Sillanpää and Jackson's (Chapter 13) account of the process of social auditing and the production of social statements at The Body Shop exemplifies the importance of process. Besides outlining their audit methodology, they also suggest that certain conditions need to be met, if it is to flourish. In particular, while aligning values is feasible, it also requires the time and patience to stimulate active dialogue and to allow values to freely evolve by means of regular conversations, focus groups and surveys. Allowing different departments and sub-units to set their own agenda is also necessary. Thus any organisation embarking upon social auditing needs to be robust enough for this to happen and needs to be prepared to meet the expectations raised among employees, whatever the economic situation facing the business.

Another example of ethical action that focuses upon processes is the development of employee charters. They are a potentially powerful instrument of ethical change within organisations if they are developed through a process of consultation and dialogue and also focus upon employee responsibilities as well as rights. Taylor and Jones (Chapter 14) outline how they have been used in a variety of organisations, illustrating the process of establishing a staff charter by reference to the experience of a specific NHS Trust. Similarly, Lewis (in Chapter 15), shows that 'whistleblowers' need more than the protection of legislation on public disclosure. There also need to be processes whereby individual employees can raise issues of concern without fear of reprisal.

Ethical action and the integrity of the actor

A focus upon processes directs attention to informal behaviour and interrelatedness. Only by focusing upon processes is it possible to shape organisational cultures within which people can find fulfillment and meaning and only through attention to processes can there be an effective management of diversity and the dilemmas posed by conflicting values. Value conflict is intrinsic to human behaviour and being ethical is not so much about finding one universal principal to govern all action, but more about knowing how to recognise and mediate between often unacknowledged differences of view. Thus ethical HRM is more than just setting standards of 'best practice', it is about knowing how to handle the tricky situations that depart from this. This is recognised by the ethics of care which draws attention to the need to take account of the particular needs and circumstances of individuals and to involve them in moral deliberation. It also involves the development of integrity based upon ethical judgement and a sense of responsibility, the development of appropriate virtues.

Thus action in this area inevitably implies the training and development of those who bear a responsibility for decisions around the management of people. This training and development does not just involve instruction on appropriate techniques, but also the development of ethical awareness and judgement. It assumes that HR professionals have an ethical stewardship for anything that touches upon the management of people within organisations.

It implies that ethics is not something that can be delegated to other functions and managers within the organisation. A major theme of this book has been that HR professionals carry a responsibility for the ethical treatment of employees. Other members of the senior management team may need to be made aware of their responsibility for ethical leadership and managing with integrity (Connock and Johns, 1995; Pearson, 1995), and there are strong argu ments for developing the ethical capacity of all managers (Maclagan, 1998; Petrick and Quinn, 1997; Snell, 1993), but, above all, it is with HR professionals that ethical sensitivity and the capacity for ethical reasoning, analysis and action must lie.

The IPD should clearly have an important role in the training of HR professionals in the ethical aspects of managing employees. We mentioned their code of conduct earlier (IPD, 1997), yet the standards on which the national system of initial professional training is based, make a glancing reference to ethical issues. The voluntary rather than mandatory basis for continuing professional development makes no reference to the desirability of ethical training. Perhaps the starting point for ethical action is then the initial and continuing education and training of HR professionals, led by the Institute of Personnel and Development and the academic institutions who are partners in the delivery of this training? In addition, the HR profession could benefit from consideration of how other 'caring' professionals address ethical issues. Professional supervision arrangements and professional ethics committees are common mechanisms and the IPD could consider ways in which it could build such support into its local professional branch infrastructure. As well as stimulating thought and debate, we hope that this book will provide the impetus for such action at the professional level.

References

Connock, S. and Johns, T. (1995) *Ethical Leadership*, London: Institute of Personnel and Development

Friedman, M. (1962) *Capitalism and Freedom*, Chicago: University of Chicago Press

Institute of Personnel and Development (1997) *The IPD Code of Professional Conduct and Disciplinary Procedures*, London: Institute of Personnel and Development

Maclagan, P. (1998) *Management and Morality: A Developmental Perspective*, London: Sage

Pearson, G. (1995) *Integrity in Organizations. An Alternative Business Ethic*, London: McGraw-Hill

Petrick, J.A. and Quinn, J.F. (1997) *Management Ethics: Integrity at Work*, London: Sage

Snell, R.S. (1993) *Developing Skills for Ethical Management*, London: Chapman & Hall

Sternberg, E. (1994) *Just Business: Business Ethics in Action*, London: Little, Brown and Warner

Sternberg, E. (1997) 'The Defects of Stakeholder Theory' *Corporate Governance: An International Review*, **5**(1): 3–10

Tyson, S. (1997) *The Practice of Human Resource Strategy*, London: Pitman, pp. 7–10, 176–7

Tyson, S. and Doherty, N. (1999) *Human Resource Excellence Report*, London: *Financial Times*/Cranfield University: London, pp. 3–14

Winstanley, D. and Stoney, C. (1997) 'Stakeholder Management: A Critique and a Defense'. Paper given at 15th Annual International Labour Process Conference, 26–28 March, University of Edinburgh, Scotland

Winstanley, D. and Stoney, C. (1999) 'Inclusion in the Workplace' in Askonas, P. and Stewart, A. *The Inclusive Society*, London: Macmillan

Index